TURNER WATERCOLORS
from MANCHESTER

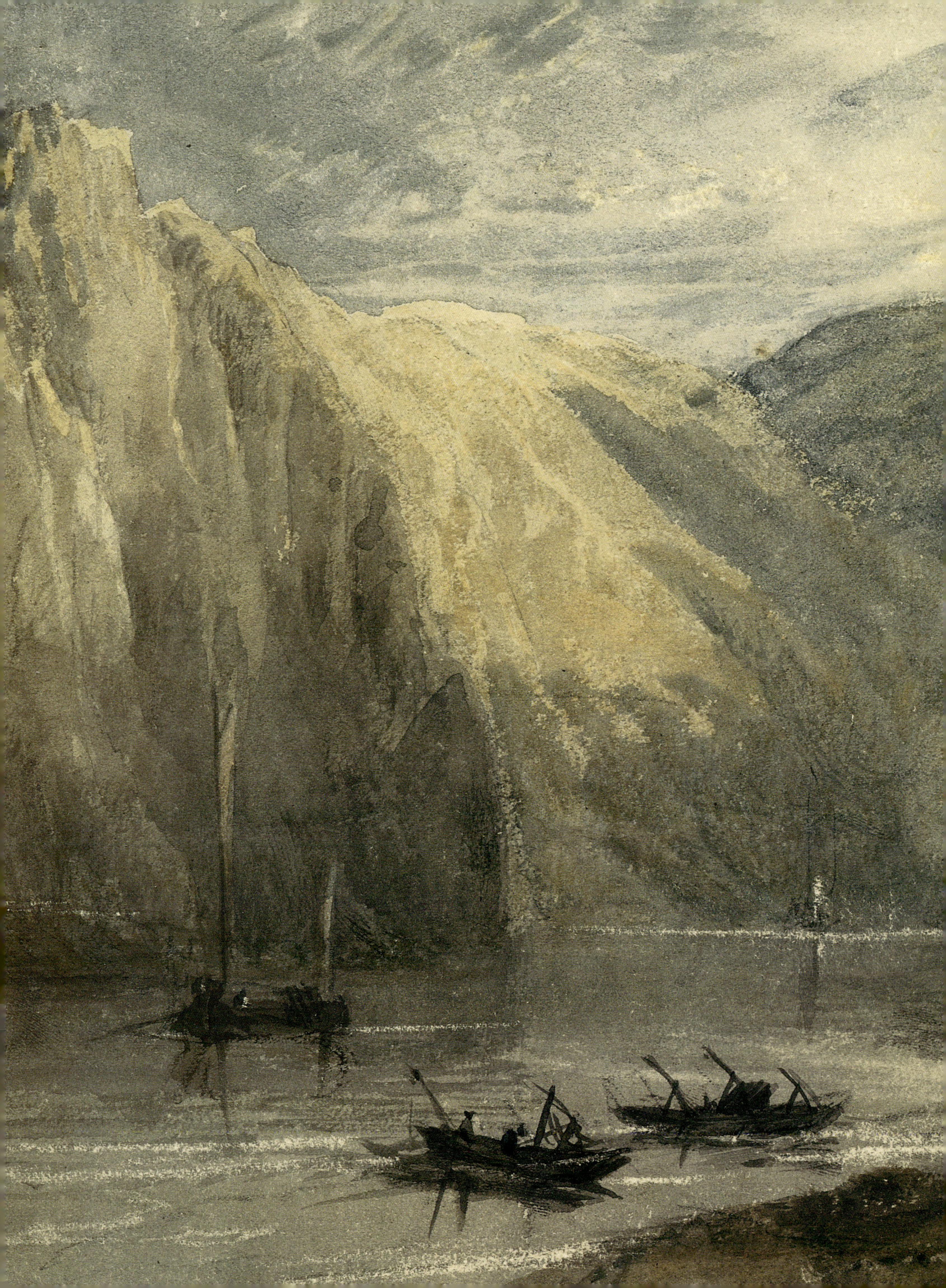

Turner Watercolors *from* Manchester

Charles Nugent

Melva Croal

The Trust for Museum Exhibitions

Designer: Judy Oser
Editor: Donald Garfield
Printed in Great Britain by Balding + Mansell

Published by The Trust for Museum Exhibitions
Copyright ©1996 by The Trust for Museum Exhibitions,
Washington, D.C., The Whitworth Art Gallery, University
of Manchester, and Manchester City Art Galleries.
All rights reserved

Library of Congress Catalog Card Number 96-061517
ISBN 1-882507-05-3

Cover image: cat. 69, *Sunset at Sea with Gurnets,* 1838-40
Frontispiece: detail, cat. 40, *The Lorelei,* 1817

CONTENTS

FOREWORD

It is the ambition of all museums to make their collections available to the widest possible public. Only a few years ago, the notion that an exhibition of British watercolors would be shown in Memphis, Indianapolis, and Omaha would have been a dream indeed, for, in our century American culture has moved more easily to Europe, rather than vice-versa. J.M.W. Turner has, however, been recognized as a precursor of some modes of American twentieth-century painting, and therefore it is apt that the United States hosts a selection of this most immediate and spontaneous part of his oeuvre.

That this has come about is due in great part to the enthusiasm and vision of Mrs. Ann Van Devanter Townsend, President of The Trust for Museum Exhibitions, whom we met through the introduction of Sir Peter Wakefield, former Director of the National Art Collections Fund, and now Director of The Trust for Museum Exhibitions, United Kingdom. It was in 1990 that she first suggested the idea of an exhibition of Turner's work, and since then staff from both the Manchester City Art Galleries and the Whitworth Art Gallery have worked closely with the Trust and the host museums to bring her idea to fruition.

The collaboration between the City Art Galleries and the Whitworth (which is the art museum of the University of Manchester)—a collaboration between "town and gown"—has been a happy one. As visitors to the exhibition will see, the collections of Turner watercolors in the two institutions ideally complement each other. The watercolors at the Whitworth are predominantly from Turner's early career, when he was learning his trade as an artist; there are some excellent examples from his later career, but they are far outnumbered by works from his early period. By contrast, the City Art Galleries have only five works from before 1820, and their collection is particularly strong in works from the later part of Turner's life. Seen together, therefore, the watercolors provide an excellent survey of Turner's development both as a draughtsman and as an individual who expresses the startling changes in the psyche of his era. In fact, Manchester boasts the largest group of Turner watercolors in public hands outside London, and we are proud to present such a group to a new audience.

During 1997 *Turner Watercolors from Manchester* will travel to the three host venues in the United States, before being shown in Manchester in early 1998. We are most grateful to the staff of the host galleries and also to the catalogue authors Melva Croal and Charles Nugent for working together to bring the exhibition to fruition.

Richard Gray, Director, Manchester City Art Galleries
Alistair Smith, Director, The Whitworth Art Gallery

Acknowledgments

An exhibition as large as *Turner Watercolors from Manchester* cannot take place without an enormous amount of preparation and forward planning. Those whose names follow represent only a proportion of all who over the last six years have provided support, advice, and encouragement, and we apologize to those whose names have been inadvertently omitted. Many people have contributed toward this exhibition and catalogue; for the errors and omissions we alone are responsible.

In the course of research for the catalogue, the staff at the Clore Gallery were unfailingly helpful; we would like to extend our thanks to them, and in particular to David Blayney Brown, Ann Chumbley, and Ian Warrell. Without their patience, understanding, and readiness to answer our queries, in the course of our many visits to the Clore Gallery Study Room, the catalogue would be altogether less substantial and scholarly.

The starting point for our research has inevitably been the two catalogues for the Turner exhibitions held in Manchester in the early 1980s, *Turner at Manchester* by Timothy Clifford of 1982 and *Turner Watercolours in the Whitworth Art Gallery* by Craig Hartley of 1984; we are grateful to both authors. Others outside our institutions who have helped with information, advice, and in other ways include Peter Bonollo, Michele Bower, Cyril Fry, David Hill, Ann Lyles, Jan Piggott, Cecilia Powell, Kim Sloan, Greg Smith, Ann Sumner, Bill Thomson, Andrew Wilton, and Andrew Wyld.

Staff at our respective institutions have also been most helpful. At the City Art Galleries, these include Richard Gray, Sara Holdsworth, Lesley Jackson, Sandra Martin, Fiona Venables, and particularly Andrew Loukes who made many helpful suggestions and contributed to the entry for Exeter, and at the Whitworth, Frances Bowers, Cliff Lomax, David Morris, who read much of the catalogue in draft and gave useful advice, Alistair Smith, Michael Simpson and John West. The conservation of the works was enthusiastically and efficiently undertaken by Jane Street at the City Art Galleries and by Nicola Walker at the Whitworth. In fact, there can be few staff members at Manchester's two main art galleries whose lives have not been touched in some way by this major project; we are grateful to them all.

Charles Nugent, Curator, Drawings and Watercolours, The Whitworth Art Galllery
Melva Croal, Curator of Art, Manchester City Art Galleries

Acknowledgments

J.M.W. Turner is among the outstanding artists I have most admired. His accomplishments in watercolor are particularly important for the formative thought processes revealed in the artist's larger paintings. Further, the exceptional beauty of these works weaves a glorious spell on audiences sufficiently fortunate to view them, endowed as they are in the artist's early period with exquisite topographical excellence, transformed in his later career into romantic symphonies of wonder, awe 'and passion.

The Trust for Museum Exhibitions is highly honored that the Whitworth Art Gallery and the Manchester City Art Galleries have collaborated to permit The Trust to offer a magnificent selection of 82 works from their collections to three distinguished American museums: the Memphis Brooks Museum of Art, the Joslyn Art Museum in Omaha, and the Indianapolis Museum of Art. The two collections from Manchester perfectly complement each other to represent the breadth and depth of Turner's entire watercolor oeuvre. The Whitworth's watercolors date primarily from his early career, with a few outstanding works from the late period, while the City Art Galleries' collection is concentrated on the later periods.

Any endeavor of the size and importance of the forthcoming Turner exhibition inevitably results in a debt of gratitude to the museums and to the many individuals involved in making the project a reality. It is a great pleasure for The Trust to acknowledge the splendid assistance and cooperation it has received from so many. Any errors or omissions in these acknowledgements are entirely the responsibility of The Trust.

The project began six years ago when Sir Peter Wakefield, Former Director of the National Art Collections Fund, and Director of The Trust for Museum Exhibitions, United Kingdom, introduced me to Alistair Smith, Director of the Whitworth Art Gallery and Richard Gray, Director of the Manchester City Art Galleries. Without their generous permission and cooperation, there could have been no exhibition. We cannot sufficiently thank Sir Peter and the two lenders. Since that propitious start, the staffs of the two Manchester museums have worked long and hard to organize the exhibition with splendid results. We thank each and everyone, even though we have not had the privilege of meeting them all. We are particularly indebted to Charles Nugent, Curator, Drawings and Watercolours of the Whitworth Art Gallery, who has been The Trust's tireless liaison with Manchester as well as one of the major authors of the catalogue, and to Melva Croal, Curator of Art of the Manchester City Art Galleries, the other major author.

Another vital ingredient in presenting any exhibition is the enthusiastic participation of the host museums. It gives me great pleasure to recognize the vital contributions of the Memphis Brooks Museum of Art, the Joslyn Art Museum in Omaha, and the Indianapolis Museum of Art.

The excellently designed and printed catalogue will be the living memory of this special exhibition. We welcome the opportunity to thank designer Judy Oser of Baltimore, the printing house of Balding + Mansell of Peterborough, England, and its excellent representative Guy Dawson, and editor Donald Garfield, for producing a beautiful book worthy of the subject and the scholarship there displayed.

Last but not least, I would like to thank those members of the splendid staff of The Trust without whose tireless and excellent work this exhibition would not have been possible. My sincere gratitude goes to Susan Peacock, Vincent Fazio, Stephanie Jacoby, and Linda Clous for a good job well done.

Ann Van Devanter Townsend
President, The Trust for Museum Exhibitions

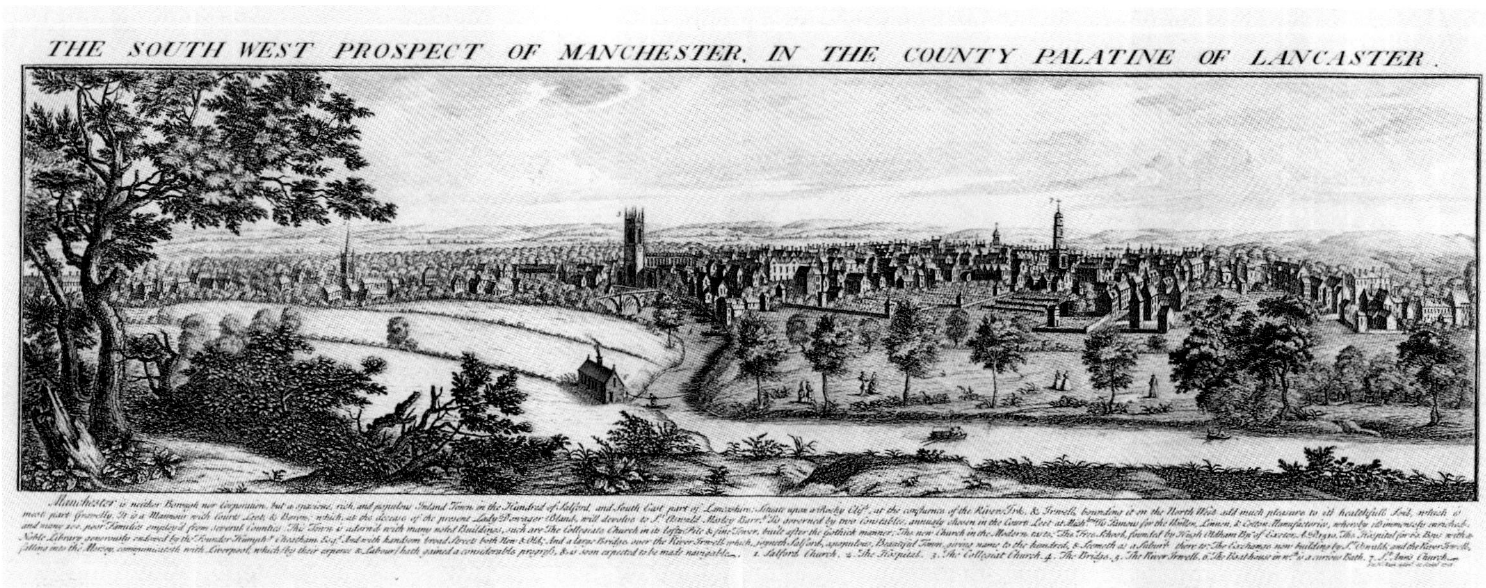

Figure 1. Samuel and Nathaniel Buck, *Southwest Prospect of Manchester* (1728), etching and engraving, Whitworth Art Gallery, University of Manchester

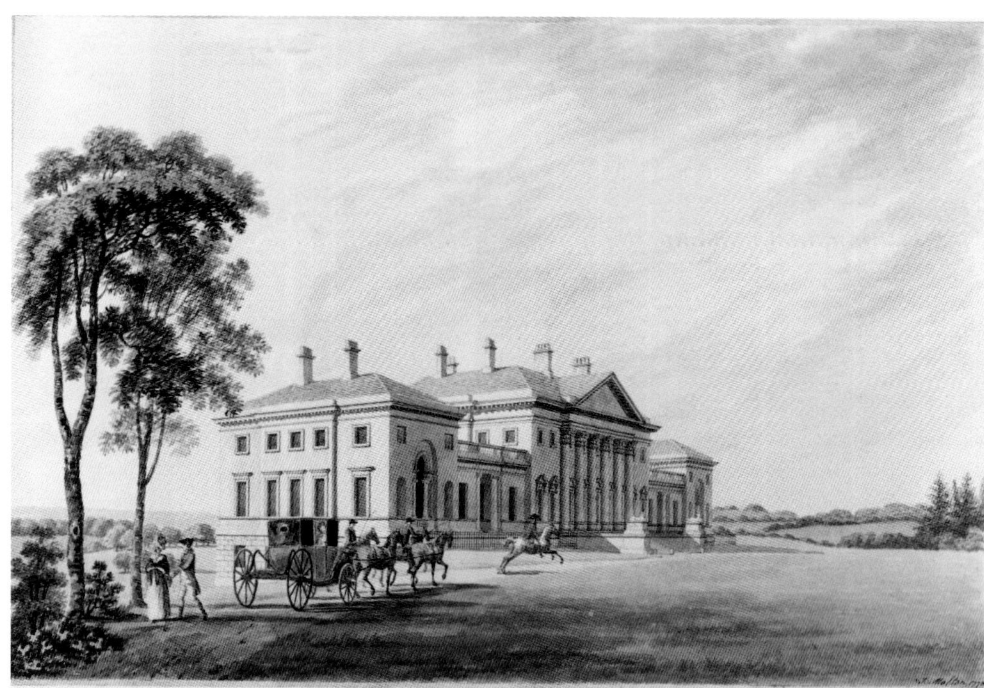

Figure 2. Thomas Malton, *Harewood House* (1778), pen and ink and watercolor, reproduced by kind permission of the Earl and Countess of Harewood, and Trustees of the Harewood House Trust

TURNER, TOPOGRAPHY, AND WATERCOLOR

CHARLES NUGENT

When one considers Turner's studies of the Venetian lagoon, which derive from his visits of the 1840s, it is hard to believe that these freely handled attempts to capture the fleeting effects of light on water are by the same hand that produced neat and precise views of houses and ruined abbeys in the 1790s. Not only is the handling of each group of drawings utterly different, but the coloring is so dissimilar, with the vibrant yellows and reds of the later studies contrasting starkly with the muted blues and greens of the earlier works. But, in spite of these apparent contrasts, Turner would have regarded both types of work as part of the same tradition and of his lifelong attempt to record the landscape and the role of humanity within it.

Turner began his career as a draughtsman working for print publishers, engravers, and antiquarians; he was what had come to be known as a topographer, and, despite appearances, his later work is just as much a part of the topographical tradition. This tradition had begun in the sixteenth century, and, from then on, meant the accurate depiction of a particular place or building; its origins were bound up with scientific illustration, cartography, and the depiction of country houses and estates, as well as with antiquarian desires to record the remains of ancient buildings. The cartographic and surveying background of watercolor painting in England is made clear by the fact that Paul Sandby, the only founder member of the Royal Academy in 1768 to be primarily a watercolorist, began his career as a military surveyor in the Scottish Highlands in the 1740s; he went on to teach military draughtsmanship at the Royal Military Academy at Woolwich one day a week for 28 years. It was part of the job of military engineers and surveyors to paint accurate watercolor landscapes recording enemy fortifications while on campaign, exemplified by the watercolors by Thomas Sandby, Paul's elder brother, of British military camps in the Netherlands and England, now in the collection of the Royal Library at Windsor Castle.

It is thus no coincidence that early depictions of country houses, towns and cities in some ways resemble maps; they frequently adopt a bird's eye view, and have a key for identifying the principal features in the landscape. This can be seen in the engravings by Johannes Kip (1653-1722) after his own and Leonard Knyff's drawings, which make up *Britannia Illustrata,* or *Views of Several of the Queen's Palaces also of the Principal Seats of the Nobility and Gentry of Great Britain,* first published in 1707 in one volume, and expanding to a third edition of four volumes in 1726. The engravings of Samuel and Nathaniel Buck, which comprise more than five hundred views of castles, abbeys, and urban panoramas, published between 1711 and 1753, frequently have an identificatory key, as may be seen in the view of Manchester from Ordsall, published in 1728 (fig. 1).

The majority of the images in these and later publications celebrate possessions (in other words, they were drawn for the person who owned the place depicted), and this remained a principal motive for topographical drawing. The practice of country-house portraiture was from an early date an important part of the topographical tradition, and Turner played his part in transforming this branch of landscape also. Comparison of two watercolors of Harewood House in Yorkshire, which remain in the collection of Lord Harewood, shows how Turner transformed this tradition of country-house portraiture, and yet remained firmly within it. The first watercolor (fig. 2) dates from 1778, and is by the leading architectural draughtsman of the day, Thomas Malton; precisely drawn, it shows a view of the house from the northeast, and with its clearly drawn pen and ink outlines represents the most refined manner of tinted drawing at this date.

Malton's manner formed the standard against which the Romantic watercolorists forged their own styles, and it is no coincidence that the greatest of these, Turner, began his career as a pupil of Malton, from whom he had lessons in architectural perspective. Turner's choice and treatment of subject matter in the 1790s frequently owe much to Malton, and it is probable that he knew of Malton's watercolor of Harewood when he was commissioned to paint the house in 1797; the similarity in viewpoint may well be deliberate in this second watercolor (fig. 3), as the pupil tries to outdo the master. Clearly, Turner's rendering of the subject is altogether more impressive than Malton's, technically more adventurous in its use of the medium and in the intensity of its color; the earlier drawing seems to belong to a different era. The manner of treating the subject matter has also changed. Malton records the house accurately, but sets it within a rather bland landscape, with token trees framing the composition on the left; a coach and four, which, with the accompaniment of two outriders, is surely the property of a gentleman, drives up to the door, while elegant figures converse beneath the trees. Turner, on the other hand, sets the house within a working landscape and includes a group of estate workers in the foreground, who have been felling a tree and digging out the stump. In contrast with Malton, who shows the house set in a landscape enjoyed by persons of refinement, Turner presents a more inclusive, yet still patrician, view of the house and estate, showing how the labors of the estate workers support the fabric of the estate and contribute toward the upkeep of the house and landscape. In terms of strict architectural accuracy, the watercolor by Malton is the more correct, but that by Turner gives much more information about Harewood House and its setting. Turner thus makes an altogether more complete statement about the role of Harewood House in the landscape, but remains within the traditions of country house portraiture.

Although in the 1790s Turner transformed the topographical tradition and reached the heights of his profession, he could only become a member of the Royal Academy, the most powerful artistic body in the land, by being an oil painter. Hence, from 1796 he began to exhibit oil paintings alongside watercolors at the annual exhibitions; he was duly elected a member of the Royal Academy in 1802. One might think that this meant that he would stop showing watercolors at the Royal Academy, but, although the numbers of watercolors that he showed did decline and eventually ceased in 1830, the truth is that he continued to assert the cause of watercolor landscape painting from within the ranks of the Royal Academy. Watercolor had traditionally been regarded as a lesser medium; it was normally associated with topographical landscape, on the lowest rung of the ladder in the Academic hierarchy of painting, as well as with being the medium most used for teaching amateurs. Turner, however, believed that watercolor could be used to treat the most serious and elevated of subject matter. This is shown by his exhibiting *Chryses* (Wilton no. 492, private collection) at the Royal Academy in 1811; it is a large watercolor and was shown along with four other watercolors and four oils. The fact that he had not shown a watercolor at the Royal Academy for five years and that he chose to exhibit a significant number in this year indicates that he may have been making a point, "showing his hand," as

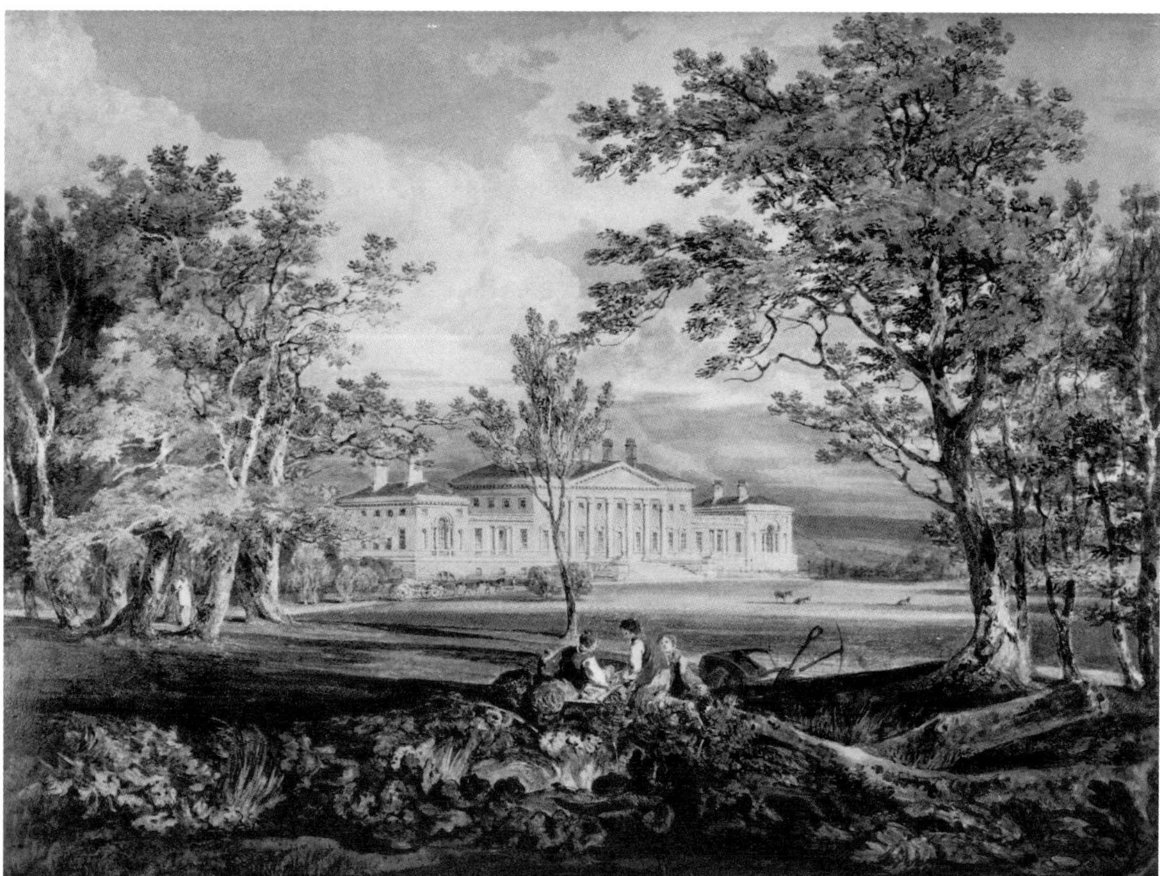

Ruskin was later to describe some of the Swiss views of the early 1840s. *Chryses* illustrates a scene in the first book of Homer's *Iliad,* where Chryses, the priest of Apollo, the sun god, prays to the god for the return of his daughter, who had been captured by the Greeks. The granting of his wish precipitates the quarrel between Agamemnon and Achilles, the story and consequences of which are the story of the *Iliad.* Thus, in *Chryses,* we have a watercolour being clearly presented as a history painting, depicting a crucial moment in a great work of literature; the way that watercolor is being used had come a long way since the 1790s. Also, the way in which the medium was perceived had changed greatly in the two decades. A review of the Royal Academy exhibition in *The Examiner* of June 1811 gave special mention to *Chryses,* ranking it with "the most celebrated painting of landscape," and another reviewer praised "the soaring property, and classical truth of Mr. Turner's imagination"; both these reviews are long and fulsome, but what is remarkable about them is not their length, but the fact that neither, at any stage, mentions that what is being described is a watercolor. This is a clear indication of how much the public view of watercolor painting had changed in the two decades. Indeed, in 1812, the following year, Rudolf Ackermann, the supplier of artists' colors, declared: "The modern art of painting in watercolors emulates the transparency of oil, and calculating its power from the highest degree of light to its deepest degree of shade, may almost vie with that mode of painting."

There often seem to be paradoxes and contradictions about Turner and his career. As is well known, he came from a humble background (his father was a barber and wig-maker in Covent Garden) and was unprepossessing in manner and appearance, but he was supremely ambitious for his art. He was a topographical draughtsman who wanted to paint history pictures, and he admired Reynolds, whose lectures he had heard as a young man, and who had placed landscape at the bottom of the hierarchy of painting, since it could never be considered a suitable vehicle for serious art. Turner, on the other hand, passionately admired landscape and wished to fight its cause from within the ranks of the Royal Academy; he wished to redefine it in terms that would admit it into the realms of serious art—his whole life can be seen as a campaign to this end. His attempts to elevate the status of landscape did not mean that he rejected his topographical background; on the contrary, he continued to stress the fundamental connection between landscape painting and the topographical tradition until the end of his life.

His espousal of the cause of landscape is intimately bound up with his espousal of watercolor painting, generally, and should be seen in the context of what may be termed the watercolor revolution that took place in the 1790s. During that decade, the way in which watercolor painting was perceived and practiced changed profoundly. At the head of the painters who brought about this change were Turner and his exact contemporary Thomas Girtin. Prior to this, the emphasis was on firm outlines and clear washes, leading to such work being described as "tinted" or "stained" drawings. During the 1790s, however, taking their cue from Turner and Girtin, painters began to build up the watercolor washes from light to dark in a highly complex and skilled manner, and to paint in watercolor rather than add color to a previously drawn outline. The progression from the carefully drawn view of Canterbury, exhibited at the Royal Academy in 1794, cat. 9 in this exhibition, to the large and ambitious views of Fonthill Abbey exhibited in 1800, such as cat. 20 in this exhibition, is readily apparent. It is clear that William Beckford, who commissioned the Fonthill watercolors, did not expect or want such technical sophistication, and the effects that Turner achieved in these works were not at all to his patron's liking (see the entry on cat. 20).

The elevation of the status of watercolor was most clearly evident in the foundation of the Society of Painters in Watercolours in 1804, which owed its origins to a group of watercolor painters who were unhappy at the way their work was being hung at the Royal Academy, either "skied" (that is, hung so high that no visitor could see it) or placed next to and dwarfed by a huge oil painting. In addition, watercolor painters were not admitted to membership of the Royal Academy. Turner was not a member of the Society of Painters in Watercolours, since, having been elected a member of the Royal Academy in 1802, he was not allowed to become a member of any other body, but he was undoubtedly an influence within the Society, and one of the founder members, William Frederick Wells, was one of his closest friends. The first exhibition of the Society of Painters in Watercolours in 1805 was a great success and became an annual event. A glance at the early catalogues of the Society shows some ambitious choices of subject matter, which clearly indicated how far watercolor painting had progressed since the early 1790s, when it was used by topographers to record ancient buildings and ruins. By the early years of the Society, watercolor painters were prepared to paint history pictures in watercolor or to deal with ambitious allegorical subjects. A good example is Stephen Rigaud's *The Genius of Painting contemplating the Rainbow,* exhibited in 1807, which is in the collection of the Royal Watercolour Society. William Henry Pyne, the artist and journalist, wrote in 1824: "The efforts that have been made in the watercolor department of landscape, and watercolor painting, before the appearance of . . . Turner and . . . Girtin amounted to little more than to produce correct views of abbeys, castles, ancient towns and noblemen's seats." There is a certain amount of exaggeration in Pyne's assertion, but it does reflect an awareness of a profound change that took place in the 1790s.

As mentioned earlier, Turner began his career as a topographer, but this did not mean that he disowned his topographical roots in his later career. If the aim of the topographer was to capture the reality and essence of the place depicted, then the mature Turner had essentially the same aims as the young artist of the 1790s. Turner's style developed at a prodigious rate and he learnt quickly from others; he consciously set himself to copy and emulate the work of other artists, in a spirit of competition that remained with him all his life. At the same time as he enrolled at the Royal Academy Schools, where he was only to be taught figure drawing, he began to work in the studio of Thomas Malton, the architectural topographer, whose influence was strongest in the early 1790s and lingered on for several years. By chance, the first watercolor that he exhibited at the Royal Academy, *The Archbishop's Palace,* Lambeth, has survived; it was shown there in 1790, when he was only fifteen, and was his only exhibit that year; it is now in the collection of the Indianapolis Museum of Art. The debt to Malton in the treatment of the architectural perspective is very apparent, but the figures that people the scene seem more lively, and certainly more diverse socially, than the token figures of elegance who are depicted in the watercolors of Malton.

In his desire to emulate and surpass the work of his predecessors and contemporaries, Turner was not averse to appropriating aspects of it that impressed him. As we have seen, many of his watercolors of the 1790s owe compositional debts to Malton, but it was the watercolorist Thomas Hearne who exercised a more lasting influence. Born in 1744, Hearne was one of the principal topographical artists of the previous generation, who unlike his rivals concentrated on the ruins of medieval buildings rather than contemporary houses; the main works by which he was known were the engravings that appeared in *The Antiquities of Great Britain.* The first volume of this work, containing 52 engravings, was published in 1786, and the second volume of 32 engravings came out in 1807. Since Dr. Monro collected Thomas Hearne's work in quantity, it is certain that Turner came across the man and his work at the Monro Academy (see cat. 3 in the exhibition). Aside from the fact that Turner watercolors resemble Hearne's at this date in style and treatment of subject (*The Old Welsh Bridge,* cat. 4 in this exhibition, is one such example), Turner is known to have copied several works by Hearne. There is an unfinished watercolor *Museum of the Priory at Haddington* (Wilton no. 73) at the Ashmolean, which is copied from a print in *The Antiquities of Great Britain,* and a second watercolor of Edinburgh Castle (Wilton no. 74) at the British Museum is also copied from a Hearne print. In addition, Turner's

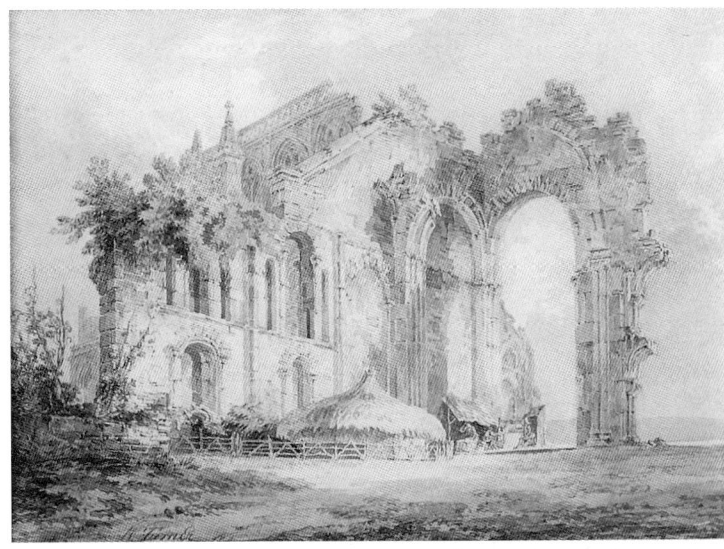

Figure 4. *Malmesbury Abbey* (1792-3), watercolor, Bury Art Gallery and Museum

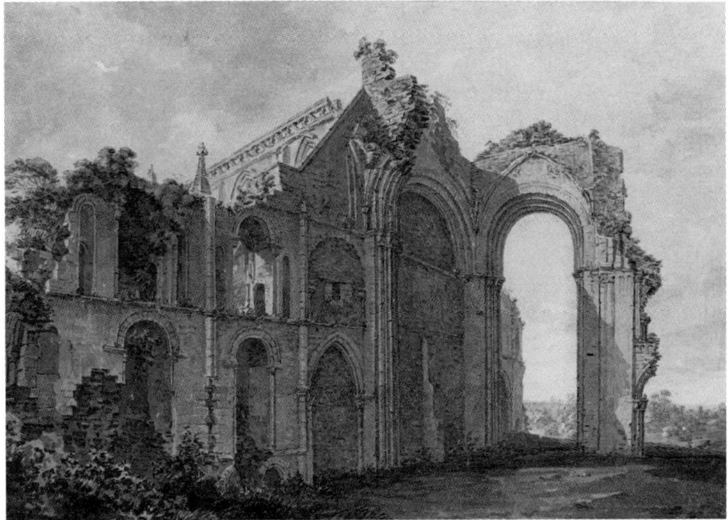

Figure 5. Thomas Hearne, *Malmesbury Abbey* (circa 1778-81), pencil and watercolor, The Syndics of the Fitzwilliam Museum, Cambridge

watercolor of *Malmesbury Abbey* (Wilton no. 26) at Bury Art Gallery (fig. 4) has exactly the same viewpoint as a Hearne watercolor of the subject in the Fitzwilliam Museum (fig. 5), which makes it hard to believe that Turner did not know of it.

Hearne's example inspired Turner not only in his formative years, but also there are aspects of his later work that show a debt to the older artist. The most extensive engraving project on which Turner worked was the *England and Wales* series between 1825 and 1837 (see cats. 48-54). It may only be a coincidence that two of the engravings, those of Barnard Castle and Ludlow Castle, are exactly the same compositions as the corresponding subjects in Hearne's *Antiquities,* but it is surely not a coincidence that the engraving of Carisbrooke Castle in the *England and Wales* series is very close to a watercolor of the subject by Hearne in the British Museum, which does not appear to have been engraved. The Hearne watercolor was presented to the British Museum by John Henderson in 1859, and almost certainly, therefore, belonged to his father, also called John Henderson, who was an amateur artist and a friend and neighbor of Dr. Thomas Monro. Like Monro, Henderson had a good collection of Hearne's work (his son's gift to the British Museum contained sixteen examples), and provided works from his own collection, as well as drawings by himself, for the copyists in the Academy to work from. Turner

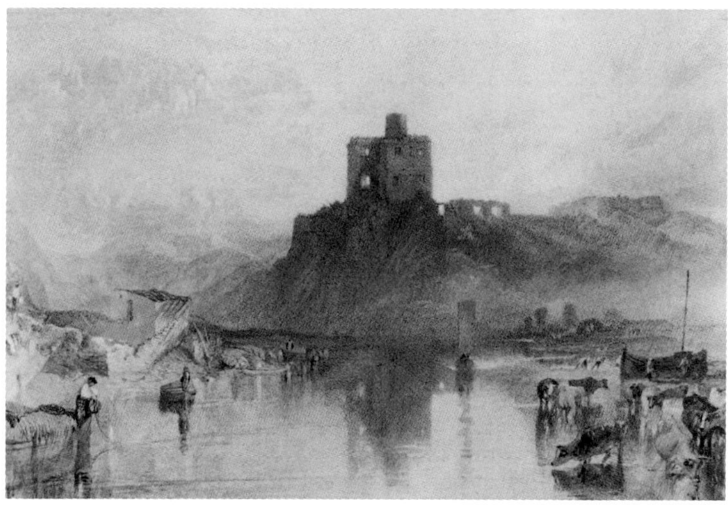

Figure 6. *Norham Castle* (1822), watercolor, Tate Gallery

probably saw the Hearne watercolor at this time, but by the late 1820s his memory of it may have been hazy, since the viewpoint for the *England and Wales* view is very slightly different.

In 1836, the young John Ruskin was moved by adverse criticism of Turner's painting *Juliet and her Nurse* to write a letter in defense of the painting, which the artist advised him not to publish. He did not actually meet Turner until 1840, but by this date was clearly already thinking about a more systematic and lengthy defense of Turner's late style; this was eventually published as *Modern Painters,* the first volume of which came out in 1843. Ruskin began *Modern Painters* with the intention of showing that Turner's late style was, in spite of first appearances, truer to nature than any other form of landscape art, which led him to examine the nature of reality, its perception and representation, and artistic truth. Ruskin refuted the idea that, although Turner trained as a topographical artist at the end of the eighteenth century, painting accurate views of towns and buildings, his later work, with its misty and atmospheric quality, its haziness that tends to obscure detail, is alien to topographical recording. Ruskin articulated the difference between simple topography (as shown in a reproduction of a drawing by Ruskin himself of the pass of Faido in Switzerland) and Turnerian topography (as shown in a reproduction of the 1843 watercolor, *The Pass of Faido,* now in the Pierpont Morgan Library, New York) in a famous passage in volume IV of *Modern Painters:* "Any topographical delineation of the facts, therefore, must be wholly incapable of arousing in the mind of the beholder those sensations which would be caused by the facts themselves seen in their natural relations to others. And the aim of the great inventive landscape painter must be to give the far higher and deeper truth of mental vision, rather than that of the physical facts, and to reach a representation which, though it may be totally useless to engineers and geographers, and, when tried by rule or measure, totally unlike the place, shall yet be capable of producing on the far away beholder's mind precisely the impression which the reality would have produced,"(*Modern Painters,* Vol. IV, in J. Ruskin, *Works,* Vol. VI, p. 35).

Thus, Turner's work from the 1790s through to the 1840s should be seen as a continuum, all part of his attempt to record the natural world and humanity's place, activities, and role within it. That Turner considered his later works to have just as much a place in the topographical tradition as his earlier renderings of the same subjects can be seen by the fact that he often reverted to sketches of an early date for reference. His *England and Wales* watercolor of Llanthony Abbey (Wilton no. 863, in the Indianapolis Museum of Art), engraved in 1836, is a reworking of a watercolor of 1794 in the British Museum (Wilton no. 65). The image of Norham Castle (figs. 6-7), which he first visited in 1797, remained with him throughout his life; all his depictions of the subject, the large watercolors of 1798 (Wilton nos. 225 and 226), the *Liber Studiorum* plate

of 1816, the watercolor of the castle of 1822 for the Rivers of England series (T.B. CCVIII - O, also recorded as Wilton no. 736) (fig. 6), and the famous late oil painting in the Turner Bequest (Butlin & Joll no. 512) (fig. 7) all derive from a sketch originally drawn in 1797 in the North of England Sketchbook (T.B. XXIV - p. 57). Andrew Wilton enlarges on the relationship between these and other treatments of the subject of Norham Castle in his Royal Academy exhibition catalogue of 1974 (pp. 172-4); his description culminates with a discussion of the final late oil painting: "Turner has dissolved his subject in sunlight, but he has not created an abstraction: the cow in the river, which he has retained from his earliest treatment of the view, reminds us that here, as always, he understood light and color as the means by which we perceive nature."

In recent years, and particularly since the opening of the Clore Gallery in 1988, no English artist has been so researched and had so many exhibitions devoted to him as Turner. His career has been analyzed from numerous perspectives, from the purely chronological to the thematic. Ever since Ruskin, there has been a tendency among art historians, critics, and amateur enthusiasts to gush when faced by a mature Turner watercolor. It may be as well to bear in mind that Turner is recorded as having said of Ruskin, "He sees more in my pictures than I ever painted," (J. Gage, *Collected Correspondence of J.M.W. Turner,* 1980, p. 281). The marvelous groups of Turner watercolors from the Whitworth Art Gallery and the Manchester City Art Galleries, which, when seen together, ideally complement one another, provide evidence of Turner's lifelong and ever-evolving attempts to record the world in which he lived. His remarks to a friend, as recorded by Ruskin, although originally spoken about the late oil painting, *Snow Storm - Steam Boat off a Harbour's Mouth* (Butlin & Joll no. 398), could equally well apply to any of the watercolors in this exhibition: "I did not paint it to be understood, but I wished to show what such a scene was like," (J. Ruskin, *Works,* Vol. XIII, p. 162).

Figure 7. *Norham Castle* (circa 1845), oil on canvas, Tate Gallery

COLLECTORS OF TURNER WATERCOLORS IN NINETEENTH CENTURY MANCHESTER

MELVA CROAL

On July 10, 1857, a large and fashionable crowd gathered in the library of Manchester's Athenaeum[1] to hear the eminent art critic, John Ruskin, give the first of two lectures on the occasion of The Manchester Art Treasures Exhibition. Works of art had been assembled from private collections throughout the land for an exhibition patronized by Queen Victoria and Prince Albert and attended by over a million visitors from England and abroad. No doubt the audience included subscribers to the exhibition, men such as John Edward Taylor, Samuel Mendel, John Pender, Thomas Ashton, and William Fairbairn, all prominent citizens and collectors of art. Also present were members of the Agnew family, the picture dealers who were largely responsible for the organization of the Fine Art section of the exhibition. They probably expected to hear some of the stirring analysis of art and praise of Turner that had made Ruskin famous. But that evening, and on the subsequent one, Ruskin chose to lecture on the political economy of art. He later published these two lectures under the title *A Joy Forever (and its price in the market)*. He explained that he took as his starting point the text that Mancunians had chosen to place over the entrance of the Great Hall of the exhibition, "A thing of beauty is a joy for ever."[2] He advised the rich citizens of Manchester to spend their money wisely and use it to preserve their heritage—the treasures they had accumulated. He urged them to encourage young artists by allowing them creative freedom in developing their work and to pay them a fair price for their labor. Reactions to his lecture in the heartland of laissez-faire capitalism were mixed, many people admiring the elegance of his style and others seeing the dangers in the implications of his message when applied to the economy in general.

Ruskin would have been known to his audience as the writer of *Modern Painters*, the first volume of which appeared in 1843. In it he praised contemporary landscape painters and particularly Turner. He was also one of a small group of friends and patrons of Turner who amassed large collections of his work during the artist's lifetime. When these collections were dispersed in the second half of the nineteenth century, they were largely acquired by a new type of collector—men from the new merchant classes, whose vigor in business was mirrored by their zeal for collecting. In their wake there emerged a powerful group of dealers to advise them. Of all the provincial centers that developed after the Industrial Revolution none was more dynamic than Manchester.

Manchester, like Leeds, Birmingham, and Liverpool, had well-established cultural roots stretching back into the eighteenth century. Its Literary and Philosophical Society was formed in 1781, by which time it also had several libraries and rising audiences for both the theater and musical performances. The visual arts were slower in becoming established, but the Royal Manchester Institution "for the Encouragement of Literature, Science and the Arts" (whose building now houses the City Art Gallery) was founded in the 1820s and became the focal point of cultural activities. It held regular art exhibitions and some of the greatest intellectuals of the century spoke in its impressive lecture theater. The Institution was initiated and supported by a group of prominent businessmen, including Turner's patron Sir John Leicester, who often contributed to the exhibitions from their own collections. In 1882 it was taken over by the City of Manchester.

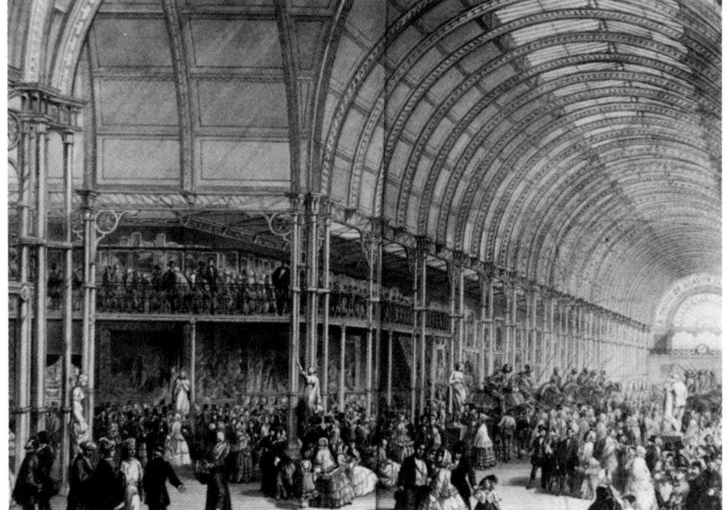

Figure 8. Interior View of Art Treasures Exhibition showing the Keats quotation above the entrance hall (1857), lithograph, Manchester Public Libraries

The new collectors were children of the original pioneers of the Industrial Revolution, coming from comfortable middle-class homes. They had enough money and leisure to take an interest in the cultural life of the community and to purchase works of art to adorn their newly built houses. The "Manchester men" as they became known were conscious that they were a new class in society whose new wealth brought responsibility as well as privilege. Their keenness to embrace British art reflected their confidence in their country which, largely due to their efforts, was becoming the richest in the world.

They were well informed both by frequent business trips to the capital, which could take in a visit to the latest exhibitions, and by the new educational institutions at home (for example, the Mechanics Institute[3] and the Royal Manchester Institution). The explosion of literature of all kinds—novels, pamphlets, travel books—was also directed at them. Far from being ill-educated and uncultured, as is often supposed, they were a new intellectual class responding to the latest ideas in literature and art criticism.

The difference between the new collectors and their aristocratic predecessors was their almost exclusive interest in contemporary art. Several of Turner's early patrons, such as Richard Colt Hoare, Sir John Leicester and Walter Fawkes, also collected Old Masters. Their taste was for art on a grand scale, with the type of elevated subject matter expounded by Reynolds in his *Discourses*, and they regarded the painting of still life and genre subjects as novelties of lesser value. Turner was also influenced by Reynolds and probably heard him lecturing in his youth, yet it was one of his principal achievements to challenge the hierarchy of the Royal Academy by campaigning for landscape to be accepted as an important subject in its own right. The new middle-class collector preferred subjects that would have direct relevance to his life; idyllic landscapes grew in popularity as towns and cities became dirtier and more claustrophobic. This trend was accelerated by the new-found ability of the

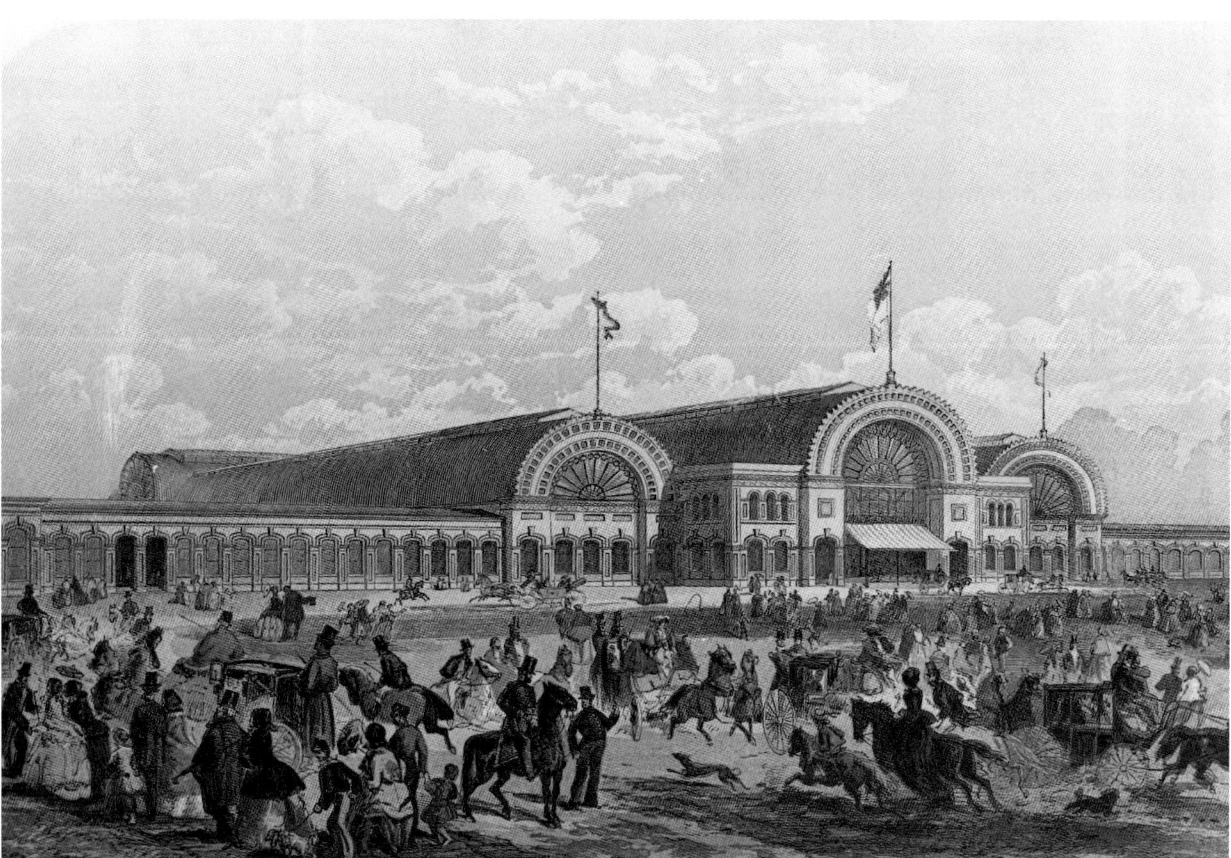

wealthy factory owner to escape to the countryside or overseas, well informed by a variety of guidebooks.[4]

The collecting of watercolors reflected a pride in a peculiarly British contemporary achievement. Although Turner's early landscape watercolors remained popular, particularly the *England and Wales* series, he had difficulty in selling his late Swiss scenes which had begun to appear dated.[5] With the advent of the Pre-Raphaelites more naturalistic and highly finished works became popular. Paradoxically this change of attitude was also due to Ruskin's preferences.

The critic's idolization of Turner meant that he often over-interpreted his works—Turner said that he saw more in his works that he had put in. Ruskin's horror of the modern blinded him to Turner's acceptance of trains, steamers, and industrial landscapes, and his imaginative proclivity meant that he was able to see in Turner's rough sketches the "workings of his mind," whereas he demanded in others a high degree of finish.[6]

The first volume of *Modern Painters* was published in 1843 and was dedicated to "The Landscape Artists of England." In this volume, and the next four, Ruskin used Turner as the yardstick by which all others, including Old Masters, were measured. A talented draughtsman himself, Ruskin saw art as the key to all other areas of study, and ultimately to communication with God. It was his evangelical zeal, his search for knowledge, and his insatiable curiosity that overflowed into his prolific publications, making him one of the most influential voices in the late nineteenth century. He lectured frequently in Manchester, a city he detested (see cat. 24). From art, his theories flowed into politics and sociology and may not, in essence, have been what Manchester audiences wanted to hear. Yet his message was idealistic enough to appeal to factory owners who, while employing men, women, and children for long hours and low pay, supported educational organizations for their workers, such as the Mechanics Institute.[7]

It was not only Ruskin's ideas that were influential, it was also how he was able to organize them which appealed to the practical Victorian mind. The way he ordered his own collection of Turners and that of the Turner Bequest to the Nation helped other collectors to formulate their own collecting patterns. His two gifts to Oxford and Cambridge Universities were selected to show Turner's progress as an artist. The way he broke down and analyzed Turner's style into five stages of development promoted a systematic approach to collecting, which was to influence the activities of both private collectors in Manchester and the formation of the Whitworth Art Gallery's collection of watercolors.

By the middle of the nineteenth century there were signs that the energy that was making Manchester so successful as a center of commerce was also making it the most important artistic center outside London. The Art Treasures Exhibition of 1857 (figs. 8-9) was a conscious attempt to emulate the Great Exhibition of 1851 in London. Later the Royal Jubilee Exhibition of 1887 was equally successful. Both these events involved collectors from the north-west whose collections were equal to those of the south. The detailed reporting of these events, and artistic matters in general, by *The Manchester Guardian*, whose proprietor John Edward Taylor was one of the greatest Turner collectors of the second half of the nineteenth century, kept the cultural life of the city in the forefront of people's minds.

Besides *The Manchester Guardian*, the other great force present in the city was that of the art dealers, Agnew's. It was a sign of the times that a skillful entrepreneur could drive a wedge between artist and collector and make a profitable living for himself. This arrangement often benefited the artist, who was pleased to make use of a dealer as an intermediary, thus saving him the tiresome business of selling his works individually and often enabling him to sell a whole studio's work as a job lot.[8] The dealer could also assist his client by searching out works that would suit him and often helped in forming his taste. The demand for reproductive prints from paintings was another lucrative sideline and the sale of copyrights went hand in hand with the works themselves. By the end of the nineteenth century the power of the dealers was such that they were allowed first refusal of paintings at major exhibitions such as the Royal Academy, thereby raising the price of paintings and dictating taste. The distinction between dealer and collector was often blurred. Joseph Gillot, the Birmingham collector who had made his fortune from the mass production of steel nibs, began by collecting rather dubious Old Masters and then diversified into collecting contemporary British works.[9] At one time he owned *Powis Castle* and *Windermere*, now in the City Art Galleries' collection but unfortunately not part of this exhibition. He mostly bought his Turners direct from the artist. He found a lucrative sideline in the buying and selling of copyrights for prints,[10] and dealt with Ernest Gambart, who was the most powerful print seller in England and evidently a fellow spirit. Following his death, the sale of his collection at Christie's in London in 1872 broke all records.

By comparison with Gillot, who was a collector who also dealt, Thomas Agnew, the founder of the firm of Agnew's was principally a dealer but also a collector of Turner. He managed to combine one of the sharpest business minds of the nineteenth-century art scene with altruism. He came from Liverpool to Manchester at the age of fifteen as an apprentice to the picture dealer Zanetti.[11] In 1817 he became Zanetti's partner and eventually took over the business himself. Zanetti had been a picture frame carver and gilder, and dealt with paintings as well other collectible items such as coins and medals, looking glasses, and scientific instruments (fig. 10).

From these diverse beginnings the firm began to achieve a higher profile in the fine art market, both through buying paintings and publishing prints.[12] They also bought seriously from the Watercolour Society's exhibitions and the Royal Academy. The first record of them buying at Christie's in London was in 1827, and from the 1850s onward they have been one of the auction house's main customers, right up to the present. They are still acknowledged as the principal dealer in Turner's work. Agnew's was almost certainly dealing in Turners in the 1830s and 1840s, although detailed records of the firm's activities were not kept until the middle of the century. The first record of them buying a Turner was in 1851. This was *Mortlake Terrace on the Thames* (Butlin & Joll no. 239), an oil painting that was sold to Thomas Ashton of Hyde, near Manchester, a cotton manufacturer whose family have been collectors for several generations and who have dealt continuously with Agnew's.

In 1861 Thomas Agnew retired and left the business in the hands of his two sons, William and Thomas, Jr. The firm's ability to take advantage of the boom years in Manchester meant that they could confidently expand into Liverpool and London. They were able to set up in London in 1860 with capital of £61,000, and on Thomas senior's retirement it was said in *The Art Journal*:

"The principal support of British art proceeds from wealthy Lancashire. Some twenty years ago, the merchant and manufacturers there were collectors of 'old masters'. They paid large sums of money for 'names' with bad pictures. Of late, however, fabrications of Titians and Raphaels made no sales in that district. Undoubtedly, the change was mainly effected by the judgment and energy of Mr. Agnew, whose perseverance has been rewarded by the knowledge that works of art are now the luxuries (they have almost become the necessities) of the rich men of that rich county; and he can justly claim the gratitude of the many who have prospered by the transfer of Art patronage from the dead to the living. . . ."

It was Thomas's eldest son William who was to become one of the most powerful men in the late nineteenth century art world, dealing in Pre-Raphaelites and other popular artists like John Linnell. His alliance with the print dealer Gambart made him even more powerful.[13] His importance as far as this essay is concerned, however, was his role in the establishment of the Whitworth Art Gallery. William was the organizer of the Fine Art Section of the Royal Jubilee Exhibition in 1887. A major international exhibition was planned with the idea of erecting a permanent institution from the profits. The exhibition was a great success and it coincided with the proposals to form a gallery with the £1,000,000 left

by the industrialist Sir Joseph Whitworth. The surplus from the Jubilee exhibition was transferred to the committee in view of their shared aspirations. It had already been proposed that the Jubilee funds should be spent on a collection that showed the development of English watercolors.

In 1891 the Whitworth Art Gallery opened with an exhibition of watercolors "illustrative of the Progress and Development of that Branch of Fine Arts in Great Britain." Fifty-four watercolors had been purchased with the Jubilee Fund including some significant works by Turner included in this exhibition (cats. 7, 14, 21, 32, 41, 37, 63, and 71).[14] From this time until the 1920s, works were bought mainly through Agnew's. William was the President of the Council of the Gallery as well as the Chairman of Agnew's. Today such an arrangement would be viewed with suspicion, but no suggestion of impropriety can be leveled at him. Indeed, the Whitworth has always acknowledged his energy and enthusiasm on its behalf.

A year later John Edward Taylor presented the gallery with a collection of watercolors that was to lay the foundation of this renowned collection. Unlike other northern collectors in this essay, Taylor was from an urbane, intellectual background. He was born in Higher Broughton, Manchester in 1830 (fig. 11) into a background of wealth and liberal enlightenment. His father, of the same name, was the founder of *The*

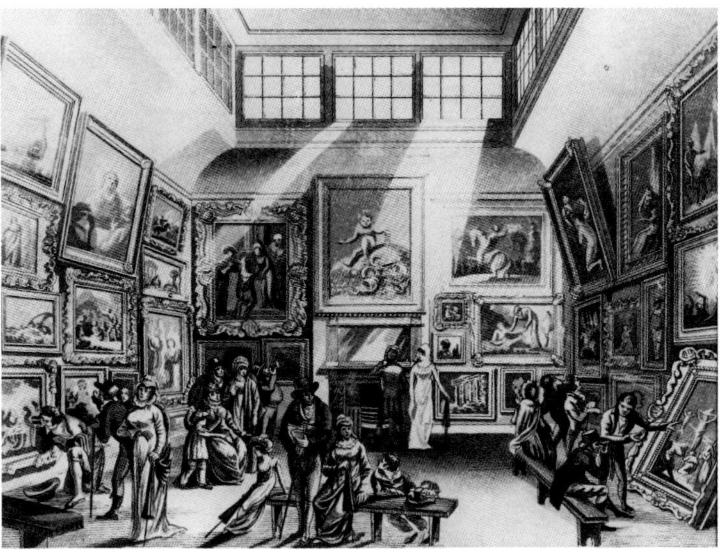

Figure 10. Zanetti's Art Gallery, Exchange Street, Manchester in the early nineteenth century, lithograph, Manchester City Art Galleries

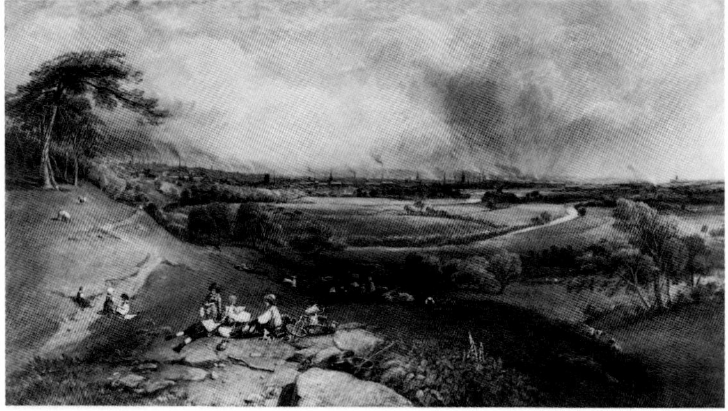

Figure 11. William Wyld, *Manchester from the Cliff, Higher Broughton* (1835), the suburban home of the Taylor family, watercolor, Manchester City Art Galleries

Manchester Guardian in 1821 (now the national newspaper *The Guardian*). After studying at Bonn University he returned to England and, by 1852, had succeeded his father on *The Guardian.* The high profile given by the newspaper to artistic matters and, by implication to collectors of art, gave much pleasure to Taylor's friend and fellow associate at the Whitworth Sir William Agnew. His magnificent collection of both fine and decorative arts showed taste and discernment, and when it was sold following his widow's death it broke auction records. After he had presented works to the Victoria and Albert Museum and the Whitworth, the residue of his collection included 101 Turner watercolors. His gift to the Whitworth Art Gallery comprised 154 watercolors, 25 of which were attributed to Turner. In 1895 Sir William Agnew, chairman of the Whitworth, reported that items had been selected "with a special regard to the aim of the Institute at developing the Exhibition of the History of Art of Watercolor Painting in England."

Taylor began collecting Turner watercolors in earnest in the 1860s, when he bought many works from Agnew's gallery in Exchange Street, Manchester. When *The Guardian* acquired additional offices in London in 1889, he moved to the capital, but by this date his collecting seemed to have lost its youthful enthusiasm. He lived in Kensington Palace Gardens (nicknamed Millionaire's Row), surrounded by his Turners, until his death in 1905. Taylor bought shrewdly and methodically. His interest in 18th century watercolors meant that he had sympathy with Turner's early works and was able to buy them cheaply when demand was low. In 1863 he bought *The Old Watermill*, 1794, now in the Whitworth collection, (not in this exhibition), which shows the influence of the picturesque style of Thomas Hearne on the young Turner, and in the same year, *Llyn Cwellyn*, c. 1798 (cat. 16). In 1864 he bought *Old Blackfriars Bridge* dating to c. 1795 (cat. 10) and a year later *Llangollen*, c. 1794 (not in the exhibition), another favorite spot for the picturesque traveler.

He then turned his attention to a group of Yorkshire scenes, perhaps because he was drawn to northern subject matter. Some of these were from the collection of Walter Fawkes of Farnley, Turner's greatest friend and one of the most important collectors of his work. He bought *Addingham Mill*, now in the City Art Galleries' collection (cat. 30) from Agnew's and also *Leeds* (now in the collection of the Yale Center for British Art). Taylor also bought two watercolors from a group of studies of birds painted for Fawkes, *Dead Pheasant* (cat. 38) and *Dead Partridge* (probably the *Grouse* now in the Indianapolis Museum of Art).

Works like *Dead Pheasant* showed his interest in odd sheets and rather obscure items. He was keen to show Turner's development, and was no doubt encouraged by his reading of Ruskin in searching for signs of the workings of the artists' mind evident in his sketches. This interest perhaps informed the purchase of works like *Sunset at Sea with Gurnets* (cat. 69), *Petworth Park, Sussex* (cat. 45), and *Sisteron* (cat. 66). Taylor also bought some of the late Swiss scenes, which Ruskin prized most highly of all Turner's works, but did not give any to the Whitworth as they did not coincide with the gallery's current collecting policy. He did, however, give a couple to the Victoria and Albert Museum. The two loosely painted sketches of sunsets are examples of a group of late works he obtained from Turner's studio after his death (cats. 79 and 80) and are further examples of Taylor's interest in Turner's late sketches.

Taylor also acquired a selection of the *England and Wales* series from Ruskin's collection. These included *Keswick Lake* (British Museum), *St. Catherine's Hill* (Yale Center for British Art), and *Warwick* (cat. 51). Some of these acquisitions, made during the 1860s, were resold very quickly, for example, *St. Catherine's Hill* and *Leeds*. Like Ruskin, Taylor often resold in order to acquire new works. His collection of the *Liber Studiorum* was most comprehensive and now forms part of the Bullard collection[15] in the Boston Museum of Fine Art. Again there was a rationale behind this, as he also collected watercolors connected with it, such as *London from Greenwich* (cat. 29), in order to show the progress of a work from its source to the finished product. Taken as a whole, his collection encompassed works of the highest quality from all periods and was particularly notable for including some of the acknowledged masterpieces from Turner's last period, for example, *The "Blue" Rigi* (Wilton cat. 1524) and *The "Red" Rigi* (Wilton cat. 525, now in the National Gallery, Melbourne).

In contrast to the systematic collecting of Taylor and Ruskin, the three donors of works in the City Art Galleries' collection, Dr. David Lloyd Roberts and James and George Beatson Blair, were more instinctive. They did, however, share Taylor's irrepressible urge to collect on a grand scale and their collections were huge. Dr. David Lloyd Roberts (1834 - 1920) said that his house was so full that he had to sell or swap works in order to house new acquisitions. This colorful character was born into a poor home in Stockport and rose to become an eminent gynecologist. W. E. Fothergill, a colleague, remembered him as standing: ". . . compact, alert, close-cropped, by his consulting room fire. There was a glass of milk warming in the fender, and amongst the instruments on the mantelpiece there were walnuts, which he cracked at intervals with explosive violence. Then there was the bowl in which all the filthy lucre he received must be washed before he would put it in his pocket on the way to the bank . . . ." His definition of gynecology as "anything either curable or lucrative" has become a classic, as well as his advice, "always take off your overcoat in a patient's house. If you are only there a few minutes they will feel you are not in a hurry."[16]

Fothergill goes on to describe Roberts' mania for collecting—that whatever their schedule and wherever they were, he would always be on the lookout for silver, china, glass, or incunabula, which he would gleefully carry home. Every working day until a month before his death he would drive in his old fashioned brougham (he never owned a car) from his home at Broughton Park to St. John Street in the middle of Manchester, "the little figure in a blue serge jacket, top hat jauntily perched on the back of his head . . . peering from the centre of the back seat" so that he

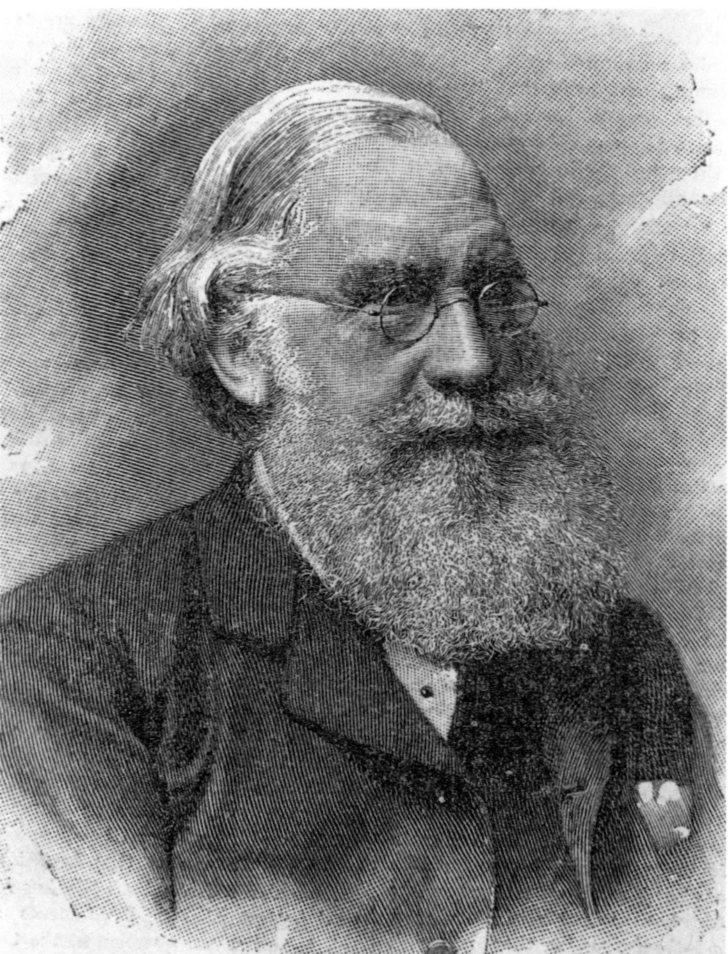

Figure 12. *Portrait of John Edward Taylor,* Manchester Public Libraries

did not miss the bookshops, silversmiths, or antique shops on the way. Even in the age of gas, his home was still lit by candles in order to protect his collection of watercolors.

In his will, Lloyd Roberts left items to the John Rylands University Library, Manchester, and the University of Wales, as well as a large bequest to the City Art Gallery including six Turner watercolors. These works, from various periods of the artist's life, were mostly bought from Agnew's at the beginning of the twentieth century. They include *River in Spate*, which is not part of this exhibition.

Compared with the exuberance of Lloyd Roberts, the City Art Galleries' other major donors, the Blair brothers, James and George Beatson, were more shy and retiring. Scottish by descent, they were partners in a cotton exporting house called Barbour Brothers, which was established in the early part of the nineteenth century in Manchester. The Blair brothers, including a third brother, Alexander, were bachelors who lived in Whalley House a few miles from the city center. Their home must have been crammed to overflowing, as following George Beatson Blair's death, the items from which the City Art Galleries were allowed to choose amounted to some 40,000.

James Blair (fig. 13) died at the early age of 54 and left all of his collection of 246 works, including 27 Turner watercolors, to the City. The collection was first shown as a whole in the City Art Gallery in June 1917 and took up four rooms. His elder brother, George Beatson Blair, gave a moving speech at the opening of the exhibition, remarking of his brother:

"In his business life he was one of the most practical and energetic workers I have ever known, and I am sure that had it not been for the relaxation and inspiration he found in his intense love for all that was beautiful in art and nature he would never have been the man he was. After a specially worrying day I would find him later in the evening in his bedroom, hung around with his whole collection of watercolours completely absorbed with his latest treasure resting on a chair in front of him."[17]

The pride of James Blair's collection was his version of *Heidelberg, Sunset* (cat. 70). The quiet sensitivity of his taste is reflected in his collection, which included works by David Cox, John Varley, and Peter de Wint, along with oil paintings by Albert Moore and Alma Tadema. His brother's collection was more adventurous in content, including works by Augustus John, Walter Sickert, and Philip Wilson Steer. Although many of their works were acquired locally in Manchester, the center of art collecting had now firmly shifted back to London and Agnew's gradually scaled down their branch in Manchester. They had decided to concentrate on their Bond Street establishment and in 1925 they opened a branch on 57th Street in New York. The last Turner collector on their Manchester books was T.A. Tatton in the 1920s and 30s.

Although Manchester benefited from the activities of some local collectors, other collections have been lost to the city. Sam Mendel was a neighbor of the Blair brothers in Whalley Range. In contrast to the modest proportions of Whalley House, Manley Hall was a palatial residence whose interior was known for its "eastern magnificence." Mendel was known as the Merchant Prince and was one of the wealthiest men in Manchester. His obituary notice in 1884 reminisces:

"On the breeziest and sweetest side of Manchester . . . Manley Hall became a palace of art treasures, with cases and cabinets filled up by the artefacts in precious metals. The flat terrain he broke into terraces and wooded heights; amidst which the lake glistened and the fountain sprouted alongside the crystal habitations of orchids and ferns."

It was said that Mendel had the largest collection of art in the northwest, much of which he acquired through Agnew's in Manchester. He had a liking for highly finished Turners but only *Carew Castle* (cat. 53) now remains of his collection in Manchester. He also owned works by

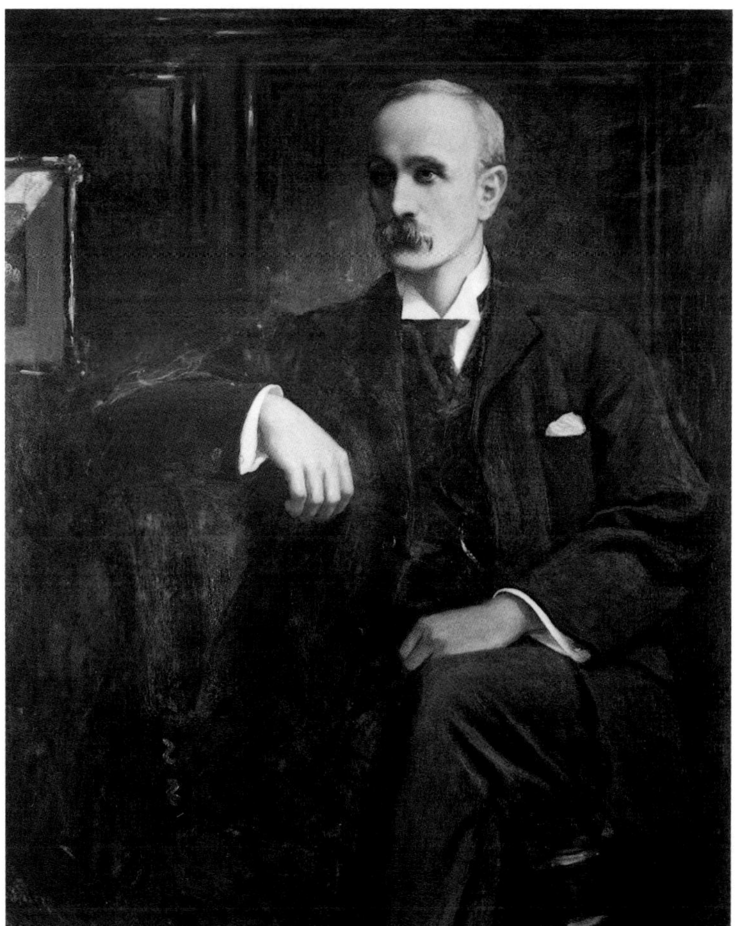

Figure 13. Thomas Mostyn, *Portrait of James Blair,* oil on canvas, early twentieth century, Manchester City Art Galleries

Rossetti, Leighton, Millais and Frith, along with many works by contemporary European artists; he took pleasure in changing his collection by buying and selling.

The Art Journal of 1870 (p. 106) describes Manley Hall: "While . . . the collections in London are literally stacked on the wall, and numbers of the gems are necessarily placed in obscure nooks, where it is impossible their beauties can be seen, Mr. Mendel's pictures are distributed in a set of spacious rooms communicating with each other, and forming a continuous gallery of considerable extent, the entire available space being covered by very valuable productions of the modern school . . . In addition to the paintings, there is a variety of water-colour drawings . . . these are arranged in portfolios, the entire hanging space being appropriated to picture in oil."

Mendel's father, Emmanuel, was one of the many Jewish immigrants who came to England from Germany after the Battle of Waterloo. He went on to make his fortune as a rope and twine manufacturer. Samuel inherited his father's fortune and flair for business. He became one of the largest shipping merchants in Manchester, but sadly the opening of the Suez Canal ruined his business and he died a broken man in Balham, London, in 1884. The sale of the contents of Manley Hall in 1875 did little to settle his debts. It started with five days for the wine cellar, two days of first editions from the library, sales of ceramics and silver, and finally the picture sale, which took four days. Manley Hall was bought by a coal merchant who tried to sell it to the city council, but they declined and the building and its park gradually deteriorated and the hall was eventually demolished.

Less spectacular in his lifestyle, and indeed known for his religiosity, was John Heugh of Firwood, Alderley Edge.[18] In Slater's *Directory* of

1863, he was listed as a merchant of Heugh, Balfour and Co., Portland Street, Manchester. As well as works by other British artists, he owned one of the largest collections of Turner watercolors in the second half of the nineteenth century. In 1861 he lent fifteen of these to the Royal Manchester Institution's Watercolors exhibition, along with the same number of works by other artists (for example, Samuel Prout and Clarkson Stanfield). He owned *Dunstanborough* (cat. 49) and, at one time, the 1798 oil version now in Melbourne. He bought *Carew Castle* (cat. 53) from Sam Mendel's sale in 1871 and also acquired works from Joseph Gillott's sale in 1872. In addition he once owned *Heidelberg, Sunset* (cat. 70).[19] In 1874 Heugh's collection was auctioned at Christie's under the name of the Holmewood collection, after the house he had moved to in Tunbridge Wells. It comprised 186 works. The 24 watercolors by Turner included *Dunstanborough* (cat. 49) and *Carew Castle* (cat. 53). The whole sale realized more than £60,000. Heugh had contributed a small piece about his collection to Thornbury's book on Turner,[20] quoting from J.E. Taylor's analysis of the progressive stages of Turner's style. Through Taylor and Ruskin, Heugh evolved a framework for his collection, although his taste seems rather conservative, concentrating on earlier works and particularly the *England and Wales* series.

Other Manchester collectors of Turner included the theater manager and entrepreneur, John Knowles; the business man and later Member of Parliament, John Pender; another Member of Parliament and owner of a major cotton spinning firm, Abel Buckley; James Worthington, who gave generously to the Whitworth and whose father-in-law, Henry MacConnell, was one of the first Manchester collectors to have acquired a contemporary collection worthy of national significance; and the Haworth and Brocklebank families who lived in nearby Cheshire but who had Manchester connections.

Finally, it is worth noting that many of the watercolors lost to Manchester now form part of America's most prestigious public collections. Few of Turner's oils or watercolors could be seen in America in the nineteenth century and those that were displayed testified to Ruskin's influence. The first exhibition of Turner's work was held in Boston in 1874 on the occasion of Charles Eliot Norton's lecture on his work.[21] By the beginning of the twentieth century American institutions began to be interested in Turner and many works from J.E. Taylor's 1912 sale were acquired by American collectors. In the following years many more Manchester watercolors were to cross the Atlantic. Of the ten Turner watercolors in the Boston Museum of Fine Art, five are from Manchester collections, while four of the ten watercolors in the collection of the Museum of Art, Rhode Island School of Design, are ex-Manchester, as are at least six from the Yale Center for British Art, four from Indianapolis Museum of Art, and three from the Taft Museum in Cincinnati. The John Herron Institute, now the Indianapolis Museum of Art, was one of the first institutions to purchase Turner's watercolors and drawings. They were acquired by the director, Professor Alfred Mansfield Brooks, in 1913, from the collection of William Ward and were part of a group intended to show the development of British watercolors. Two of the five early Turners from this group had been in J.E. Taylor's Manchester collection. Ward had been Ruskin's most able copyist and had later become a collector and dealer (see cat. 24). Professor Brooks knew of him from his former teacher, Charles Eliot Norton, Harvard Professor of Art History and an intimate friend of John Ruskin.

Ruskin and Norton had met in 1855 and formed an intimate friendship that was to last until Ruskin's death. In May 1857 Norton stayed with Ruskin in Oxford while the latter was preparing the two Manchester lectures with which this essay began. When Ruskin concluded by encouraging the merchants of Manchester to use their wealth and power to pre-serve the world's heritage, it was as if he were describing not the power of money but a sublime Turner sunrise: "Wealth well used is as the net of the sacred fisher who gathers souls of men out of the deep. A time will come . . . when this golden net of the world's wealth will be spread abroad as the flaming meshes of morning cloud are over the sky; bearing with them the joy of light and the dew of the morning, as well as the summons to honourable and peaceful toil."

It was this imaginative approach to Turner's painting that Norton was to take back to America and that inspired future generations to collect and enjoy Turner's watercolors.

Notes

1. Now part of Manchester City Art Galleries.

2. John Keats, *Endymion*, I, i.

3. The Mechanics Institute was founded in 1837 as an educational institution for the working classes and financed by local employers.

4. Far from being parochial and backward-looking as is often inferred, the demand for a more relevant and more naturalistic subject matter paralleled the Realist movement in France although the results were often quite different.

5. See Gerald Reitlinger, *Economics of Taste,* 1961. "What happened in the 1850s was something quite new. The conviction that Turner had been underrated in his own lifetime became so strong that even his followers achieved old-master status. This did not, however, include his later works." By the 1860's the prices of Turner's paintings had multiplied fifteen times and for watercolors the rate of increase doubled.

6. See David Blayney Brown, "Rule, Britannia? Patriotism, Progress and the Picturesque in Turner's Britain," in the recent *Turner* exhibition, Canberra, 1996.

7. For example see Julian Treuherz "Henry McConnell, Cotton Spinner," *Turner Studies*, vol. 6 no. 2.

8. See Evan R. Firestone, "John Linnell and the Picture Merchants," *Connoisseur*, no 182 (Jan-April 1973), for a good account of the relationship between artist and dealer.

9. In May 1848 he bought from Gambart six pictures including a Ruisdael and a Cuyp, for 2,018,880 pen nibs.

10. He owned half the copyright for Holman Hunt's *The Light of the World* (the Keble College version), which he called "that man with his lantern." For information on Gillott, see Jeannie Chapel in *Turner Studies*, vol. 6, no. 2.

11. His fellow apprentice was later his rival, John Clowes Grundy, who also had premises in Exchange Street, Manchester. Another relative of Grundy's had premises in Liverpool.

12. An early artist working for Agnew's at this time was Arthur Fitzwilliam Tait, who came into the firm at the tender age of twelve in 1831, and worked there for twenty years before leaving to become one of the most famous artists working for the American print-makers, Currier and Ives.

13. He shared his father's sharp business acumen combined with a strong sense of public spirit. An example of this is his purchase of Holman Hunt's *The Shadow of Death* (Manchester City Art Galleries) which he bought from the artist for £10,500 making it one of the most expensive pictures sold at that time. He and his brother made a huge profit from exhibiting the painting round the country and selling engravings of it. After having made their profit, they presented it to Manchester City Art Gallery.

14. Cat. 71 was not purchased from Agnew's.

15. Francis Bullard was the nephew of Charles Eliot Norton (see later in text). Norton encouraged him to collect prints of the *Liber Studiorum* and his collection eventually numbered some three hundred works.

16. William Brockbank, *Honorary Medical Staff of the Manchester Royal Infirmary 1830-48,* Manchester University Press, 1965.

17. *Manchester City News* of May 26, 1917.

18. See John Guille Millais, *Life and Letters of Sir John Everett Millais*, 1899, vol. II, p. 41. Millais said that the family was so religious that even the parrot said "let us pray."

19. Heugh was a friend of Walter Dunlop, a businessman from Bingley, Yorkshire, and a fellow Turner collector, (who owned *Landscape* [formerly called St. Martin's Precipice] (cat. 64), and their names often appear together in records. They were both patrons of Rossetti, who called Dunlop the "devil Dunlop." He became hostile to them in one of his more manic periods, mostly because he had not fulfilled his commissions for them.

20. Walter Thornbury, *The Life of J.M.W. Turner*, 2nd edition, 1897, p. 595.

21. The exhibition consisted mostly of Charles Eliot Norton's own collection, including prints and copies after Turner, and was held at the Parker Memorial Hall, Boston, April 23, 1874.

CHRONOLOGY

1775 Joseph Mallord William Turner born at 21 Maiden Lane, Covent Garden, London. The eldest son of a barber and wig-maker.

1789 aged 14 First known sketchbook (T.B.II) The *Oxford* sketchbook. Admitted to the Royal Academy Schools and at about the same time began working with Thomas Malton, known for his architectural watercolors.

1790 aged 15 First watercolor, *The Archbishop's Palace, Lambeth,* exhibited at the Royal Academy, London.

1794 aged 19 First Midland tour in order to make sketches for engravings. He and Thomas Girtin employed to copy drawings for Dr. Monro for about three years.

1795 aged 20 South Wales tour in the summer. Commissioned by Richard Colt Hoare to make a series of drawings of Salisbury Cathedral.

1797 aged 22 On his first summer tour of the North of England he painted Norham Castle for the first time as well as amassing material that he was to use for the next thirty years.

1801 aged 26 First tour of Scotland from June to August.

1802 aged 27 Elected a full member of the Royal Academy. Exhibited eight works including the oil paintings *Fishermen upon a Lee-shore in Squally Weather* and the *Egremont Sea-Piece.* First continental tour, visiting France and Switzerland. Sketched and took notes in the Louvre, Paris.

1804 aged 29 Death of his mother in Bethlem Hospital. Opened a gallery at 64, Harley Street, London to display his works. Acquired Sion Ferry House on the Thames at Isleworth. During the next five years the Thames was to become a constant source of inspiration for a series of naturalistic oils and watercolors.

1807 aged 32 First volume of *Liber Studiorum* published.

1808 aged 33 Probable first visit to the home of Walter Fawkes at Farnley Hall. Fawkes was to be one of his most important patrons as well as a good friend.

1809 aged 34 First visit to Petworth House.

1815 aged 40 Oil paintings *Dido Building Carthage* and *Crossing the Brook* exhibited at the Royal Academy.

1817 aged 42 Toured Belgium, Holland, and the Rhine.

1818 aged 43 Traveled to Scotland to research his illustrations for the *Provincial Antiquities of Scotland.*

1824 aged 49 Began *Picturesque Views in England and Wales.*

1825 aged 50 Death of Walter Fawkes, a bitter blow for Turner.

1829 aged 54 The oil painting *Ulysses deriding Polyphemus* exhibited at the Royal Academy.

1830 aged 55 First recorded purchase of a painting by H.A.J. Munro of Novar, *Venus and Adonis,* painted circa 1804.

1836 aged 61 Toured France and Switzerland with H.A.J. Munro of Novar. John Ruskin's first letter to Turner.

1838 aged 62 Oil painting *The Fighting 'Téméraire'* exhibited.

1840 aged 65 Met Ruskin for the first time. Third visit to Venice. The oil painting *Slavers throwing overboard the Dead and Dying* exhibited at the Royal Academy.

1841 aged 66 Visited Switzerland this year and in the summers of 1842, 1843, and 1844.

1842 aged 67 The oil painting *Peace - Burial at Sea* and *Snow Storm Steam Boat off a Harbour's Mouth* exhibited at the Royal Academy.

1845 aged 70 Brief visit to French coast.

1847 aged 72 The oil painting *The Dogano, San Giorgio, Citella, from the Steps of the Europa* purchased from the Royal Academy exhibition by Robert Vernon and presented to the National Gallery, London.

1851 aged 76 Died at 119 Cheyne Walk, Chelsea, and buried in St. Paul's Cathedral, London.

1 North-east View of Malmesbury Abbey, Wiltshire, 1792

inscribed: Malmsbury Abby [sic] on the reverse
pencil and watercolor
186 x 257 mm.
Purchased from Thomas Agnew & Sons by Charles E. Lees in 1891
Presented by Charles E. Lees in 1894
(WAG.D.1894.2)

In the summer of 1791, Turner went to stay at Bristol with the Narraway family, who were friends of his father. It was his first extended visit outside the London vicinity. On this visit, he spent much time sketching in the Avon Gorge at Clifton, and also traveled to Bath and Malmesbury. The sketches he produced on this tour are mainly in the *Bristol and Malmesbury* sketchbook (T.B. VI); this drawing is based on a pencil and pen and brown ink sketch on page 21 of the book, and was probably painted early in 1792. The Whitworth drawing, in turn, formed the basis of a finished watercolor of circa 1794, which was on the London art market in 1931 and is now untraced; it is not included in Wilton's catalogue, but was engraved in aquatint by R.G. Reeve in 1809 (Rawlinson no. 816).

Both the Whitworth drawing and the finished watercolor are illustrated and discussed by Robert Yardley in *Turner Studies*, Vol.5, No. 1, pp. 56-7. Sketches in the *Bristol and Malmesbury* sketchbook formed the basis for one of Turner's two Royal Academy exhibits of 1792, *Malmesbury Abbey* (Wilton no. 25), now in the Castle Museum, Norwich. In the following years, Turner produced a number of finished watercolors of Malmesbury based on the 1791 sketches; one that is close in style and size to the Whitworth drawing is the *Malmesbury Abbey* in Bury Art Gallery (Wilton no. 26), see fig. 4. Turner visited Malmesbury again in 1798 (several drawings of it are in the *Hereford Court* sketchbook T.B. XXXVIII), and the abbey, taken from a similar angle, was the subject of a watercolor in the *Picturesque Views in England and Wales* series (Wilton no. 805), painted circa 1827.

2 A Shipwreck on a rocky Coastline with a ruined Castle, 1792-3

pencil and watercolor
169 x 236 mm.
Bequeathed by Hector J. Towlson in 1969
(WAG.D.1970.54)

This watercolor was executed soon after Turner's first extended visit to Wales in the summer of 1792. It came after an initial brief crossing of the Severn to the mouth of the Wye in September 1791. Turner traveled up the Wye to Monmouth, across to Abergavenny on the Usk, and then north to Llanthony Abbey in the Black Mountains; he rejoined the Wye at Hereford and continued past its source into central Wales. His tour is attested by the survival of surprisingly few drawings, but one that survives (T.B. XII - H) shows that he ventured as far as Devil's Bridge over the Mynach river in Cardiganshire.

Whatever records he may have made at the time, this was the London-born artist's first visit to a mountainous region, and he was clearly impressed by what he saw. The watercolor provides evidence of this, and of the influence of the Alsatian-born painter Philippe-Jacques de Loutherbourg, who came to England in 1771 and was elected a member of the Royal Academy in 1781. De Loutherbourg, whose Christian names are usually Anglicized to Philip James, visited Wales in 1786. He had a fondness for dramatic subject matter such as stormy seascapes and rocky coastlines, generally with a dwarfed human element. His manner of painting was very unlike contemporary English work in its drama and scope, and Turner's attempt to embrace it is indicative of his ambition to transcend pure and simple topography.

This is one of several watercolors on sheets of similar size and subject matter executed in the winter of 1792-3; others are in the Turner Bequest (T.B. XXIII - Q, R, and V). The watercolor was bequeathed to the Whitworth as the work of de Loutherbourg in 1970 and was only correctly identified in 1993.

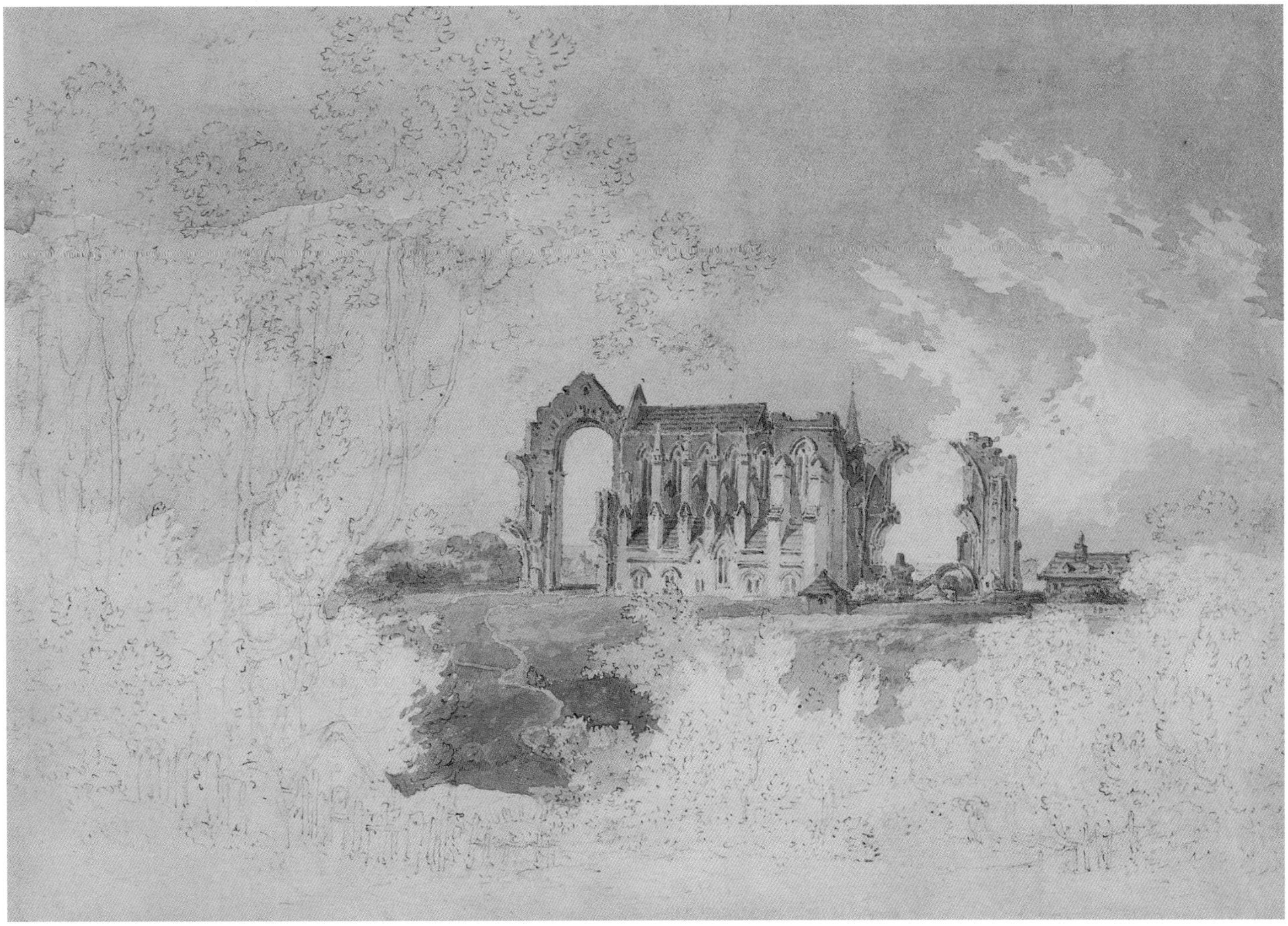

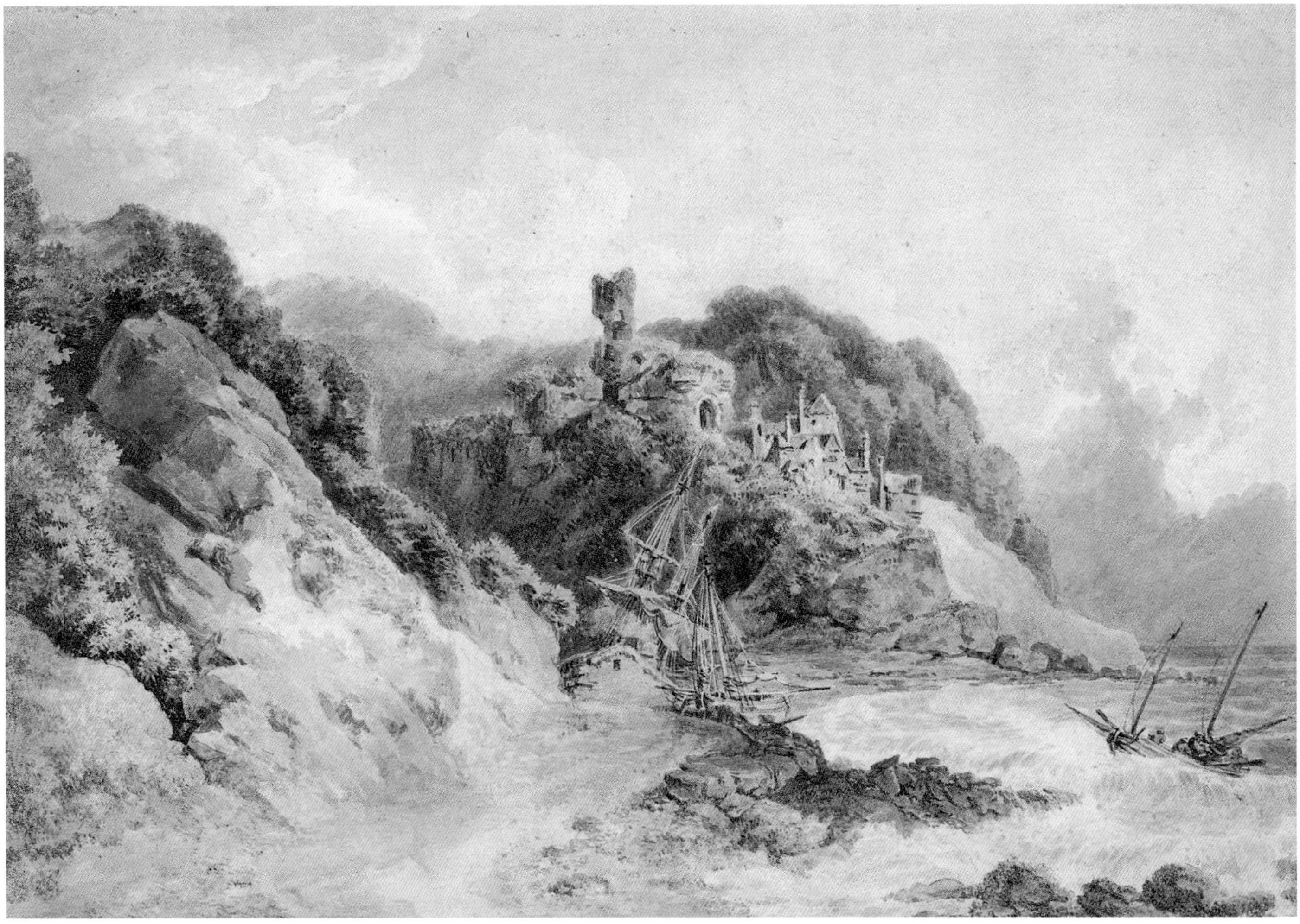

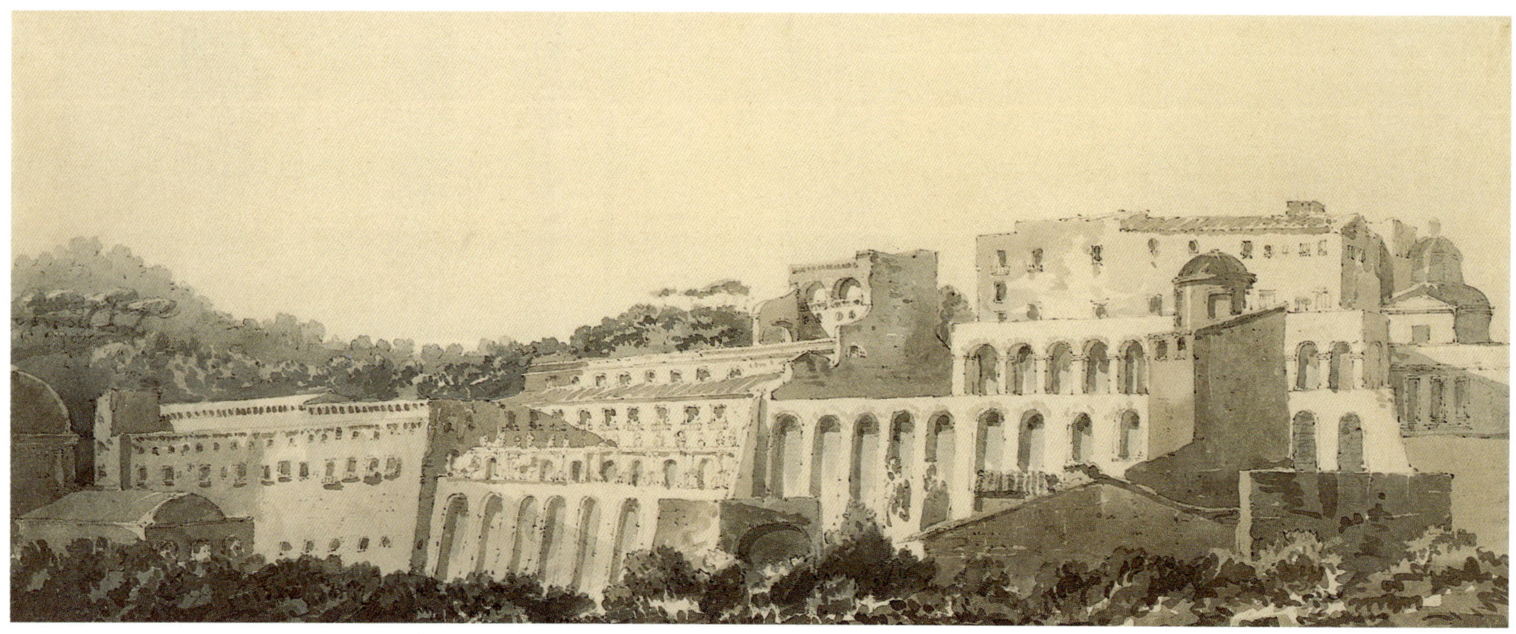

3   Thomas Girtin and Joseph Mallord William Turner, Convents near Capo di Monte, 1794-7

pencil and blue and gray wash, on
Whatman paper
177 x 417 mm.
Purchased from Thomas Agnew & Sons by
W. Langton in 1869
Presented by Miss F. M. Langton (via the
National Art Collections Fund) in 1963
(WAG.D.1963.1)

This drawing dates from the period in the 1790s when the young Turner was working for Dr. Monro in his so-called Academy. Dr. Thomas Monro (1759-1833) specialized in mental illness; he was also an accomplished, if repetitive, amateur artist and a rapacious collector of drawings. Farington recorded in his Diary (December 1, 1795): "Dr. Monro's collection of drawings by modern artists is larger than any I have before seen," and (April 14, 1797): "Dr. Monro's house is full of drawings. In the dining Parlour 90 drawings framed & glazed are hung up, and in the Drawing room 120." Probably in 1794, Monro moved to a house in Adelphi Terrace, London, and invited young artists to come there on winter evenings to study and copy his collection of paintings, drawings, and prints. He did this partly in order to help them learn, but mainly in order to increase the size of his own collection, since he kept the drawings that they produced. Some, at least, of the artists were paid for their evening's work, and Farington noted in his Diary: "Steers says Dr. Monro's house is like an Academy in an evening. He has young men employed in tracing outlines made by his friends &c. Henderson, Hearne &c. lend him their outlines for this purpose."

The romantic artist John Robert Cozens had gone mad in 1792 and had been consigned to Dr. Monro's care; at this time, his sketches became available to Monro, who used them as a source for the copyists at his Academy. Most of the Monro School foreign views therefore derive from Cozens' sketches, either in the six sketchbooks which record part of a journey to Italy in 1782-3 and are in the collection of the Whitworth Art Gallery, or ones now lost. This example is copied from a sketch on page 3v and 4 of Volume V of the sketchbooks (see fig. 14). The problem of authorship of many Monro School drawings, which vary substantially in quality, has been a source of confusion and contention, ever since they were included in Monro's posthumous sale at Christie's in 1833, which lasted five days. At the sale and since, many have had Turner's name attached to them, because he was the most famous artist known to have worked in the Academy. There were, however, many other artists involved in what may almost be termed a production line for watercolors, where little time was spent on each drawing. We know the names of some of the professional artists, such as Thomas Girtin and Henry Edridge, but there were in addition amateurs, members of Monro's family, and students whose names probably will never be known.

Also, to confuse the matter further, some at least of the Monro School watercolors are collaborative. Farington recorded that he had met Turner and Girtin at dinner on November 12, 1798, and they "told us they had been employed by Dr. Monro 3 years to draw at his house in the evenings. They went at 6 and staid till Ten. Girtin drew in outlines and Turner washed in the effects. They were chiefly employed in copying the outlines or unfinished drawings of Cozens &c&c of which Copies they made finished drawings." Although previously thought to be by Turner alone, it is now thought that the Whitworth watercolor falls into this collaborative category; the dot-and-dash technique of the pencilwork is very characteristic of Girtin. There are also other Monro School drawings in the Turner Bequest that have pencil outlines by Girtin. In particular, T.B. CCCLXXV - 20 is of similar proportions to this drawing and is a copy of the sketch *Convent at Naples* on the preceding pages of the same sketchbook.

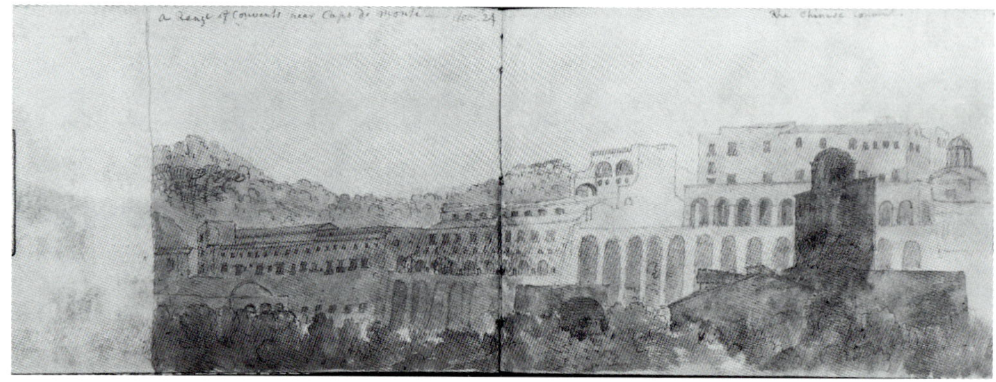

Figure 14. John Robert Cozens, *Convents near Capo di Monte* (1782), pencil and gray wash, Whitworth Art Gallery, University of Manchester

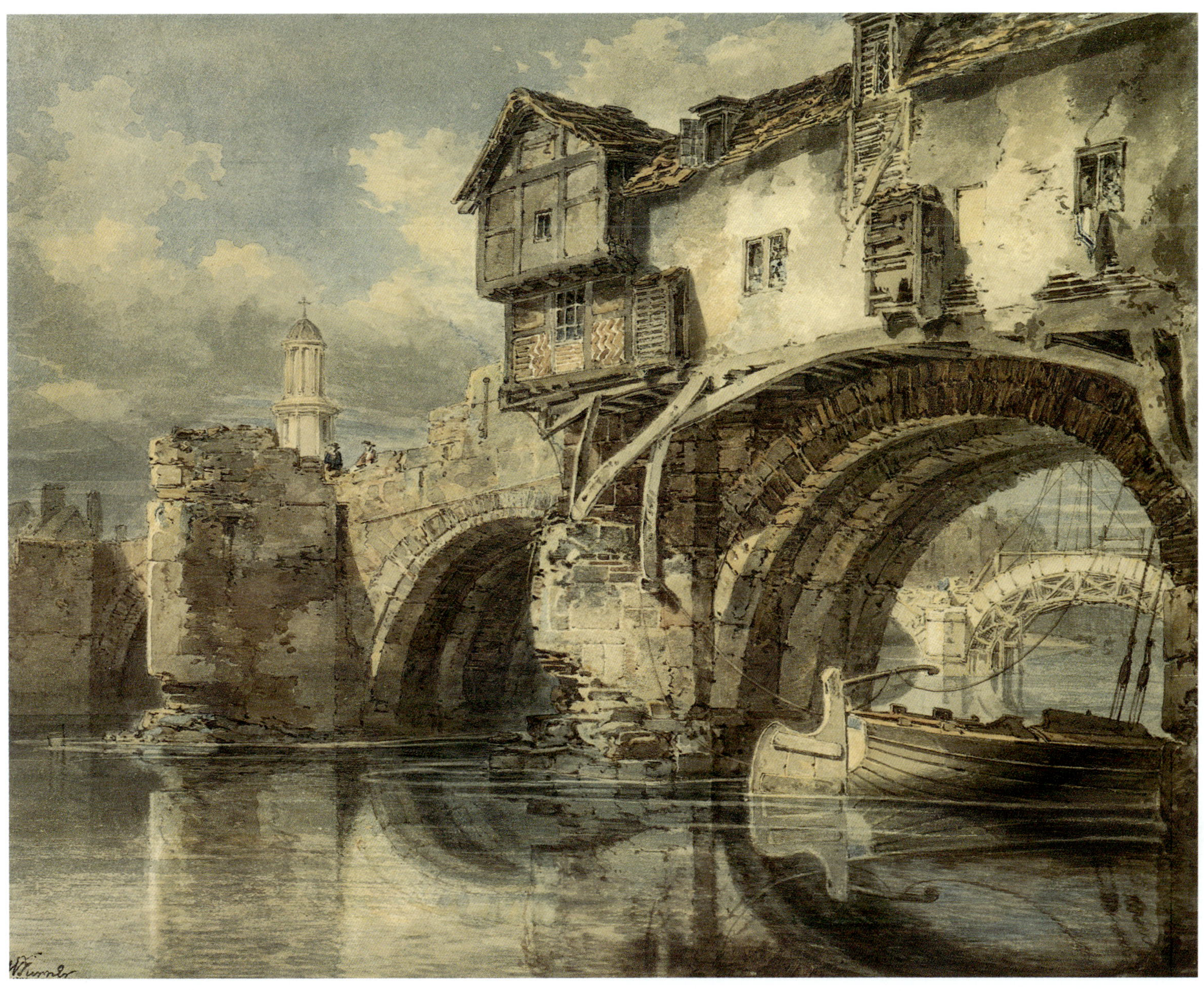

4   The Old Welsh Bridge, Shrewsbury, 1794

signed and dated: WTurner / 1794
pencil and watercolor
224 x 274 mm.
Presented by John Edward Taylor in 1892
(WAG.D.1892.90)

In 1793, Turner was approached by John Walker to furnish topographical views to be engraved in his *Copper-Plate Magazine*. Thus began a series of tours around England and Wales in search of material. His tour of 1794 took him through the Midland Counties and into north Wales, where he ventured as far as Valle Crucis Abbey, Chester and Flint Castle. The tour is recorded in the *Matlock* sketchbook (T.B. XIX), which has an itinerary at the front of it, and on loose sheets comprising T.B. XXI and XXII. The sketch for this watercolor (T.B. XXI- D) omits the figures on the bridge and shows no indication of the sky or water. The subject here is the Old Welsh Bridge (demolished 1795-8), while through the right-hand arch can be seen the New Bridge under construction (1791-5).

The idea of viewing a subject through an arch is taken from Canaletto's famous painting *Westminster seen through an arch of Westminster Bridge*, published as an engraving in 1757, which Turner would certainly have known in the collections of either John Henderson or Dr. Monro. Turner also made a sketch (T.B. XXI - E) of the other bridge in Shrewsbury, the English Bridge, which, although at the opposite end of the town, is frequently confused with the Welsh Bridge. Both bridges were favorite subjects of Paul Sandby. Turner's finished watercolor of the English Bridge (Wilton no. 136) is in a private collection. By the time of Turner's visit in 1794, the medieval gatehouse which figures in many of Sandby's drawings had been demolished, so Turner concentrated instead on the buildings at the other end of the bridge, deliberately juxtaposing their dilapidation with the building of the new bridge beyond. Turner's emphasis on the crumbling masonry, the coloring and careful depiction of the architectural detail reflect his knowledge of Thomas Hearne (1744-1817), the foremost topographer of the preceding generation, whose work he would certainly have come across at Dr. Monro's house.

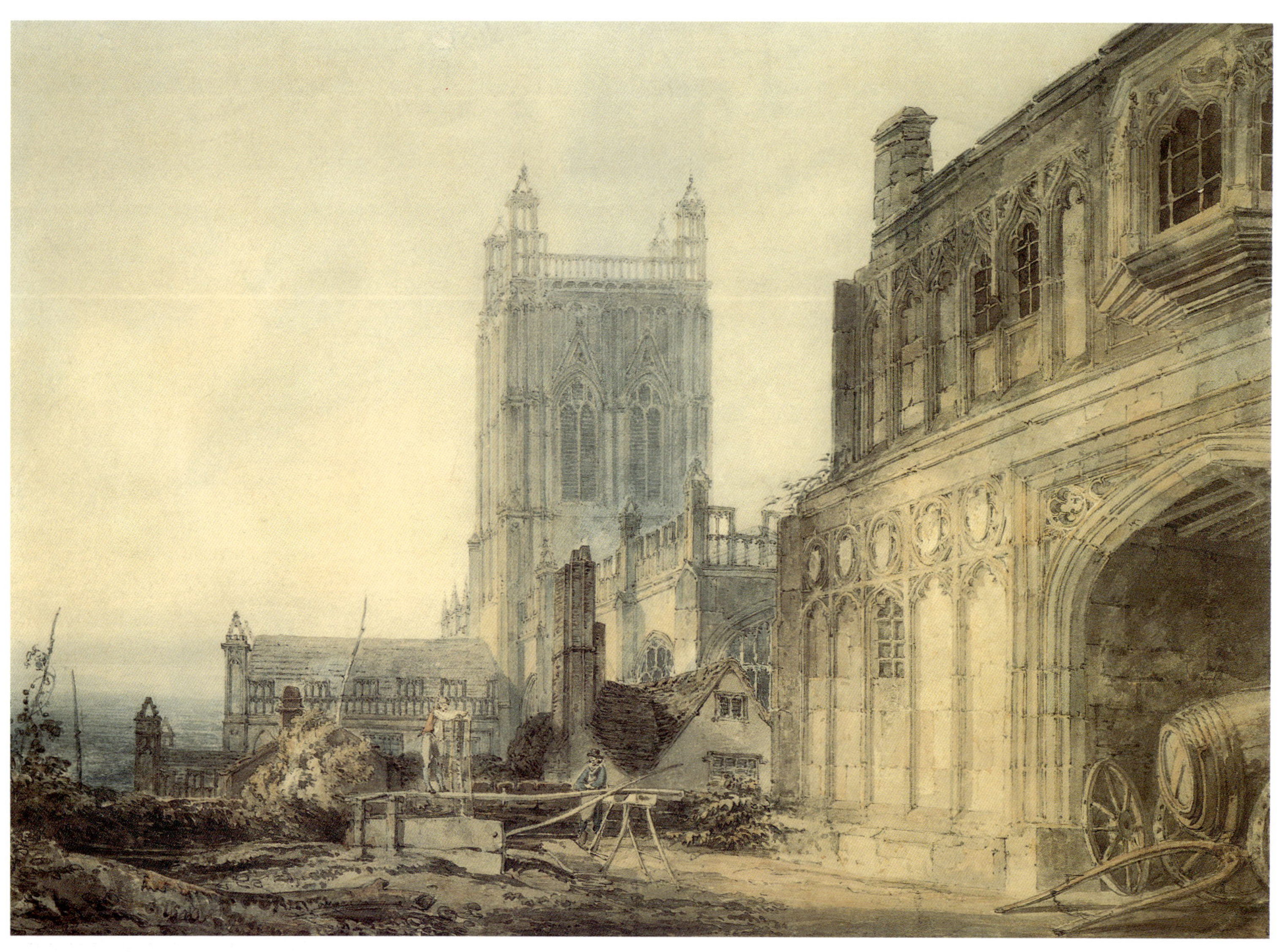

<table>
<tr><td>

5

</td><td>

Great Malvern Priory and Gatehouse, Worcestershire, from the North-west, 1794

pencil and watercolor
305 x 414 mm.
Presented by Theodora Winter
(in memory of her father Sir Thomas
Barlow) in 1984
(WAG.D.1984.2)

</td></tr>
</table>

This most recent addition to the Whitworth's Turner collection derives from Turner's tour of Worcestershire, Herefordshire, and Monmouthshire in the summer of 1793. Unlike the watercolor of the Porch (see cat. 8 in this exhibition), which shows the priory from the other side and therefore omits the tower, this watercolor derives from sketches, which did not form part of the Turner Bequest and were last seen when they were sold at Sotheby's on November 28, 1922, lots 127 and 128. Another very similar version of this composition, signed and dated 1794, was offered at Christie's on April 12, 1994, lot 53 (Wilton cat. 50); it also shows men sawing wood in the foreground but has an additional cartwheel lying on its side and a basket in front of the gatehouse. Interestingly, Turner used this composition some thirty years later for a watercolor commissioned by Charles Heath for publication as part of the *Picturesque Views in England and Wales* series (Wilton no. 834). The *England and Wales* watercolor is in the collection of Manchester City Art Galleries, and appears as cat. 50 in this exhibition. The earlier and later versions are shown here together for the first time.

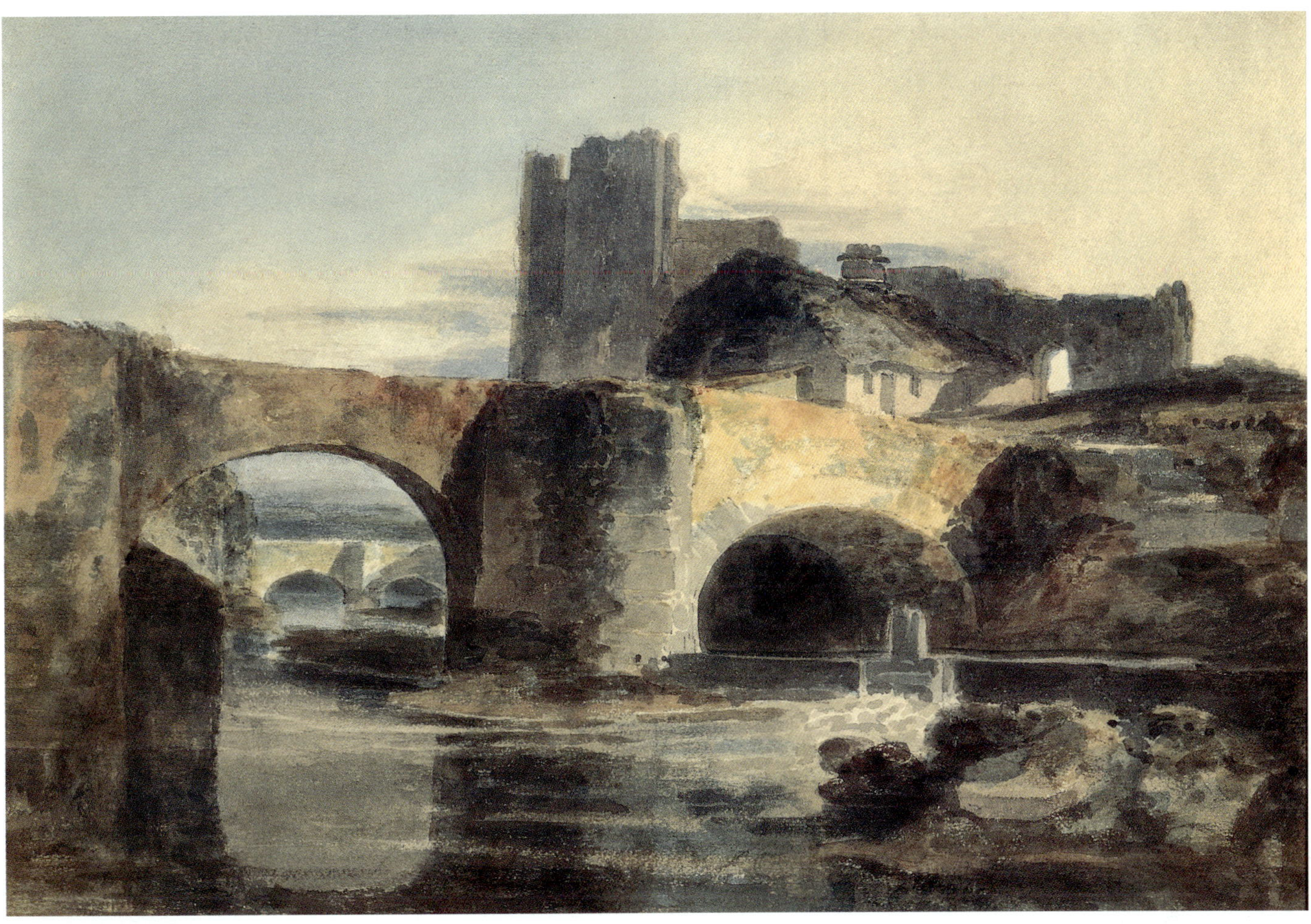

6 Brecon Bridge and Castle, c. 1795

pencil and watercolor
230 x 340 mm.
Bequeathed by James Blair
(MCAG 1917.92)

Previously catalogued as *A River and Castle with Two Bridges*, this watercolor can now be positively identified as a view of Brecon, South Wales, through a pencil drawing in the *South Wales* sketchbook (T.B. XXVI p. 91—fig. 15) and a finished watercolor *Brecon Bridge* that was recently sold on the London art market and is now in a private collection.

Brecon is an ancient site with a settlement dating to Roman times. The ruined castle, situated on the confluence of the Usk and Houdhy rivers was a favorite picturesque motif in Turner's time. The artist used the traditional spelling Brecknock he would have been familiar with in Boswell's *Antiquities*, a book which he had hand-colored as a young man.

The *South Wales* sketchbook was one of two Turner took with him on his 1795 tour of Wales. Andrew Wilton, in his catalogue *Turner in Wales*, 1984, has pointed out that it was on this trip that he began a practice which he continued throughout his life. This was the use of a small sketchbook for quick jottings and a larger one for more considered work, often in color, which he could show to prospective clients. The covers and first pages of the *South Wales* sketchbook are filled with notes in two different hands and include details of commissions. It would appear that Turner got a friend or relative to copy information from guidebooks that he would later annotate. He therefore used his sketch books not just as a visual aid but as a practical record of places and commissions that he gradually built up as a reference library. Against "Brecknock" on page three of his itinerary he noted "3 bridges and a castle x Golden Lion Inn." The commissions were presumably noted on his return. On page five among the "order'd drawings" there were five works for a Mr. Lambirt including "Brecknock" which was to be made the "size of the sketch." None of the other four works has been traced but orders for Mr. Lambirt are also noted by Turner after his 1797 North of England tour.

Given that there is a pencil drawing and a finished watercolor ("the size of the sketch"), Manchester's version, which is slightly larger, is a puzzle. Because of its heavy, opaque style and its size, it was previously thought to be one of the missing pages of the *Hereford Court* sketchbook of 1798 (see cats. 15 and 22), but in view of its identification and probable earlier date this is no longer tenable. Parts of the work are clumsily executed, particularly the bottom right hand side. It is possible that this is the work of one of Turner's students he had at the time, or a combined effort, but the feeling for form and light, particularly as it plays on the old stonework of the bridge in the foreground, has a sensitivity and authority which has led to its acceptance as part of Turner's oeuvre. It could be seen as an intermediary stage between the rather fussy, picturesque style of the pencil drawing and the classical grandeur and simplicity of the finished work, which, with its sunset glow and addition of two Italianate figures on the bridge, is reminiscent of the work of the Welsh artist, Richard Wilson, whom Turner much admired and who is often seen as the father of British landscape painting.

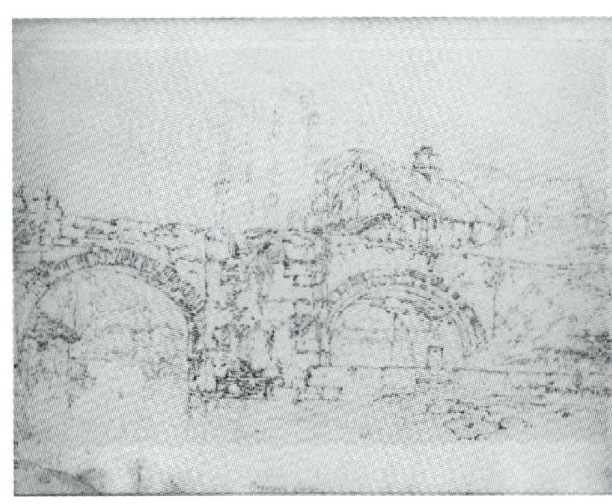

Figure 15. J.M.W. Turner, *Brecon Bridge and Castle,* pencil, Tate Gallery

7   **Magdalen Tower and Bridge, Oxford, 1794**

signed and dated: 1794 Turner
pencil and watercolor
286 x 222 mm.
Purchased from Thomas Agnew & Sons in 1891 with a fund presented by the Guarantors of the 1887 Manchester Royal Jubilee Exhibition
(WAG.D.1887.6)

This is one of several watercolors of Oxford based on sketches made in the summers of 1792 and 1793 (Wilton nos. 68-72). The quite slight pencil sketch for this watercolor (T.B. XI - B) is inscribed "Magdalen Colledge" and "Water Dark"; it is mainly architectural, does not include the boat or the figures, and shows no indication of the sky or water apart from the written inscription. A watercolor of the same composition, which is virtually identical in size, is in the British Museum (Wilton no. 70); it came from the collection of John Henderson, who was Dr. Monro's neighbor in Adelphi Terrace and whom Turner certainly knew.

Wilton (1979) suggested that the Whitworth drawing is a replica of the one in the British Museum, but Hartley (1984), following Finberg (1909), contended that the reverse is the case. The Whitworth drawing fol-lows the pencil sketch more closely, especially in the architectural detail. Also, the tree on the left spreads its branches further to the right in the pencil sketch. These branches are visible as pencil marks in the sky of the Whitworth drawing, but they have not been painted in watercolor; the British Museum drawing merely reproduces the watercolor of the Whitworth version, suggesting that it is later. As in the *St. Anselm's Chapel* watercolor (cat. 9), Turner's training under Thomas Malton is recalled here by his getting right under the motif and his bold juxtaposition of verticals and diagonals. Turner was later to produce between 1798 and 1804 a series of watercolors of Oxford subjects for reproduction in the *Oxford Almanack* (Wilton nos. 295-304, now in the Ashmolean Museum, Oxford), and two oil paintings of the city in 1810 and 1812 (Butlin & Joll nos. 102 and 125).

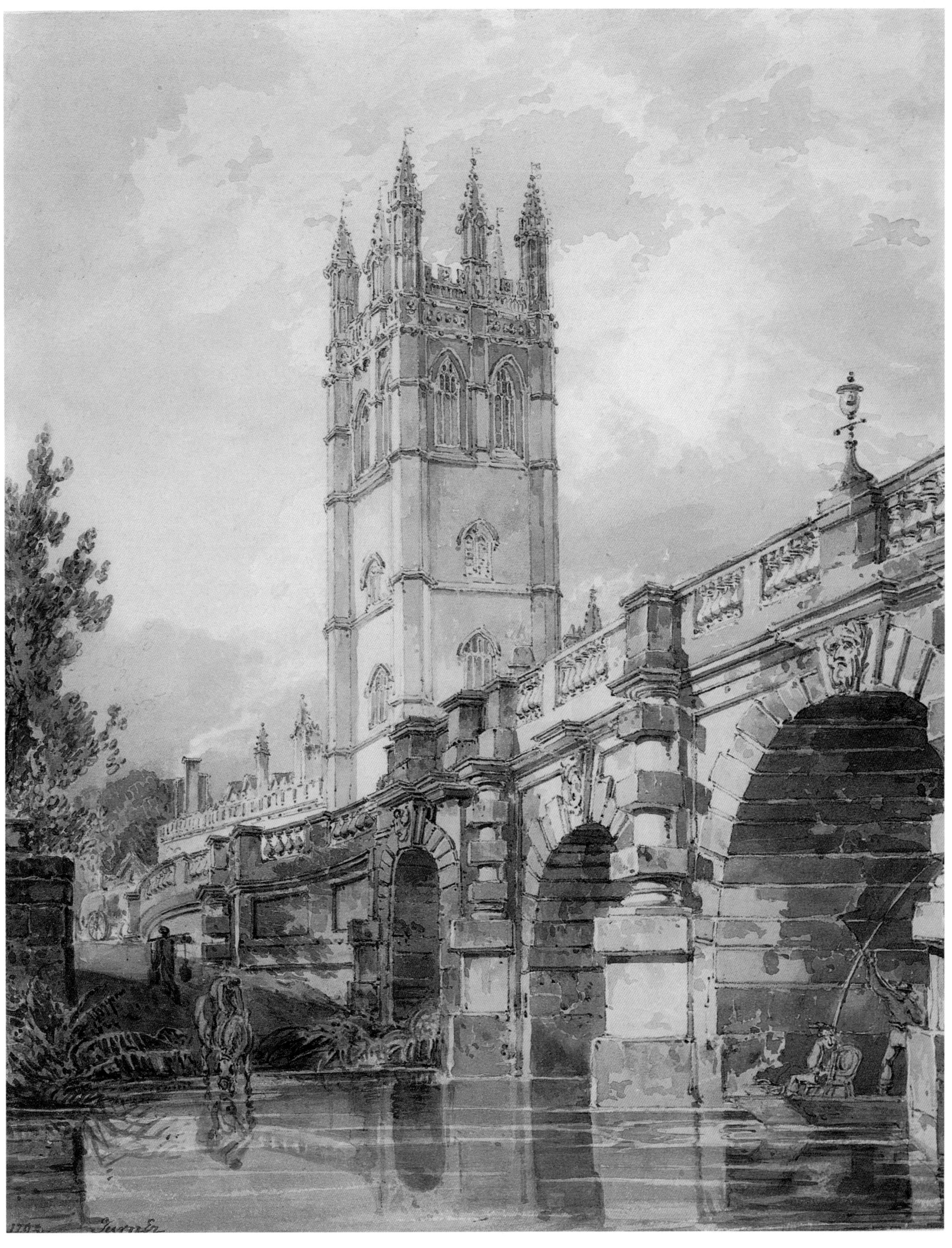

29

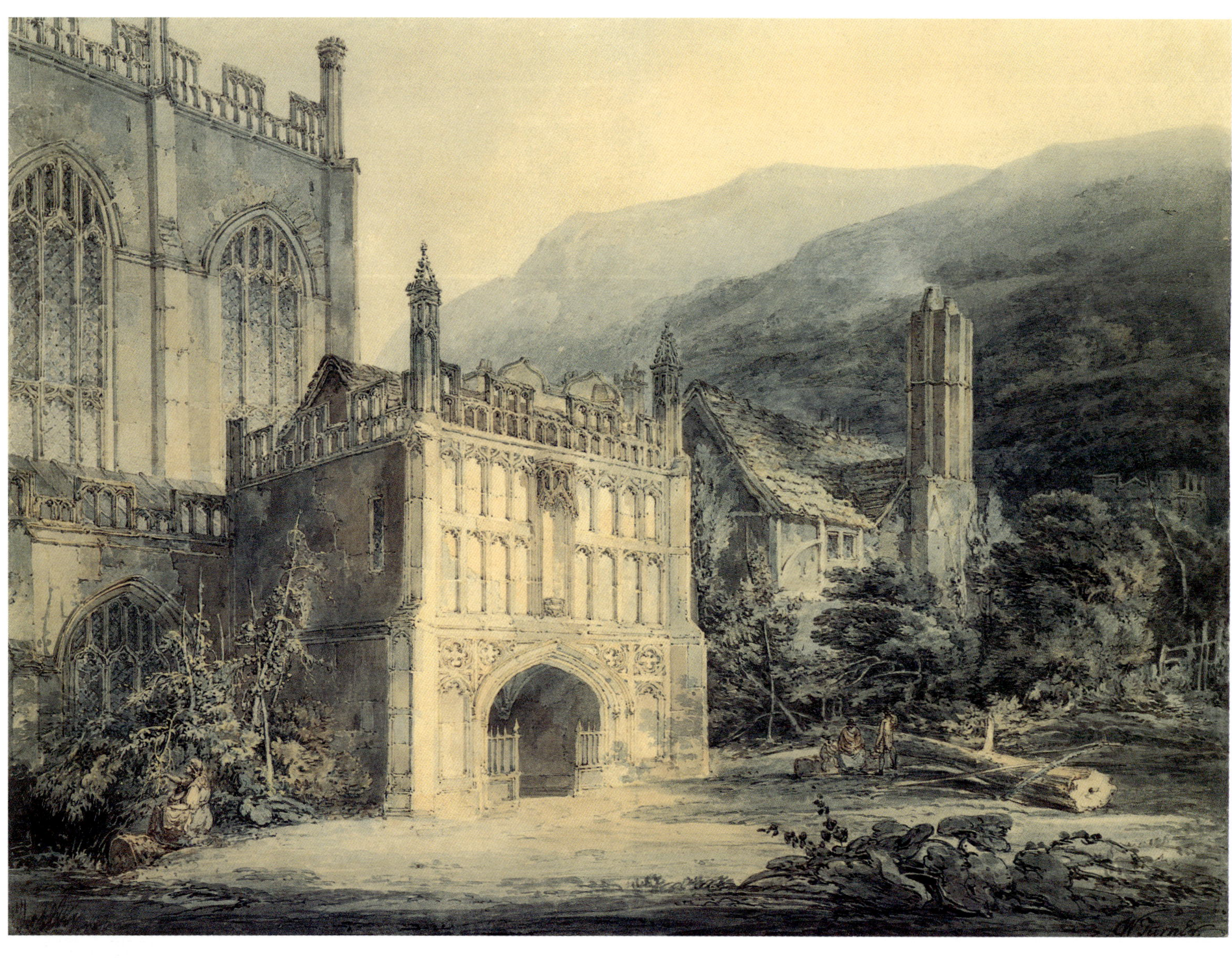

8   The Porch of Great Malvern Priory, Worcestershire, 1794

signed: WTurner
pencil and watercolor
231 x 429 mm.
Probably purchased from John Heugh by
Thomas Agnew & Sons in 1862
Purchased from Thomas Agnew & Sons by
J. Smith in 1862
Purchased from J. Smith by Thomas
Agnew & Sons in 1870
Purchased from Thomas Agnew & Sons by
James Worthington in 1870
Bequeathed by Mary Worthington in 1904
(WAG.D.1904.10)

This drawing also derives from Turner's tour of
Worcestershire, Herefordshire, and
Monmouthshire in the summer of 1793; no
sketchbooks survive from this tour, although a
number of the drawings listed by Finberg
under T.B. XII and XIII were probably made
during the course of it. This watercolor derives
from a large pencil sketch (T.B. XIII - D) and
was exhibited at the Royal Academy in 1794,
no. 336, along with four other watercolors, one
of which was *St. Anselm's Chapel, Canterbury
Cathedral, with part of Thomas-a-Becket's Crown*—
cat. 9 in this exhibition.

There are a number of other watercolors
of Great Malvern Priory, including cat. 5 in this
exhibition and a watercolor offered at Christie's
on April 12, 1994, lot 53. At least three other
drawings of the subject are recorded in nineteenth century collections, but remain untraced
and are not mentioned in Wilton's catalogue.
Turner's Royal Academy exhibits of 1794
attracted the attention of the press for the first
time, and the *Morning Post* reviewer called them
"among the best in the present exhibition: they
are the productions of a very young artist, and
give strong indications of first-rate ability; the
character of Gothic architecture is most happily
presented, and its profusion of minute parts
massed with judgment and tinctured with truth
and fidelity. . . . This present effort evinces an
eye for nature, which should scorn to look to
any other source."

9   St. Anselm's Chapel, Canterbury Cathedral, with part of Thomas-a-Becket's Crown, 1794

signed: Turner
pencil and watercolor
517 x 374 mm.
John Edward Taylor, by 1873
Presented by John Edward Taylor in 1892
(WAG.D.1892.113)

Turner first exhibited at the Royal Academy in 1790, showing one work. He did not exhibit an oil painting there until 1796. This water-color was one of the five exhibits of 1794 and featured as no. 408; another exhibit of that year is cat. 8, *The Porch of Great Malvern Priory*. The group attracted the first comments from the reviewers (see entry for cat. 8). Turner seems to have first visited Canterbury in the autumn of 1792, and his *Gate of St. Augustine's Monastery, Canterbury* (Wilton no. 31 or 32) was exhibited at the Royal Academy in 1793, no. 316. The Whitworth watercolor may derive from sketches made in 1792, or perhaps from a second visit in the autumn of 1793, although no sketch connected with this watercolor survives among those known to have been executed on these visits to Canterbury (T.B. XV - A, E, and F).

St. Anselm's Chapel ranks as one of the most accomplished of Turner's early architectural studies and is an impressive achievement for an artist who was still a teenager. The precise wording of the title, which is taken from the 1794 catalogue, is evidence of the artist's intention to produce an exact architectural likeness. Turner has deliberately chosen one of the most architecturally complex parts of the building, so that his skills in capturing spatial recession and complicated perspective are tested to the utmost. As Andrew Wilton has observed, Turner has taken the compositional device of the low viewpoint from the work of his teacher Thomas Malton, and, by placing himself near to the base of the building, has thus emphasized the structure's soaring monumentality.

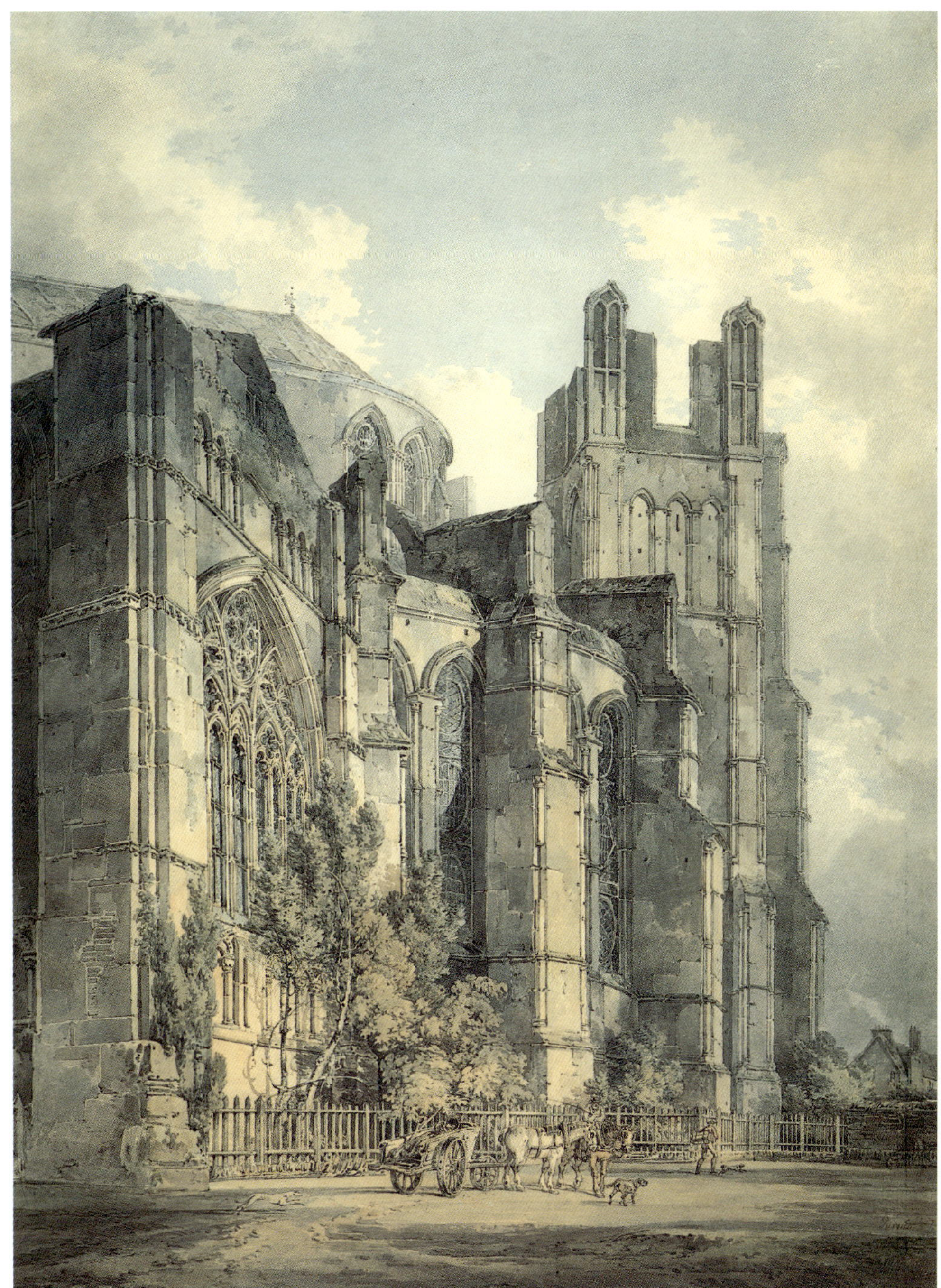

10 Old Blackfriars Bridge, London, 1795-6

pencil and watercolor
262 x 171 mm.
Purchased from Thomas Agnew & Sons by
John Edward Taylor in 1864
Presented by John Edward Taylor in 1892
(WAG.D.1892.89)

Taken from a boat in the Thames this view along Old Blackfriars Bridge looking south toward the Surrey shore has compositional similarities with *Magdalen Tower and Bridge* (cat. 7) and, along with *St. Anselm's Chapel* (cat. 9), shows the extent of the young artist's debt to Thomas Malton, who gave him lessons in architectural perspective from the end of 1789. It dates from 1795-6, a time when Turner was producing small drawings for engraving in the *Copper-Plate Magazine* and other publications. These included two other London subjects, *Westminster Bridge* (Wilton no. 96), taken from a similarly oblique angle, and the *Tower of London* (Wilton no. 103). Old Blackfriars Bridge was built in 1760-9 and replaced by the present bridge in 1869. The *Copper-Plate Magazine*, June 1796, described the bridge as "before any other in point of taste and elegance" and noted "at each end of the bridge, flights of stone steps, defended by iron rails, for the convenience of taking water." Another contemporary but slightly smaller version of the Whitworth watercolor was sold at Christie's, November 17, 1992, lot 66.

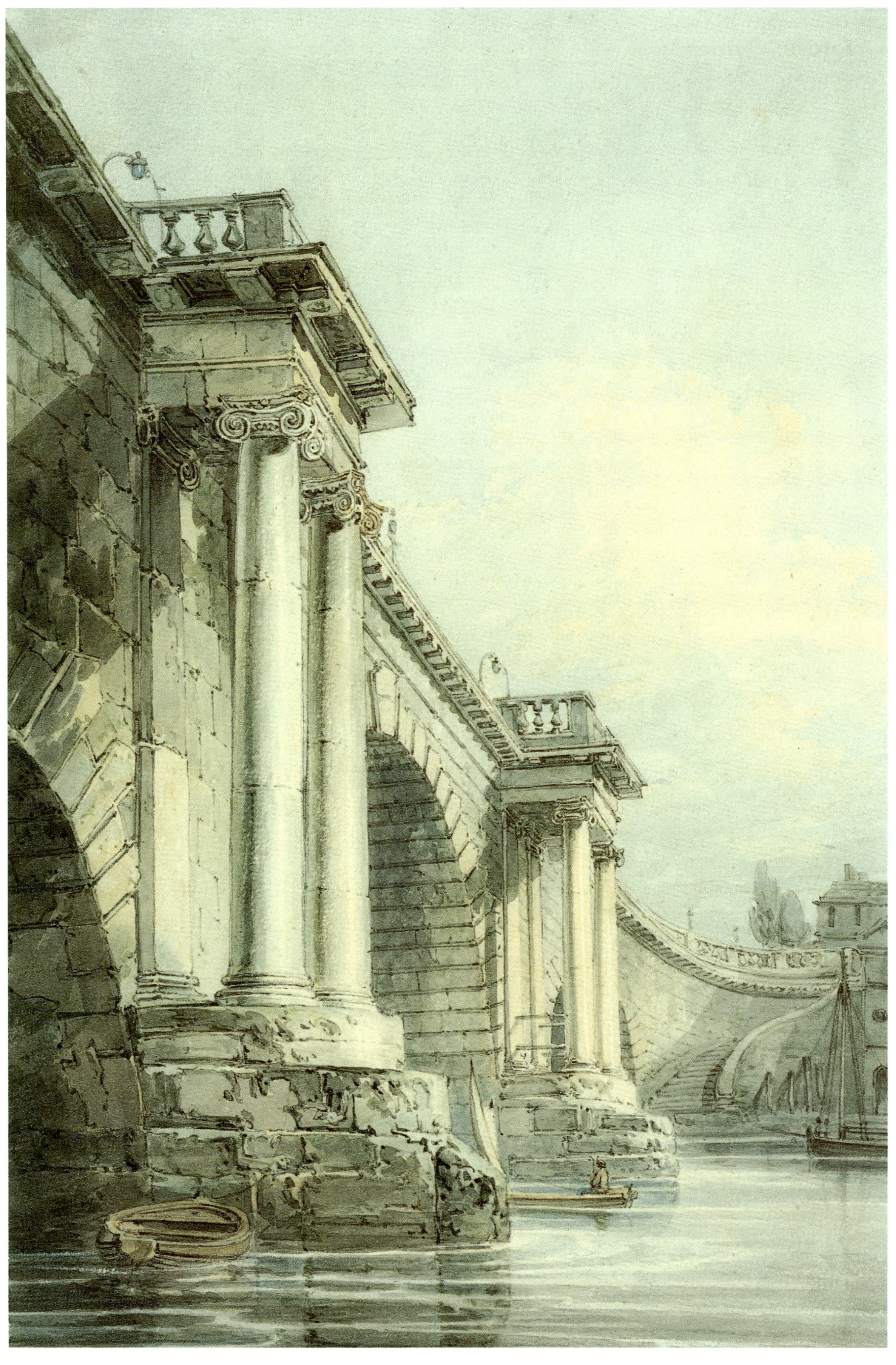

11 View of Hampton Court, Herefordshire, from the North-west, 1795-6

pencil and watercolor
320 x 425 mm.
Viscount Malden, later 5th Earl of Essex
John Edward Taylor, by 1873
Presented by John Edward Taylor in 1892
(WAG.D. 1892.96)

In 1795, Viscount Malden, who was to inherit the title of the Earl of Essex in 1799, commissioned from Turner five drawings of Hampton Court in Herefordshire, a property that he had inherited in 1781. Soon after his marriage in 1786, Malden decided to remodel the house, possibly with the help of James Wyatt, who was working not only at nearby Hereford Cathedral but also at the principal seat of the Earls of Essex, Cassiobury Park, near Watford in Hertfordshire. Turner's drawings of Hampton Court record these alterations. He made a note about Malden's commission in a list at the beginning of the *South Wales* sketchbook (T.B. XXVI): Cascade "Hampton" [this word added and then smudged out]/ Oak /Chaple. 13.17 / N.Front / S.Front. The Whitworth watercolor, deriving from a sketch on page 53 of the sketchbook, is the N.Front, and the Whitworth also owns two others from this commission— *Oak,* not included in this exhibition (Wilton no. 184), and *Chaple* (Wilton no. 185, see cat. 12). The *Cascade* watercolor is in the Victoria and Albert Museum, and *S.Front* remains untraced. The whole set was probably worked on in late 1795 and early 1796; the Victoria and Albert watercolor is dated 1795.

The history and identity of the various Hampton Court watercolors has been confused by the existence of another watercolor of the north front of the house, also in the Whitworth's collection but not included in the present exhibition (Wilton no. 182); this was at one stage thought to be the lost *S.Front* of 1795, but in fact derives from a sketch in the *Hereford Court* sketchbook (T.B. XXXVIII p. 67), made on Turner's later visit to the house in 1798. An engraving of the south front of Hampton Court appeared in the *Copper-Plate Magazine* in 1797 (Rawlinson no. 12) and derives from a small watercolor, recorded in Wilton (1979) as untraced (Wilton no. 98), which was with the Albany Gallery in 1986 (*Fifty Watercolor Drawings*, no. 13). A further note on the same page in the *South Wales* sketchbook records a commission from Sir Richard Colt Hoare for watercolors of the north and south fronts of the house, which were not made until circa 1806 (Wilton nos. 215 and 216) and are now in the Yale Center for British Art. The first of these repeats the composition of this drawing, while the second reproduces that of the Albany Gallery watercolor.

An already confused and confusing situation was further complicated by the appearance of a watercolor of the south front of the house at Sotheby's on March 14, 1985, lot 61. In spite of the claims of the auction catalogue's note for that sale, the watercolor in question is not to be associated with the 1795 commission, but relates to the later visit of 1798 (the sketch for it is in the *Hereford Court* sketchbook T.B. XXXVIII p. 66) and the Whitworth watercolor of that date (Wilton no. 182), since it is very similar in technique and almost exactly the same size. Not long after inheriting the title of Earl of Essex, Turner's patron lost interest in Hampton Court and turned his attention to Cassiobury Park, his main seat, commissioning improvements from James Wyatt and four watercolors of the house from Turner (Wilton nos. 189-192). Hampton Court was sold to Richard Arkwright in 1810.

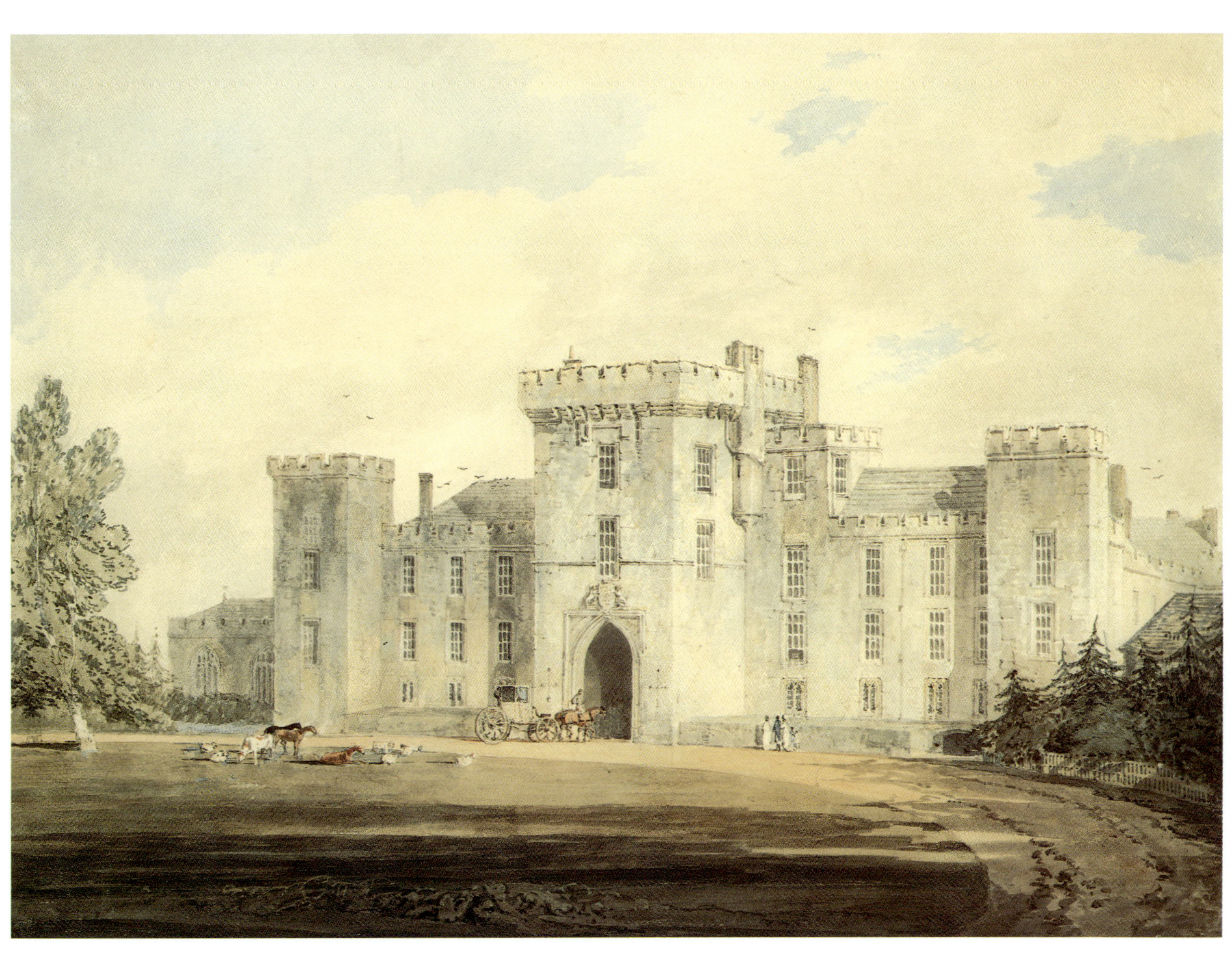

12 The Chapel, Hampton Court, Herefordshire, 1795-6

signed: WTurner
pencil and watercolor.
318 x 424 mm.
Viscount Malden, later 5th Earl of Essex
Bequeathed by Mary Worthington in 1904
(WAG.D.1904.11)

This is one of the five drawings commissioned by Viscount Malden in 1795, and noted on page 5 of the *South Wales* sketchbook (T.B. XXVI). For details of the commission and an attempt to disentangle the confusions that have arisen over the various different Turner watercolors of Hampton Court, see the entry for cat. 11. This watercolor is the only one of the series for which a size is specified (13.17 is to be interpreted as 13" x 17", and all the known drawings for the commission are slightly smaller than this). As with the other watercolors for the series, this example is based on a pencil drawing in the *South Wales* sketchbook, the sketch appearing on page 52.

13 A View in Kent, 1796

pencil and watercolor
222 x 359 mm.
Purchased from Charles Stuart Bale by Thomas Agnew & Sons for John Edward Taylor in 1881
Presented by John Edward Taylor in 1892
(WAG.D.1892.95)

One of a group dating from circa 1796, this drawing is generally associated with a visit by Turner to Norbury Park in Surrey, the home of the scholar, artist, and patron William Lock. Turner traveled to Surrey in connection with a commission he received from Lock to draw his fernhouse, the finished watercolor of which was exhibited at the Royal Academy in 1798, no. 640, but is now untraced. The unifying characteristic of all the "Norbury" Turner watercolors is that they are dominated by large trees and often show park land. Wilton (1979) lists some of the watercolors from the group, this one included (Wilton nos. 152-163), and describes them as being "executed in a uniform style, finer and more delicate than most of Turner's work hitherto; in particular, the foliage of the trees is rendered with a feathery, almost feminine touch."

While the Whitworth watercolor has much in common with the largest and most impressive of the group, that now in the Vaughan Bequest at the National Gallery of Ireland, it is also similar in its handling of foliage, its low horizon, and hint of habitation in the distance, to a watercolor of an *Oak Tree* from the collection of David Rolt, sold at Christie's, March 18, 1986, lot 94, and now in an American private collection. The title of the Whitworth watercolor is a traditional one, but is given some support by the fact that the drawing may have belonged to Turner's friend, the watercolorist William Frederick Wells, who had a cottage at Knockholt near Tunbridge Wells in Kent. In the drawing, the harvesters are dwarfed by the huge trees, which dominate the landscape and the distant church tower, so that nature seems more enduring than humanity in spite of the transience of the seasons.

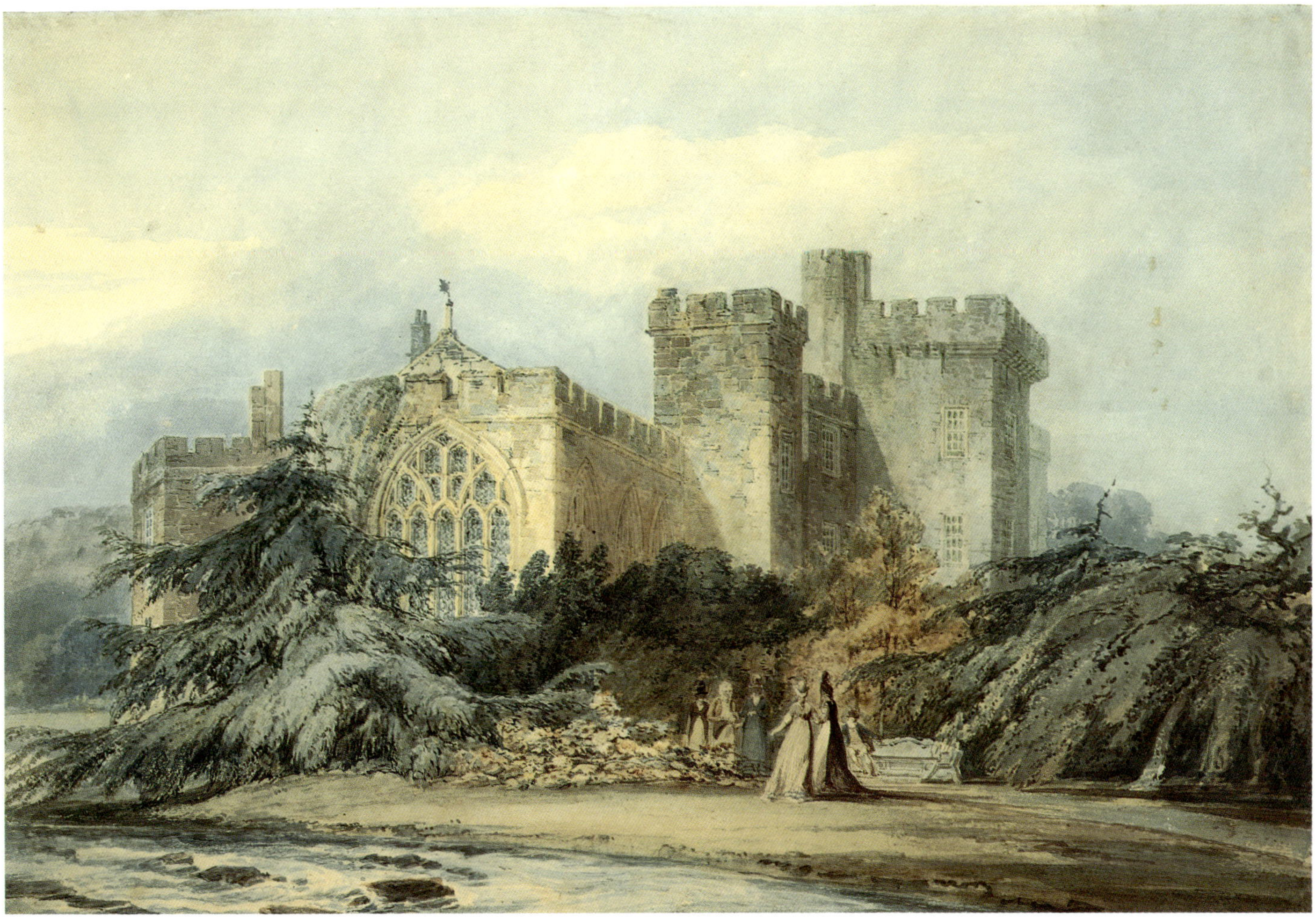

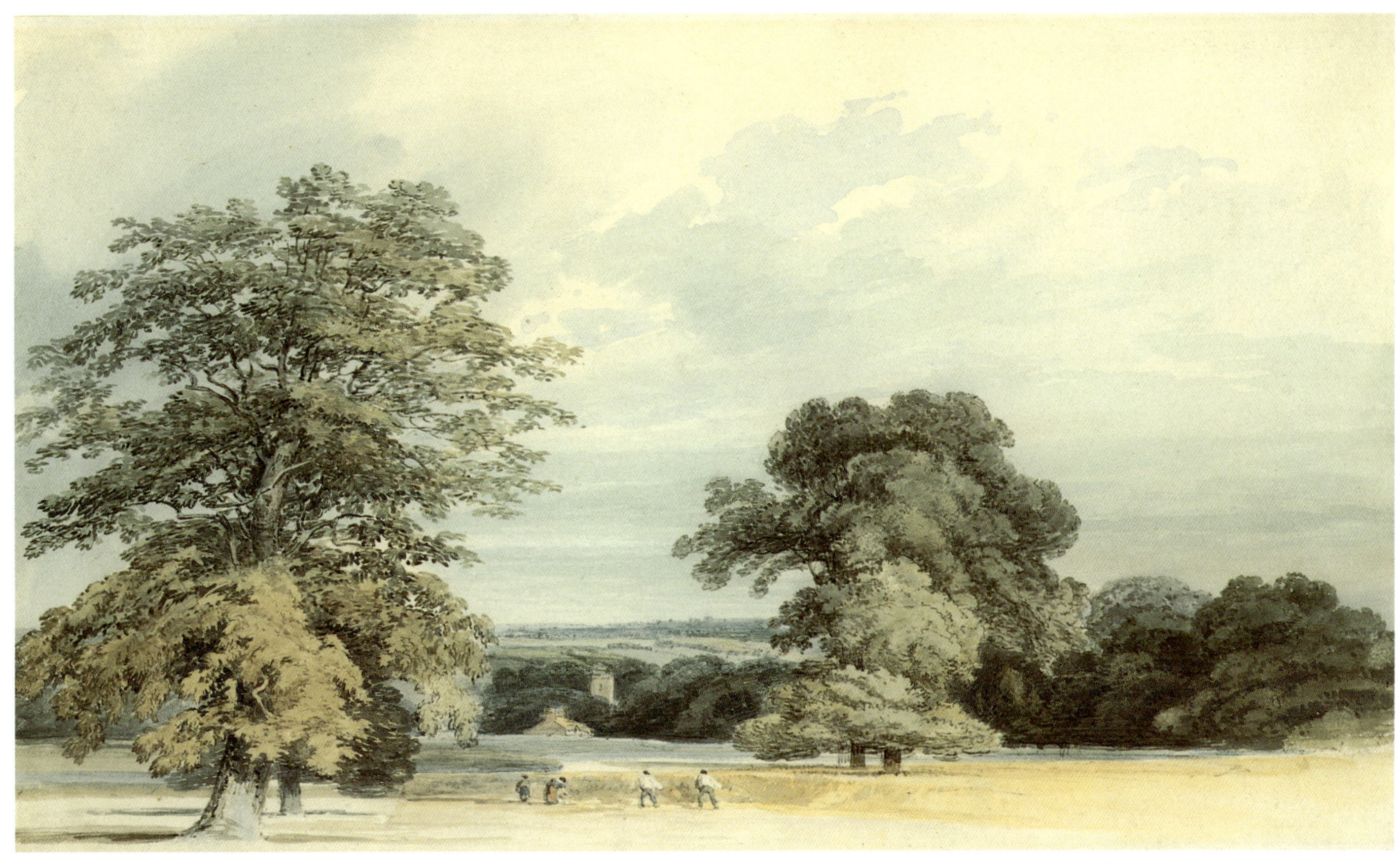

14 The Interior of Buildwas Abbey, Shropshire, 1797

inscribed on the reverse: Buildwas Abbey - near Shrewsbury (over previous inscription)
pencil and watercolor
481 x 328 mm.
Purchased from W. Leech by Thomas Agnew & Sons in 1887
Purchased from Thomas Agnew & Sons in 1891 with a fund presented by the Guarantors of the 1887 Manchester Royal Jubilee Exhibition
(WAG.D.1887.10)

Pages 2 to 6 of the *Matlock* Sketchbook (T.B. XIX) contain an itinerary in Turner's hand for his 1794 tour, and Buildwas Abbey is mentioned on page 3: "At the foot of a mountain call'd Wrekin, near the Severn, Buildews Abby [sic]." A pencil sketch showing a different view of the interior of Buildwas Abbey is in the Turner Bequest (T.B. XXVII - A), but no sketch connected with this watercolor has been located. Like many of the Whitworth's early acquisitions, which were put on permanent view, this watercolor has suffered seriously from fading and the blues have disappeared completely. However, the original appearance can be judged from the line around the edges of the watercolor, where an old mount covered a tiny area, so that it did not fade along with the rest of the watercolor. On this basis, the drawing can be related to others of circa 1797. The compositional device of placing the viewer in an arched interior with a central pillar from which arches radiate is undoubtedly taken from Piranesi, whose work Turner would have encountered when he began to frequent the Monro Academy in 1794.

A Monro School copy, attributed to Turner, of Plate 2 in Piranesi's *Prima Parte di Architettura . . .* of 1743 is in the Metropolitan Museum of Art, New York, and from 1794 Turner began to exhibit architectural watercolors at the Royal Academy that owe compositional debts to Piranesi. These include *The Inside of Tintern Abbey, Monmouthshire* (Royal Academy, 1794), in the Victoria and Albert Museum (Wilton no. 57), *Transept of Tintern Abbey, Monmouthshire* (Royal Academy, 1795), either the watercolor in the Ashmolean Museum, Oxford, or the one in the British Museum (Wilton nos. 58 and 59), *St. Erasmus in Bishop Islip's Chapel* (Royal Academy, 1796), in the British Museum (Wilton no. 138), *Transept of Ewenny Priory, Glamorganshire* (Royal Academy, 1797), in the National Museum of Wales, Cardiff (Wilton no. 227), and *Refectory of Kirkstall Abbey* (Royal Academy, 1798), in Sir John Soane's Museum, London (Wilton no. 234). Before fading, the Whitworth watercolor must have shown the same interest in the contrasts between sunlight and shade that is vividly evident in the 1797 watercolor at Cardiff.

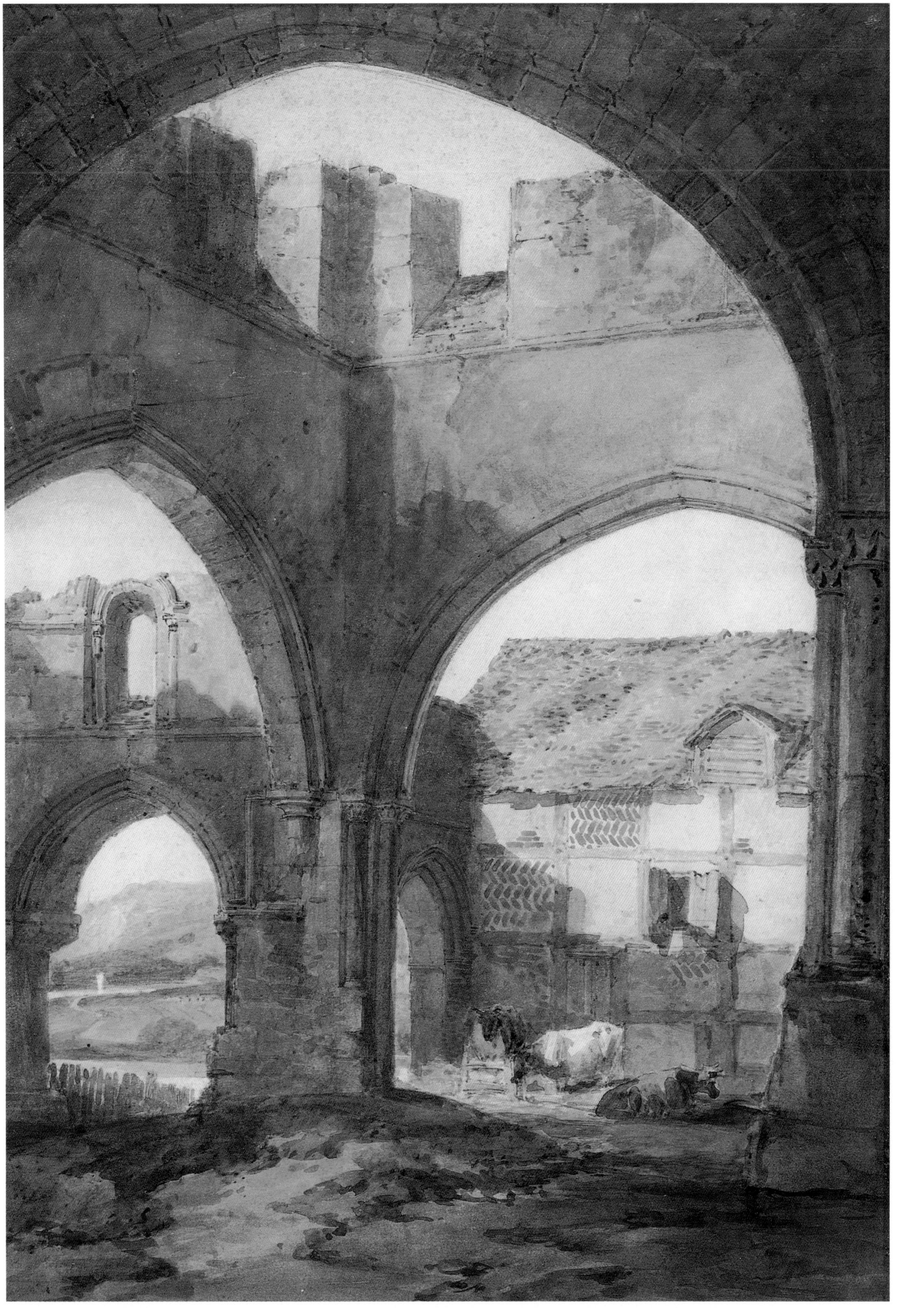

**15 Kilgarran Castle,
Pembrokeshire, c. 1798**

signed: W Turner
watercolor
274 x 374 mm.
Owned by John Ruskin after 1878
Bequeathed by George Beatson Blair
in 1947
(MCAG 1947.114)

Kilgarran Castle is situated on the Twyvey river near to the south-west coast of Wales. Turner visited it on his fourth tour of Wales in 1798. Sketches he made in the *Hereford Court* sketchbook (T.B. XXXVIII) are the basis for a series of oil paintings and watercolors, the principal oil painting being *Kilgarran Castle on the Twyvey, Hazy Sunrise, previous to a Sultry Day* exhibited at the Royal Academy in 1799. The watercolor in the City Art Galleries' collection is very similar to this oil and there is a watercolor sketch relating to both on page 88 of the *Hereford Court* sketchbook.

The castles of Wales had an irresistible attraction for Turner at this time and Kilgarran, in particular, had been singled out by his friend and benefactor, Richard Colt Hoare, who wrote in his journal: "I was so delighted with this enchanting spot that I visited it three times, and visited it in every possible direction—it can only be seen to advantage by water . . ." Turner also sketched it from several directions. He probably took a boat trip up the river from Cardigan, a popular excursion at the time, and sketched it, like Colt Hoare, from several viewpoints. Although the view on page 88 appears to be observed from the water, in the finished watercolor Turner added the dark profile of the near-side bank to lead the eye into the work.

He may also have been drawn to Kilgarran Castle by his admiration for the Welsh artist Richard Wilson. There is no documentary evidence that Turner saw Wilson's version of *Kilgarran Castle,* which was recorded by Joseph Farington on his tour of Wales in 1800 and which had been engraved in 1775, but the similarity in composition makes it highly likely. Both works are based on the drama of steep dark diagonals and the exaggeration of the height of the river banks. Turner was at his closest to Wilson in the late 1790s and adopted the dark brooding colors and melancholic atmosphere of his mentor in both oils and watercolors.

It was around this time that the theme of the ruined castle was being transformed by young artists from a picturesque, antiquarian motif into a symbol of brooding melancholy. It was seen by Turner as a metaphor for the fleeting nature of power and the fall of great civilizations. Kilgarran Castle was built in 1110 and changed hands between the English and the Welsh until it fell into disrepair in the seventeenth century. The transience of power is contrasted with monotony of everyday life as represented by the fishermen with their nets. Another view of the castle, on p. 100 of the *Hereford Court* sketchbook, shows a smoldering forge that could well account for the spiral of smoke in the distance in this watercolor and is possibly another reference to the transience of life and power.

**16 Llyn Cwellyn, North
Wales, 1798**

pencil and watercolor
255 x 362mm.
Purchased from F. Halsted by John
Edward Taylor in 1863
Presented by John Edward Taylor in 1892
(WAG.D.1892.88)

This watercolor, now rather faded, is based on a sketch in the *Hereford Court* sketchbook (T.B. XXXVIII p. 97), made during Turner's extensive tour of North Wales in 1798 (see also cat. 22). The reverse of the sketch is inscribed "Castle Kiljahwm (?) / Quathlyn Pool" and below "Hon Mr Lacelles," and also, probably relating to the sketch on the following page of Caernarvon Castle, "Pope / Jan.1799." The first part of the inscription refers to Castell Cidwm, the large cliff (here seen on the left of the composition), which dominates the northern end of Llyn Cwellyn, a lake to the west of Snowdon on the road from Beddgellert to Caernarvon. Llyn Cwellyn was and is a popular starting point for the ascent of Snowdon. The viewpoint in the Whitworth watercolor is taken from beside the main road near to where the modern youth hostel now stands.

The reference to "Hon Mr Lacelles" suggests that Turner received a commission for a version of this composition, possibly this watercolor, from Edward Lascelles, his patron at Harewood House. In the sketch, which has remained in the sketchbook and not been mounted separately, the colors are substantially clearer and stronger, and not surprisingly the Whitworth watercolor is faded by comparison. It is, however, so close in style and technique to the sketch that it must date from the same year. The dark coloring and the stopping-out in the foreground can be compared with other Turner watercolors of circa 1798, such as *Kilgarran Castle*, in the Manchester City Art Galleries, cat. 15 in this exhibition.

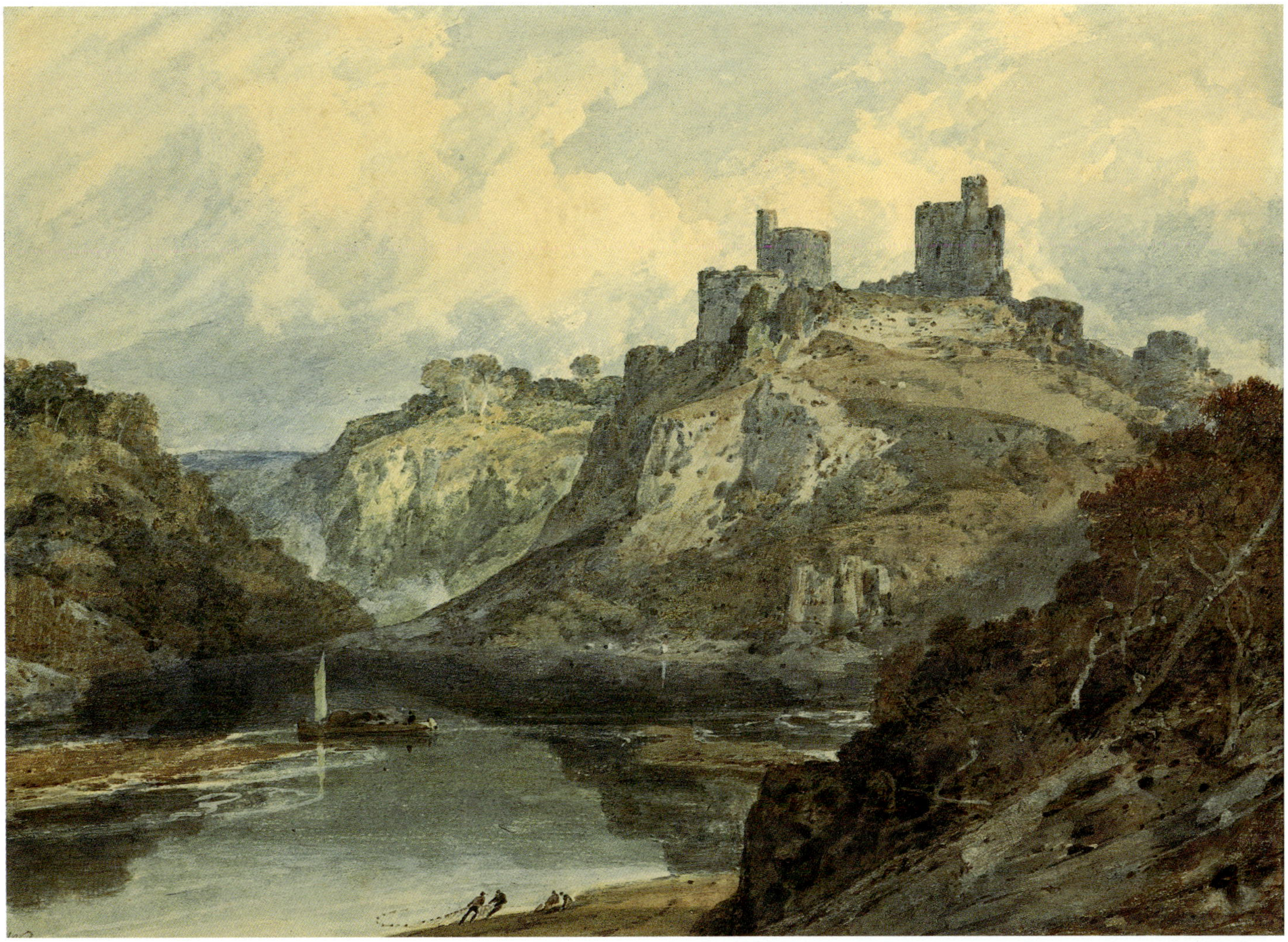

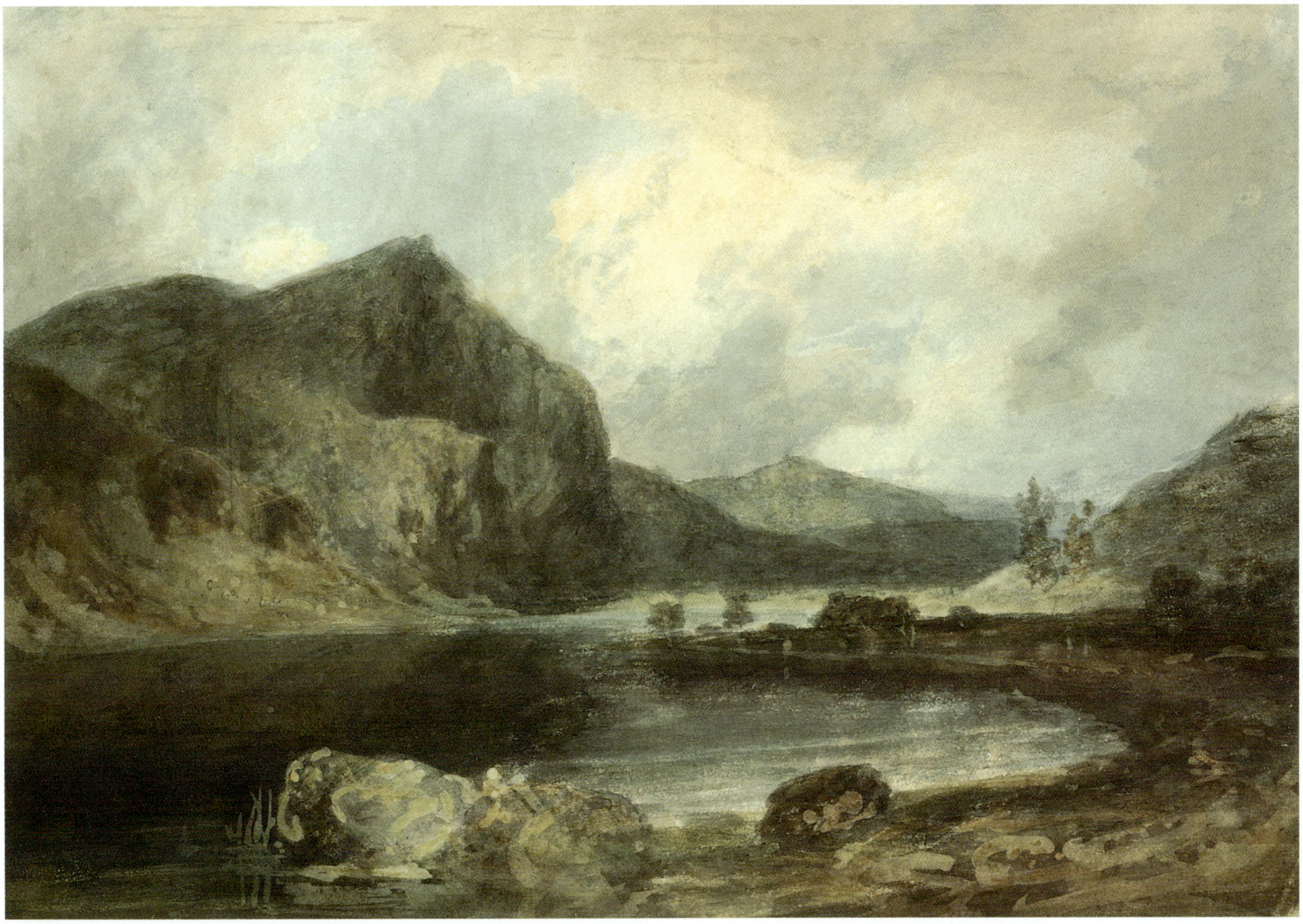

17 The Chapter-House, Salisbury Cathedral, 1798-9

pencil, pen and ink and watercolor
645 x 512 mm.
Sir Richard Colt Hoare
Presented by Sir William Agnew in 1891
(WAG.D.1889.3)

This watercolor is one of a series ultimately intended to include ten views of the cathedral and ten of the city of Salisbury. They were commissioned from the artist by Sir Richard Colt Hoare, Bart. (1758-1838), the antiquarian and collector, and carried out between 1797 and 1805. Turner visited Salisbury in 1795, making drawings in the *Isle of Wight* sketchbook (T.B. XXIV). The first knowledge that we have of the Colt Hoare commission is a penciled note on the fly-leaf of this sketchbook, where the name "Sir Richard Hoare" appears beside two titles "Salisbury Porch" and "Front of Salisbury." These were to be "Size of Ely," which presumably refers to the large interior view of Ely Cathedral that Turner was to exhibit at the Royal Academy in 1796 (Wilton no. 194), and that Hoare had seen and may have owned. That the commission was originally conceived in terms of just two watercolors is suggested by the fact that the *Isle of Wight* sketchbook contains sketches only of the north porch (p. 17, relating to the watercolor sold at Christie's on July 9, 1985, lot 98, Wilton no. 196) and the west front (p. 16, relating to the watercolor now in the Harris Museum, Preston, Wilton no. 198). No sketch has been discovered for the Whitworth watercolor.

The enlargement of the commission firstly to eight and finally to ten drawings is documented by further evidence in the Turner Bequest. A list possibly written by Turner but more probably by Sir Richard, on the reverse of the mount of a watercolor by John Robert Cozens (T.B. CCCLXXX) gives the subjects as "2 Chapter. 2 inside. 1 Cloyster. 2 outside. 1 general." Another list (T.B. CCCLVIII - A) records the expansion of the commission to include a series of ten smaller watercolors of the city, together with another two views of the cathedral, one internal and one external, to bring the set of cathedral views up to ten (five

on the list, including both *Chapter-House* watercolors, are listed as already paid for). The extra two watercolors (an *East Front*, no. 5, and an *Entrance from the West Door*, no. 10) were presumably never executed, as only eight watercolors of the cathedral were sold when the collection was dispersed at Christie's in 1883.

Following the list on the reverse of T.B. CCCLXXX, the watercolors are: (1) the Whitworth example, exhibited at the Royal Academy, 1799, no. 327, Wilton no. 199; (2) *Chapter-House, Salisbury*, exhibited at the Royal Academy, 1801, no. 415, and now in the Victoria and Albert Museum, Wilton no. 201; (3) *Interior looking toward the North Transept*, in the Salisbury and South Wiltshire Museum, Wilton no. 203; (4) *Choir*, exhibited at the Royal Academy, 1797, no. 450, and now also in the Salisbury and South Wiltshire Museum, Wilton no. 197; (5) *South View from the Cloisters*, in the Victoria and Albert Museum, Wilton no. 202; (6) *West Front*, exhibited at the Royal Academy, 1799, no. 335, and now in the Harris Museum and Art Gallery, Preston, Wilton no. 198; (7) *North Front*, sold at Christie's on July 9, 1985, lot 98, Wilton no. 196; and (8) *View from the Bishop's Garden*, in Birmingham City Museum and Art Gallery, Wilton no. 200. The critic of the *St. James's Chronicle*, reviewing the 1799 Royal Academy exhibition, praised the Whitworth drawing for its "forcible and rich" color, and its "solemn and grand effect." These have now totally disappeared, as the watercolor hung with the others from the set on the wall at Stourhead (Colt Hoare's house) until they were all sold in 1883 and is now badly faded. Some of the watercolors in the smaller set of town views (Wilton nos. 204-8 and 211-14) have fared better, because they remained in an album until being sold in 1927.

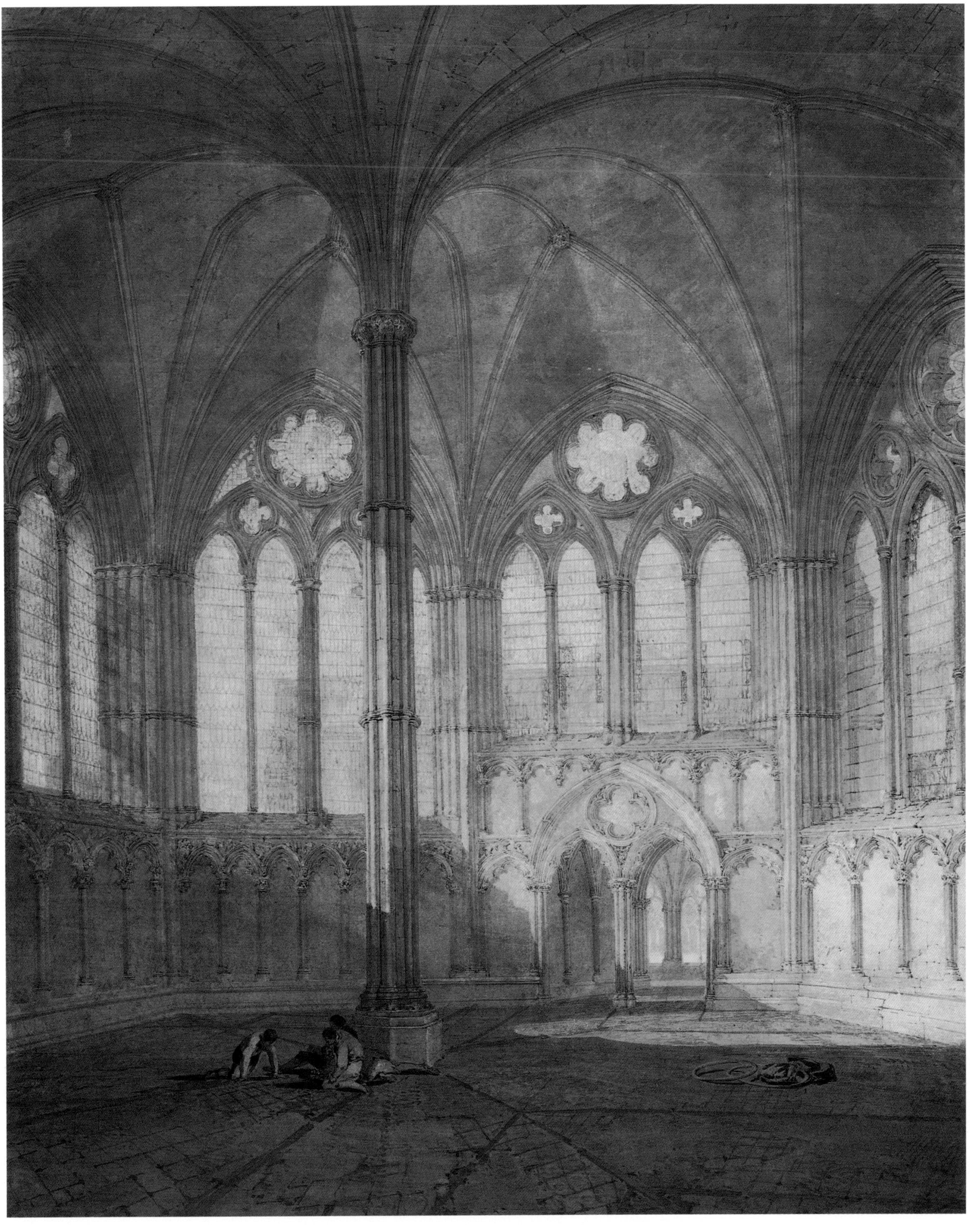

18 A River Landscape with a Castle on a Hill, 1798-9

pencil and watercolor
432 x 610 mm.
Bequeathed by Mary Worthington in 1904
(WAG.D.1904.20)

From its acquisition until 1982, this watercolor was known as *Norham Castle on the Tweed*, but, as a result of research for the *Turner Watercolours in the Whitworth Art Gallery* exhibition of 1984, it was realized that this title was incorrect. The buildings shown here are unlike those at Norham, and the course of the river differs from that of the Tweed at Norham. Turner made two large watercolors of Norham (Wilton nos. 225 and 226) from a sketch on the *North of England* sketchbook (T.B. XXXIV p. 57), and both show the castle as a different building from the one in the Whitworth drawing. Since 1982, there have been various attempts to identify the scene, with suggestions that it may not derive from the northern tour of 1797 at all, but that it shows a view in Wales, which Turner had visited on several occasions before 1799, the latest possible date for this drawing.

The recent discovery by Ian Warrell of a very slight outline pencil sketch for the Whitworth watercolor in the Turner Bequest has brought identification tantalizingly closer, but still not established it with any certainty. The drawing in question is T.B. XXXVI - V, a watercolor of Richmond, Yorkshire, which has the pencil sketch on its reverse. The sketch was too slight to have been recorded by Finberg, and the view is not identified. While the fact that the sketch is on the reverse of the Richmond view does not necessarily mean that the view depicted is near Richmond, it is at least possible. David Hill has suggested that it may be Ellerton Priory in Swaledale, a few miles from Richmond, so that the tower in the distance on the right may be that of Marrick Priory. However, Hill acknowledges that, if this is the case, Turner has used an enormous amount of artistic license, which would be unusual for this date. The jury must therefore remain out on this most perplexing question.

19 St. Agatha's Abbey, Easby, from the River Swale, Yorkshire, 1798-9

pencil and watercolor
630 x 890 mm.
James Worthington, by 1873
Bequeathed by Mary Worthington in 1904
(WAG.D.1904.18)

The scale of this finished watercolor suggests that it was either exhibited or executed on commission or both. But no private commission is known and it cannot be located in any contemporary exhibition. It is based on a sketch in the *North of England* sketchbook (T.B. XXXIV p. 25) made on Turner's tour of Yorkshire, Northumberland, and the Lake District in the summer of 1797. The sketch does not include the river bank to the left and extends farther to the right to include a house, which is omitted in the final watercolor, where the height of the abbey buildings is also greatly exaggerated. Turner followed a similar composition in a later watercolor of circa 1819 for Dr. Whitaker's *History of Richmondshire*, now in the British Museum (Wilton no. 561).

Finberg (1909) identified the North of England sketch as forming the basis for the Richmondshire watercolor also, but the compositions are slightly different. It, in fact, derives from a sketch on page 112 of the *Yorkshire 2* sketchbook of 1816 (T.B. CXLV). A smaller watercolor of Easby Abbey, of a similar date to the Whitworth watercolor but showing the building from the other direction, is also in the British Museum (Wilton no. 274). The scale of the Whitworth watercolor is typical of those exhibited at the Royal Academy in 1798 and 1799, and in technique it may be compared with other works executed in those years, such as the Norham Castle view, sold at Christie's on July 14, 1987, lot 190 (Wilton no. 225) or the Abergavenny Bridge watercolor, sold at the same location on November 17, 1992, lot 63 (not in Wilton).

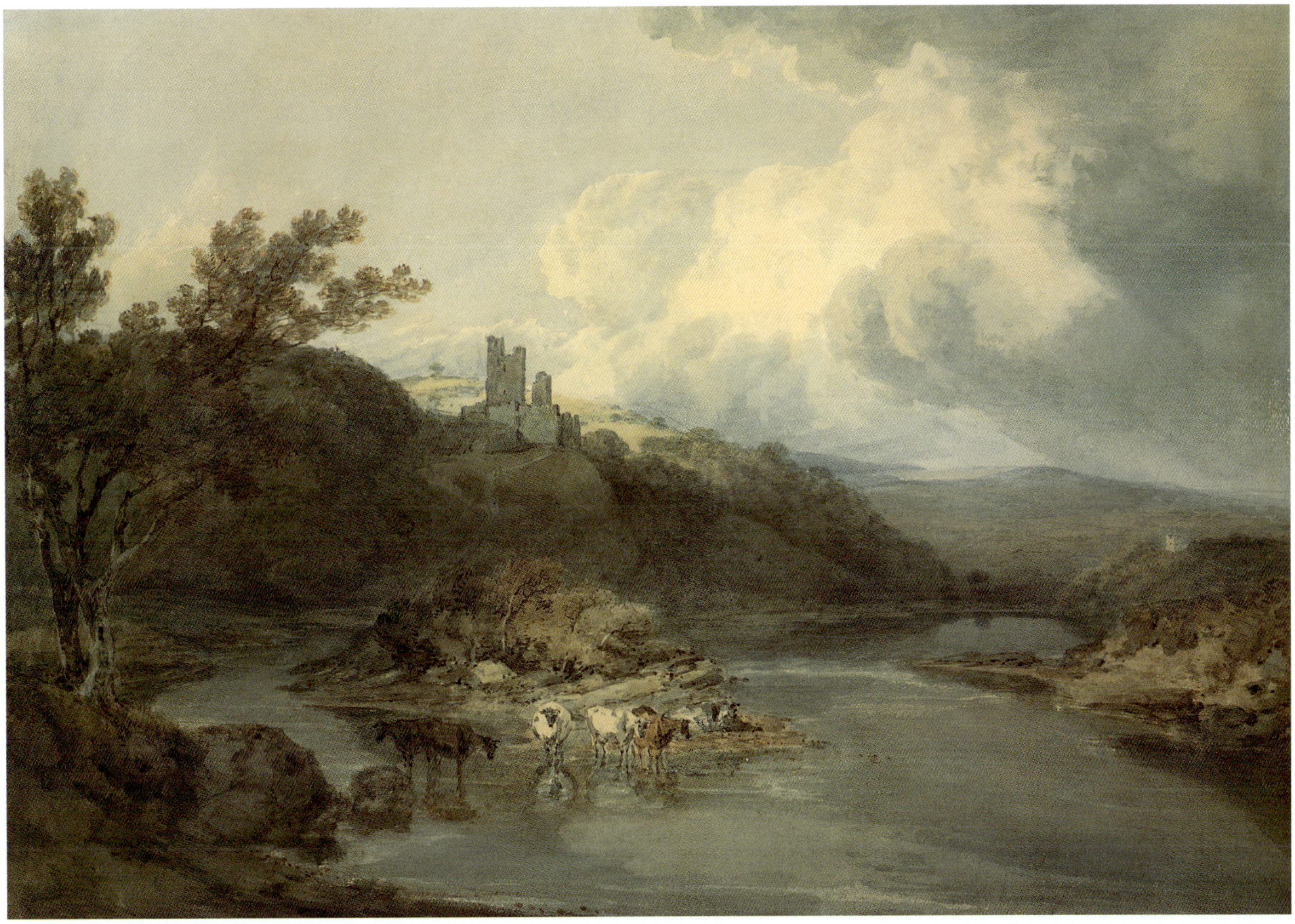

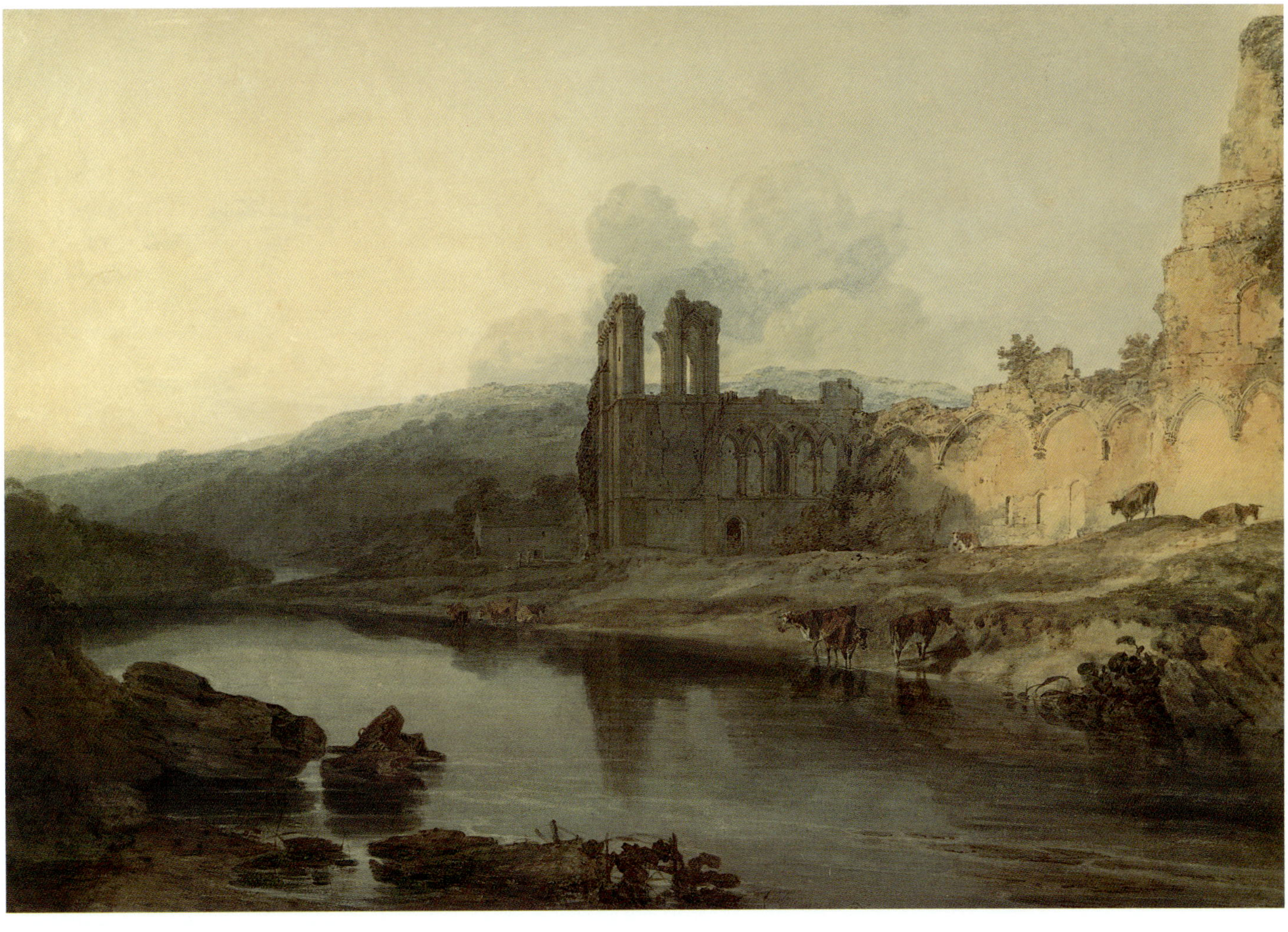

20 North-east View of Fonthill Abbey, Sunset, 1800

pencil and watercolor
696 x 1035 mm.
William Beckford
Purchased from Thomas Agnew & Sons by
James Worthington in 1870
Bequeathed by Mary Worthington in 1904
(WAG.D.1904.19)

Fonthill Abbey in Wiltshire, one of England's most remarkable buildings, was the home of the eccentric millionaire William Beckford (1760-1844), who commissioned James Wyatt to design the house in 1793. Work continued on the vast Gothic abbey for many years, building material coming from the demolition of the Palladian mansion in the valley below built by Beckford's father. The building was not finished until 1813. Owing to financial difficulties, Beckford sold the Abbey in 1822, and the central tower collapsed in 1825, resulting in the almost total demolition of the building. In the early years of the project, however, Beckford was very proud of his creation, and in 1799 commissioned several artists to come to Fonthill and record the building's appearance,

as was noted by Joseph Farington, who first mentioned Turner's visit there on May 27, 1799: "Turner called on me . . . He has been at Fonthill 3 weeks, - Tresham, West, Hamilton & Wyatt there part of the time. - He is to make several drawings, - views near the Abbey & c."

Five large watercolors of the Abbey resulted from this commission, which Turner worked on over the winter and spring and exhibited at the Royal Academy in 1800. Farington mentioned two other watercolors of Fonthill (July 10, 1800), which, if they were ever made, were presumably not completed in time for the Royal Academy exhibition and are now untraced. The watercolors were designed to show the Abbey from different angles at different times of day, although they have now all faded very badly and their light effects can no longer be distinguished. The other watercolors are *Morning* (Art Gallery of Ontario, Wilton no. 336), *Noon* (Brodick Castle, National Trust for Scotland, Wilton no. 338), *Afternoon* (Private Collection, Wilton no. 335), and *Evening* (Montreal Museum of Fine Arts, Wilton no. 337). Turner made studies for the Beckford commission in the *Fonthill* sketchbook (T.B. XLVII) and the *Smaller Fonthill* sketchbook (T.B. XLVIII); the sketch for the Whitworth drawing is T.B. XLVII p. 11, which is much more dramatic and colorful than the finished version and gives some idea of the original effects.

Beckford paid only 35 guineas for each of the watercolors, and soon tired of them, since he had sold all but the *Noon* view by 1818.

The reason for his unhappiness with at least one of them is recorded in *Recollections of the late William B.*, 1893, p.15, where it is claimed that Beckford thought one of the series "a very fine drawing, but rather too poetical , too ideal, even for Fonthill. The scenery there is certainly beautiful, but Turner took such liberties with it that he entirely destroyed the portraiture, the locality of the spot." In all the Beckford watercolors, the tower of the Abbey is shown complete (except Wilton no. 335, which is so faded that the tower has disappeared), although the sketches show that it was incomplete at the time of Turner's visit. He therefore almost certainly had access to Wyatt's plans; this is not unlikely, since Turner had been working for several architects, including Wyatt, as an architectural draughtsman over the previous few years. An intermediate Wyatt design for the Abbey in Turner's hand is in Bolton Museum and Art Gallery (Wilton no. 332) and the *North-West View of Fonthill*, exhibited at the Royal Academy in 1798 as by Wyatt, is also by Turner, Wilton no. 333, Yale Center for British Art.

21 The Abbey Pool, 1800-1

signed: WTurner
pencil and watercolor
514 x 762 mm.
Purchased from Thomas Agnew & Sons by
John Heugh in 1873
Purchased from Thomas Agnew & Sons in
1891 with a fund presented by the
Guarantors of the 1887 Manchester Royal
Jubilee Exhibition
(WAG.D.1887.15)

There has in the past been some confusion over the title of this watercolor, which has been erroneously identified as St. Agatha's Abbey, Easby. This probably arose from the fact that both this drawing and cat. 19 in this exhibition, which does show Easby Abbey, were in the same 1864 sale at Christie's. The title given here is the first recorded title, under which the drawing was engraved with Turner's participation in 1844 (Rawlinson no. 640). The ruins depicted have not been identified, nor have any preparatory sketches been located with certainty. Studies of about the same date with cows in water and ruins beyond (T.B. LXX - H and J) show different locations—the combination of cows and architecture may be seen in *The Refectory of Kirkstall Abbey,* exhibited at the Royal Academy in 1798 and now in Sir John Soane's Museum (Wilton no. 234).

Stylistically, the watercolor can be dated circa 1800-1, and related to other works such as the *Study of a Group of Cows* in the Ashmolean

Museum, Oxford (Wilton no. 409) and the studies in the *Cows* sketchbook (T.B. LXII). The pose of the cow second from the left in the watercolor is similar to the left hand sketch on page three of the book and the watercolor on page six. Turner later developed an oil painting from the watercolor, which is known as *The Quiet Ruin, Cattle in Water; A Sketch, Evening*, and is now in the Tate Gallery (Butlin & Joll no. 83). The oil painting was probably exhibited at Turner's Gallery in 1809. Many of the details of the watercolor have been altered. Although Ruskin thought that the oil preceded the watercolor in date, it is certainly later: "The subject was completed afterwards in a careful, though somewhat coarse, drawing, which defines the Norman window in the ruined wall, and is one of many expressions of Turner's feeling of the contrast between the pure rustic life of our day, and the pride and terror of the past," (J. Ruskin, *Works*, Vol. XIII, p.121).

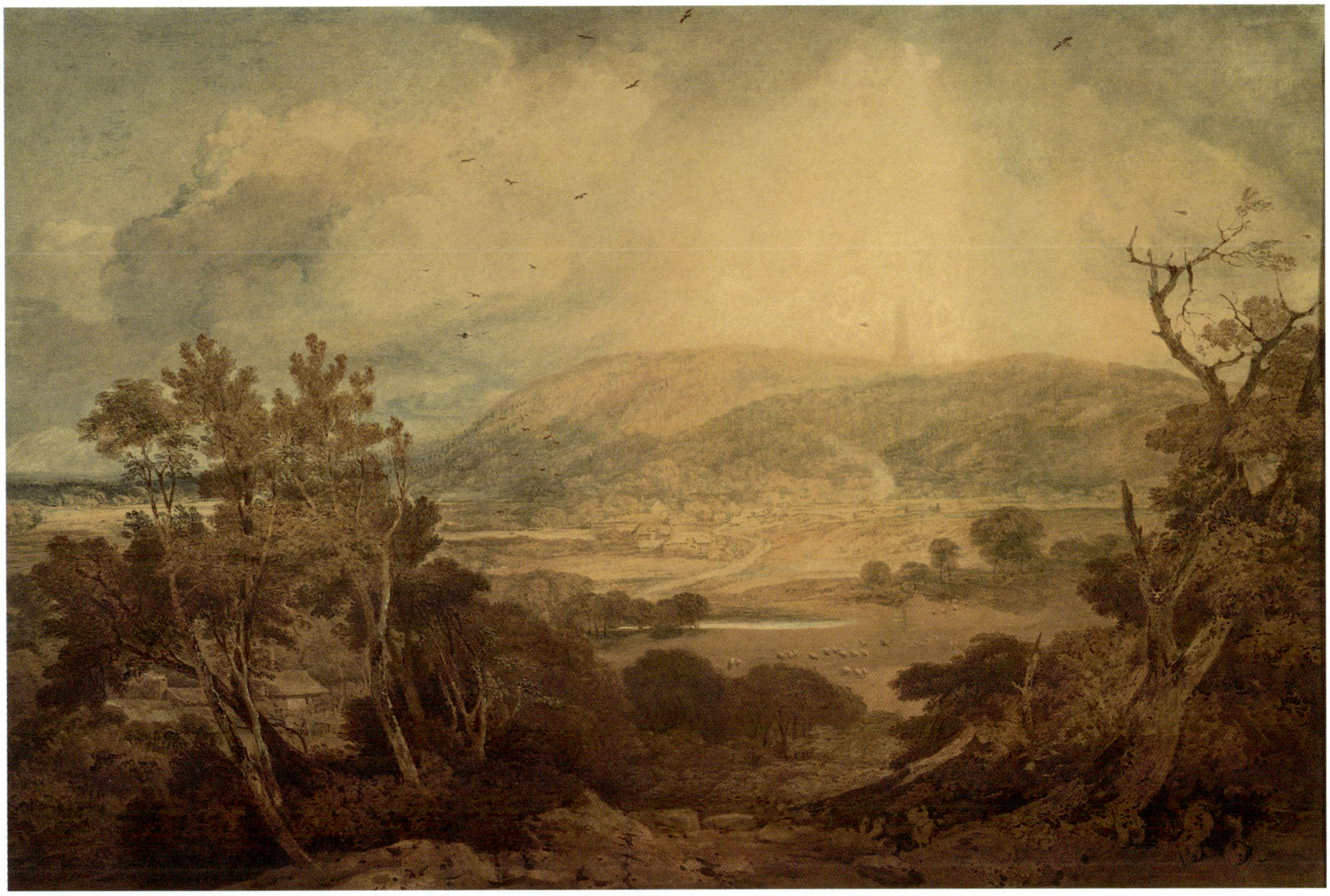

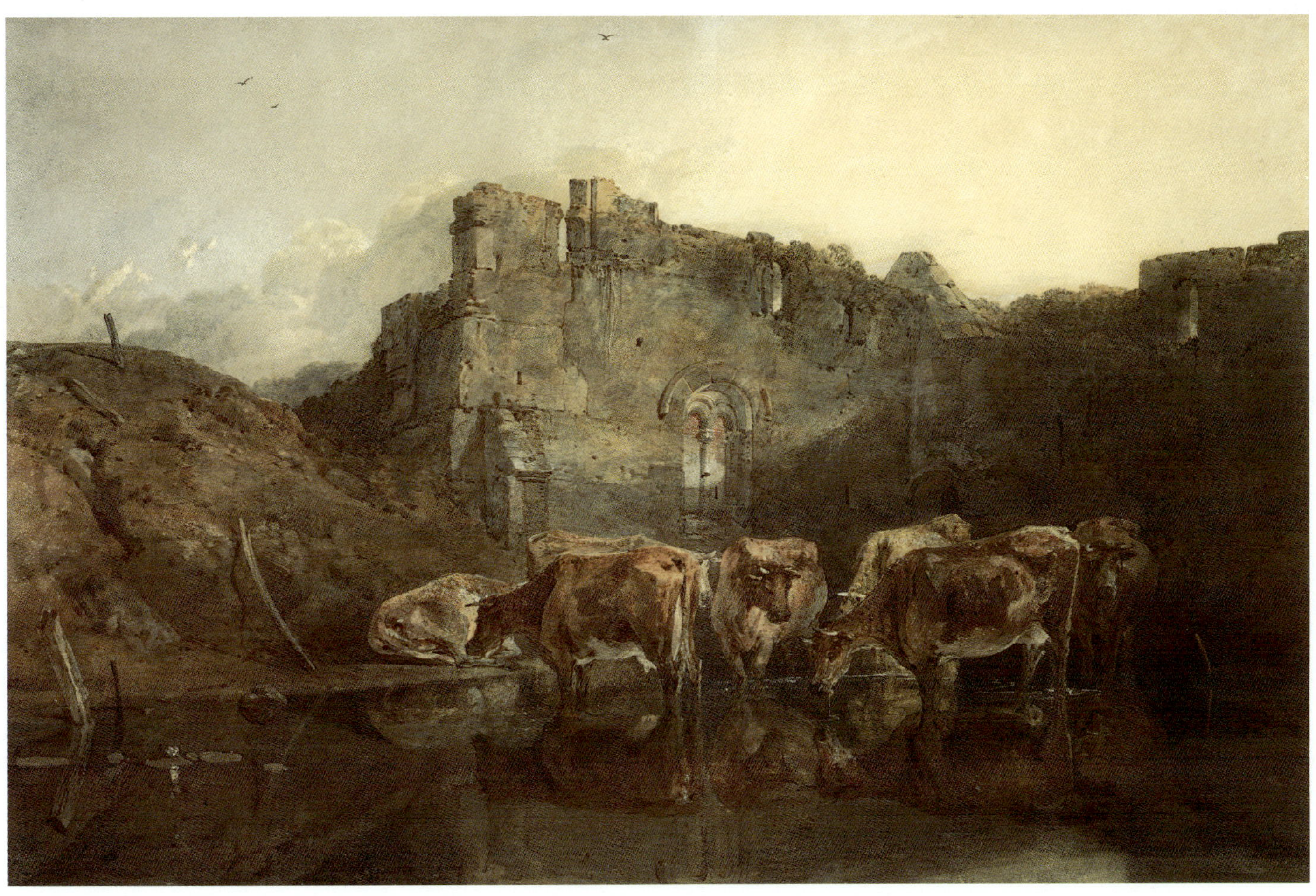

22 Conway Castle, North Wales, 1801-2

signed with initials: JMWT.RA
pencil and watercolor
427 x 629 mm.
Purchased by Thomas Ashton in 1863
By descent to Mrs. P.W. Kessler
Presented by her daughters in 1948
(WAG.D.1948.18)

Turner visited Wales five times in eight years during the 1790s, but after his visit to Switzerland in 1802, he noted that it "on the whole surpasses Wales; and Scotland too" (*Farington Diary* October 1, 1802. He only visited Wales once after 1802. This watercolor derives from the extensive tour of 1798, after which Farington noted in his diary (September 26, 1798): "Wm. Turner called on me. He has been in South & North Wales this Summer - alone and on Horseback - out 7 weeks. Much rain but better for effects." This watercolor is one of at least five large watercolors of Conway, which derive from sketches in the *Hereford Court* sketchbook (T.B. XXXVIII) and which have, over the years, become very confused. The Whitworth watercolor derives from a composition on page 52 of the sketchbook with the following names inscribed on its reverse: "Revd. Mr. Lancaster / Barrington / Revd. Mr. Dunford / Revd. Mr. Ogle," probably the names of prospective clients for finished versions of the view.

Another watercolor, based on the same sketch, was recorded by Armstrong (1902) as being in the possession of Humphry Roberts, who sold it at Christie's in 1908. It recently reappeared at Christie's on July 13, 1993, lot 33. Neither of these two versions can be associated with the patrons named on the reverse

of the sketch. The other versions of Conway Castle derive from sketches on pages 50a and 51 of the book: Wilton no. 268, commissioned by the artist's pupil William Blake of Newhouse and by descent until sold at Christie's on June 30,1981, lot 55, Wilton no. 269, ex collection Mrs. Charles Lupton and G.D. Lockett, sold at Christie's on November 16, 1982, lot 124, and Wilton no. 270, sold at Sotheby's on April 11, 1991, lot 46, and now in the J. Paul Getty Museum, Malibu, California. A large oil painting of the same composition as Wilton nos. 268-70 is in the collection of the Duke of Westminster (Butlin & Joll no. 141).

Watercolors of Conway Castle by Turner are recorded in various nineteenth century collections and sales, but it is not always possible to link them to versions known today. All of them were worked on between 1798 and 1802. Because the Whitworth watercolor has the initials RA after the signature (Turner was elected a full member of the Royal Academy in February 1802), it must date from the very end of this period, and can be compared with other watercolors of 1801-2, such as *Kilchern castle with the Cruachan Ben mountains, Scotland: Noon*, exhibited at the Royal Academy in 1802 and now in the City Museum and Art Gallery, Plymouth.

23 The Coniston Fells, Cumbria, 1801-2

pencil and watercolor
251 x 412 mm.
Presented by John Edward Taylor in 1892
(WAG.D.1892.93)

This drawing, which has a pencil sketch of a rocky waterfall among trees on the reverse, has been identified as originally forming part of the *Smaller Fonthill* sketchbook (T.B. XLVIII). The artist used this sketchbook from 1799 to 1802. It was broken up so that only seven loose leaves remain in the Turner Bequest. Finberg (1909) identified "at least five leaves" (p. 123) in J.E. Taylor's collection, of which this is one, a further six in the Ruskin Drawing School at Oxford (later transferred to the Ashmolean Museum), two in the National Galleries of Scotland, and two in the National Gallery of Ireland. Wilton (1979) identified several more, but only listed in his catalogue those that make use of watercolor (Wilton nos. 314-26). He mentioned the others in passing, and pointed out that others remain to be discovered, as occurred when a previously unknown cloud study from the sketchbook was sold at Christie's on November 17, 1992, lot 64.

Some of the drawings from the sketchbook were made in connection with the 1799 Fonthill commission for William Beckford (Wilton nos. 335-9 and see also cat. 20 in this exhibition), but most were executed during

Turner's journey to Edinburgh via Yorkshire and Durham in 1801. Turner returned from Scotland via the Lake District, an itinerary recorded in the *Tweed and Lakes* sketchbook (T.B. XXXV) and certainly visited Coniston, exhibiting a famous oil painting of the Coniston Fells at the Royal Academy in 1798 (Butlin & Joll no. 5). But the title of the Whitworth watercolor is a traditional one. For the 1984 exhibition, *Turner Watercolours in the Whitworth Art Gallery,* a tentative identification of the watercolor as "a view of the Coniston Fells, with Black Comb showing in the distance on the left, from somewhere between Windermere and Coniston" was suggested, but this has not been confirmed and the scene has still not been identified with any certainty. Whatever the location, and in spite of its considerable fading (notable in the fade line along the right edge), the watercolor may still be compared with other watercolors from the sketchbook, such as *Durham Castle* (Leeds City Art Gallery, Wilton no. 315) and *Durham Cathedral* (National Galleries of Scotland, Wilton no. 316).

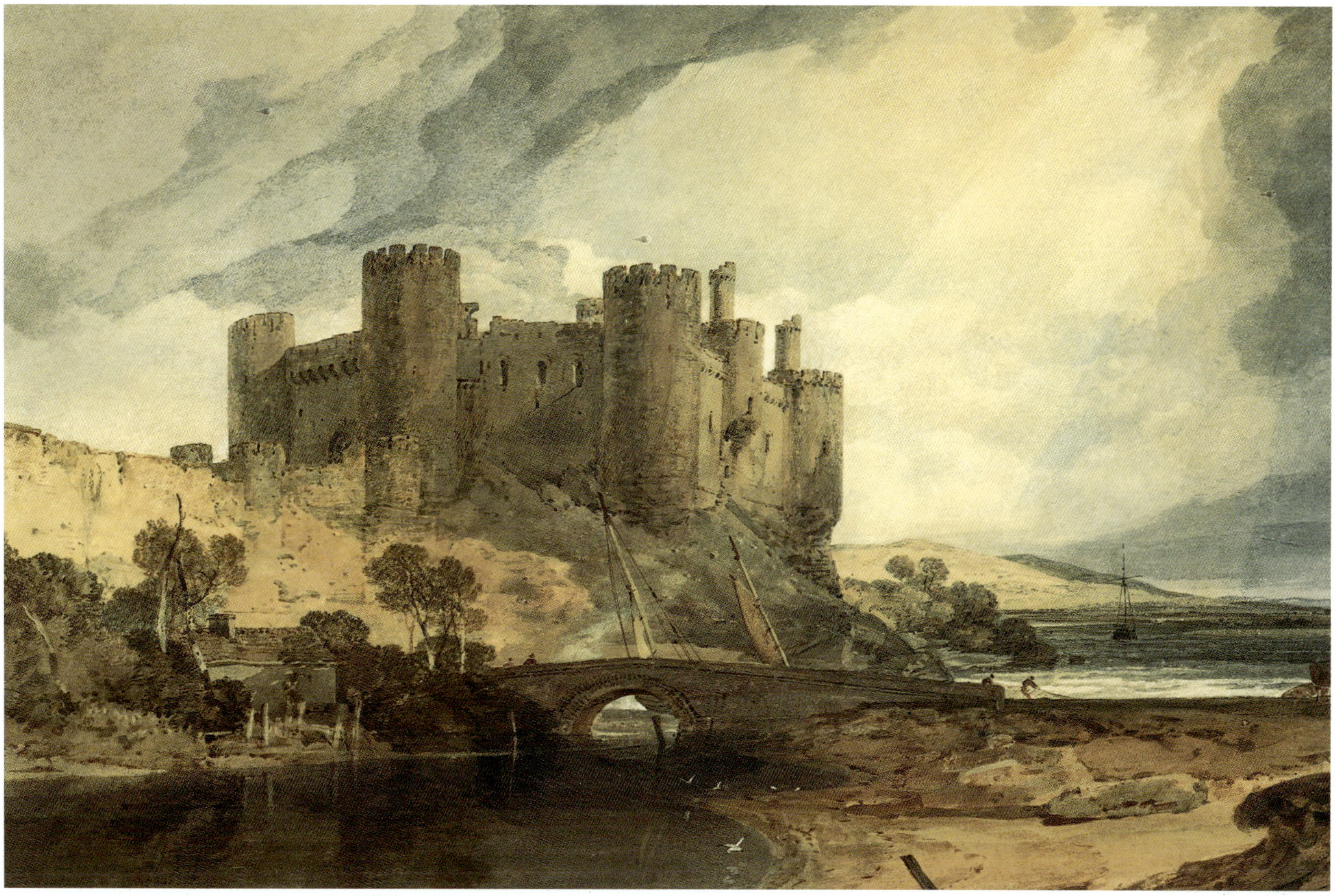

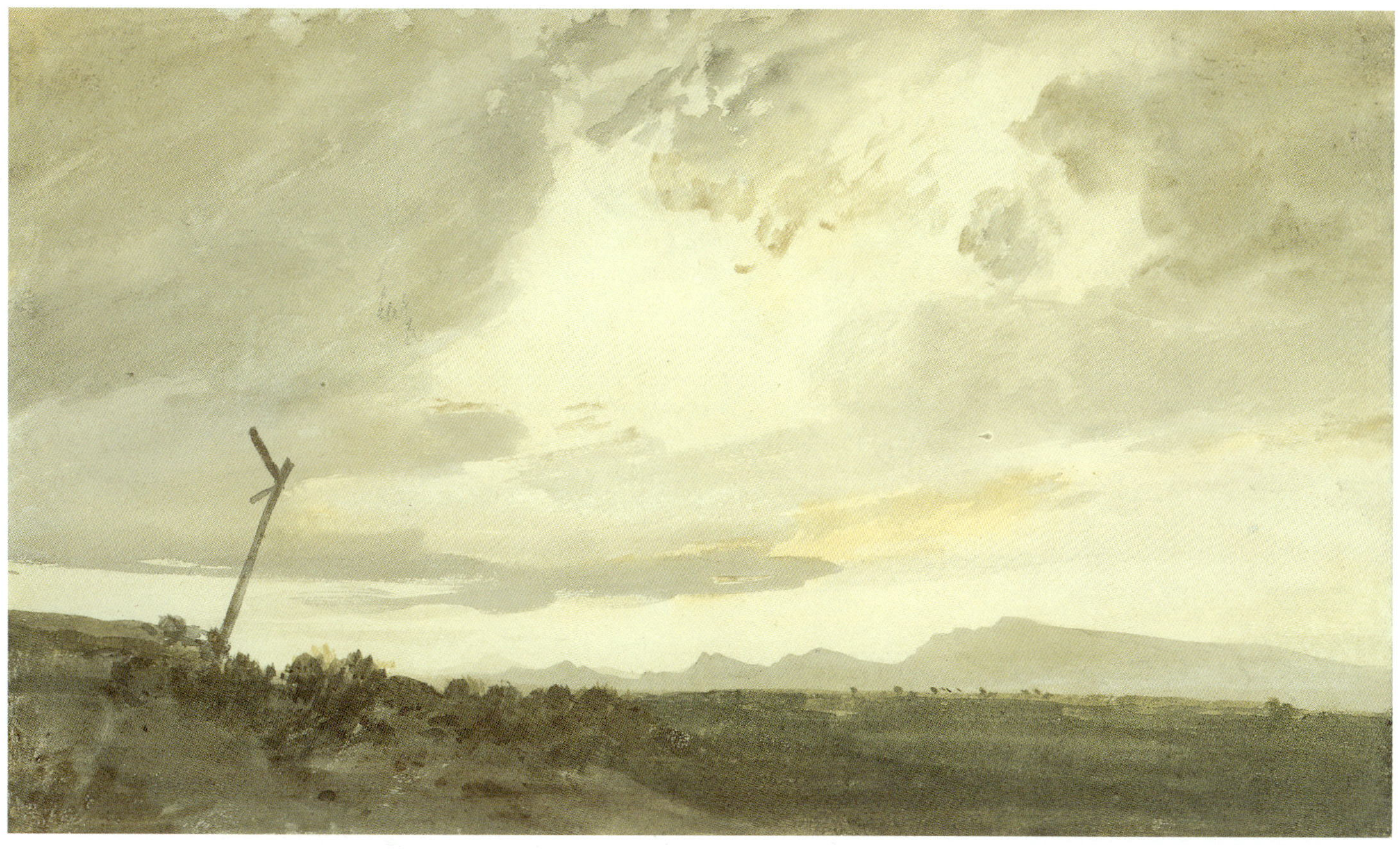

THE ALPINE TOUR OF 1802

Turner, along with many other English artists, took advantage of the Peace of Amiens of October 1801, which briefly halted the war between England and France, to cross the Channel and visit the Continent, his first journey abroad. He traveled from mid-July to mid-October 1802. Although he stopped in Paris, his main destination was the Alps. By the time he got there, he had a traveling companion, Neweby Loweson, a young gentleman of independent means from near Bishop Auckland in County Durham, who acted as paymaster for the journey. He also had a Swiss servant who made the travel arrangements. Turner told Farington on his return that he had hired this servant in Paris, and that they "paid [him] 5 livres a day, & He bore his own expenses," (*Farington Diary* November 23, 1802). It is not known whether he met up with Loweson in Paris or had traveled with him from London, but it was probably the former. For this journey, Turner used nine sketchbooks, four of which he brought with him from England; the remaining five he bought on the Continent, two in Paris and three in Switzerland.

24 The Aiguillette, Valley of Cluses, 1802

pencil, black chalk and watercolor,
on prepared gray paper
447 x 322 mm.
John Ruskin, by 1873
By descent to Arthur Severn
Purchased from Arthur Severn by Thomas Agnew & Sons in 1925
Purchased from Thomas Agnew & Sons in 1925
(WAG.D.1925.56)

This drawing is a sheet from the *St. Gothard & Mont Blanc* sketchbook (T.B. LXXV), which has the watermark J. Whatman 1801; Turner prepared this sketchbook specially for the journey by covering each sheet with a gray wash, and dismembered it soon after his return for mounting in a presentation album for prospective patrons. Fifty-six sheets from the book are now locatable in the Turner Bequest, but nine leaves, of which this is one, were apparently not included in it and are now widely scattered. This sketch served as the basis of a finished watercolor of circa 1806, which is now in a private collection. It was presumably among the sketches Turner showed to William Daniell and Joseph Farington at his house on November 22, 1802. The latter described them in his diary entry for that day as "slight on the spot, but touched up since many of them with liquid white, & black chalk."

Ruskin, who took a special interest in Turner's Alpine studies, owned both the sketch and the finished watercolor. The latter has a special connection with the city of Manchester, as Ruskin allowed it to be copied by William Ward for presentation to the Ancoats Art Museum. This museum was the brainchild of Thomas Coglan Horsfall, a wealthy Manchester card manufacturer, who believed that exposure to art would have a civilizing effect on the working classes of Manchester, and turn them away from drinking, gambling, and crime. Although Ruskin declared himself "furious at anybody's thinking that any good whatever can be in, by or for such a place as Manchester," Horsfall was undeterred and founded the museum, which was housed at Ancoats Hall from 1885. The Ward copy, together with the other contents of the museum, was transferred to the Manchester City Art Galleries in 1918.

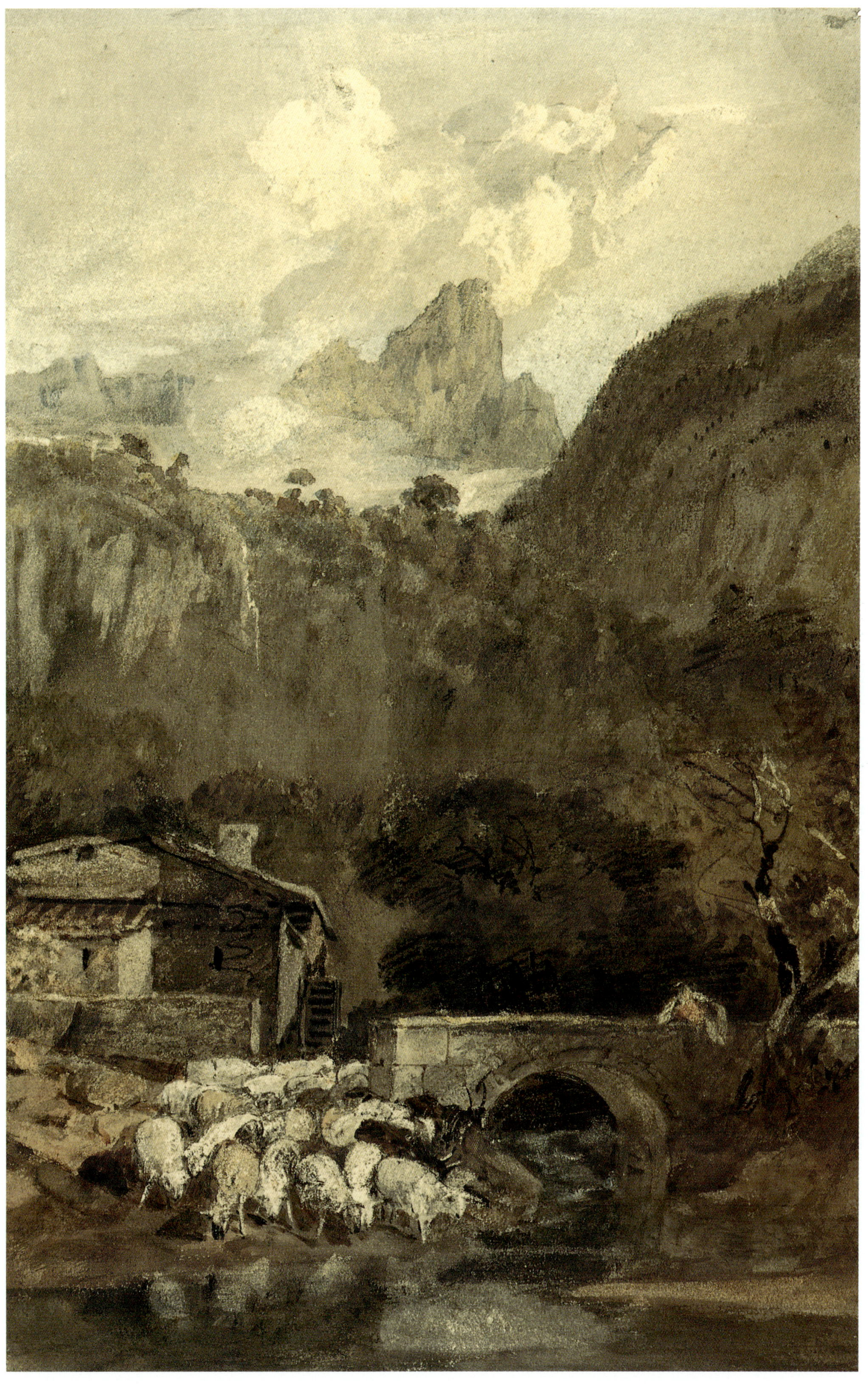

25 Lake Thun from the Landing-place at Neuhaus, 1802

pencil, black chalk and watercolor, on
prepared gray paper
325 x 478mm.
John Ruskin, by 1878
By descent to Arthur Severn
Purchased from Arthur Severn by Thomas
Agnew & Sons in 1925
Purchased from Thomas Agnew & Sons
in 1925
(WAG.D.1925.58)

This drawing, like cat. 24, is also a sheet from the dismembered *St. Gothard & Mont Blanc* sketchbook (T.B. LXX), deriving from Turner's Alpine tour of 1802. Both this drawing and *The Aiguillette* were almost certainly bought directly from the artist by Ruskin; they were exhibited as part of Ruskin's collection at the Fine Art Society in 1878, for which the famous critic wrote the catalogue. Both drawings descended to Arthur Severn, who, together with his wife Joan, Ruskin's cousin, was the main beneficiary of Ruskin's will. It was from Arthur Severn that Agnew's bought the drawings before selling them to the Whitworth in 1925. Ruskin was particularly interested in Turner's Alpine studies, and, of the nine sketches from the *St. Gothard & Mont Blanc* sketchbook, which are not in the Turner Bequest, six are known to have belonged to Ruskin, who probably bought them directly from the artist.

In his entry on this drawing in the 1878 Fine Art Society catalogue, Ruskin described the group generally: "This drawing begins the series which I hold myself greatly fortunate in possessing, of studies illustrative of the first impression made on Turner's mind by the Alps. To most men of the age . . . they are entirely delightful and exhilarating; to him they are an unbroken influence of gloomy majesty, making him thenceforth of entirely solemn heart in all his work, and giving him conceptions of the vastness and rock-frame of the earth's mass," (J. Ruskin, *Works*, Vol. XIII, p. 417). The *St. Gothard & Mont Blanc* sketchbook contains other views similar to this, but without color, on pages 44 and 46. Other views are in the *Lake Thun* sketchbook (T.B. LXXVI), in particular pages 60 and 61, which are narrower than this drawing but from almost the same viewpoint. The lake also figures as plate 46 in the *Liber Studiorum*, which was developed from a finished watercolor of circa 1806, formerly in the Newall collection, sold at Christie's on December 13, 1979, lot 74, and now in an English private collection (Wilton no. 373).

26 The Valley of Chamonix, Mont Blanc in the Distance, 1809

signed and dated: JMWTurner RA pp
1809
watercolor and bodycolor
279 x 395mm.
Walter Fawkes
By descent in the Fawkes family until 1937
Purchased from Thomas Agnew & Sons by
E.E. Cook
Presented by the executors of E.E. Cook
(via the National Art Collections Fund)
in 1955
(WAG.D.1955.18)

This watercolor, which is unusually signed in full, is based on a sheet in the *St. Gothard & Mont Blanc* sketchbook (T.B. LXXV). The Whitworth possesses two sheets from this now dismembered sketchbook, although the majority remain in the Turner Bequest (see the entries for cats. 24 and 25). The finished watercolor derives from page 18 of the sketchbook and was commissioned by Walter Ramsden Fawkes of Farnley Hall near Otley in Yorkshire. Fawkes had purchased from the Royal Academy exhibition of 1803 a watercolor of the *Glacier and source of the Arveron, going up to the Mer de Glace*, Wilton no. 565, now in the Yale Center for British Art, and, until his death in 1825, was Turner's most important patron, becoming a close friend of the artist and eventually owning six oils and some 250 watercolors by the end of his life. Fawkes was extremely fond of Turner's Alpine subjects, and most of the finished watercolors that Turner worked up from his Alpine sketches (Wilton nos. 371- 397) in the years after 1802 were painted for Fawkes.

The sketch in the Turner Bequest is gloomy and somber, a mood that is absent from this watercolor, which is bright and enlivened by the addition of a figure and several grazing goats; the view is taken from the Montanvert, and shows Mont Blanc in the distance. The initials 'pp' after the signature and before the date stand for Professor of Perspective, an office at the Royal Academy to which Turner had been elected in 1807. He was very proud of this honor and did a great deal of research into his subject in preparation for a series of lectures he began to give in 1811. He continued to give these lectures, to mixed critical response, until 1828, and finally resigned the office in 1837. (An exhibition on this hitherto-neglected area of Turner's work took place at the Clore Gallery in 1992-3, and a book, *Turner as Professor: The Artist and Linear Perspective*, was published.)

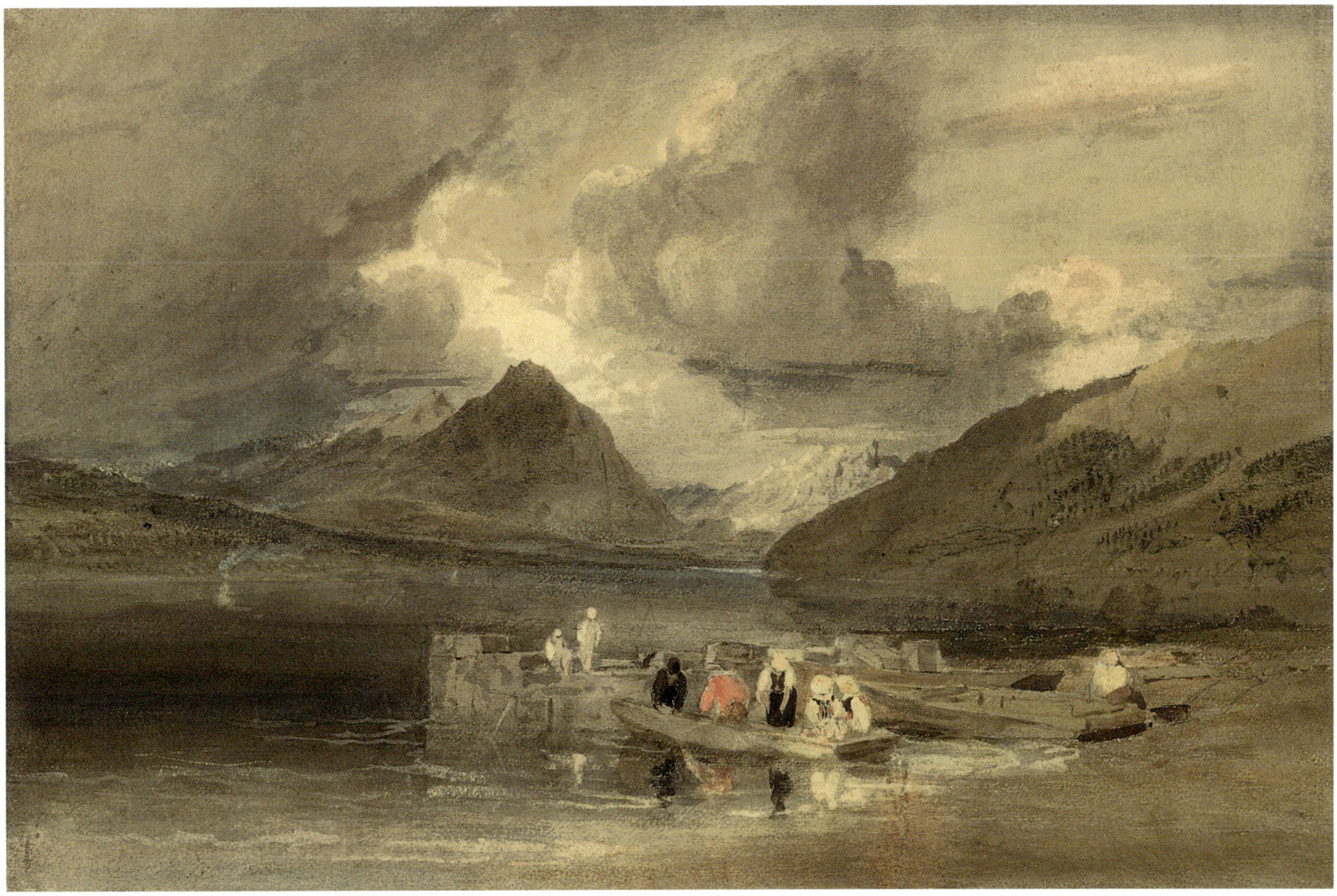

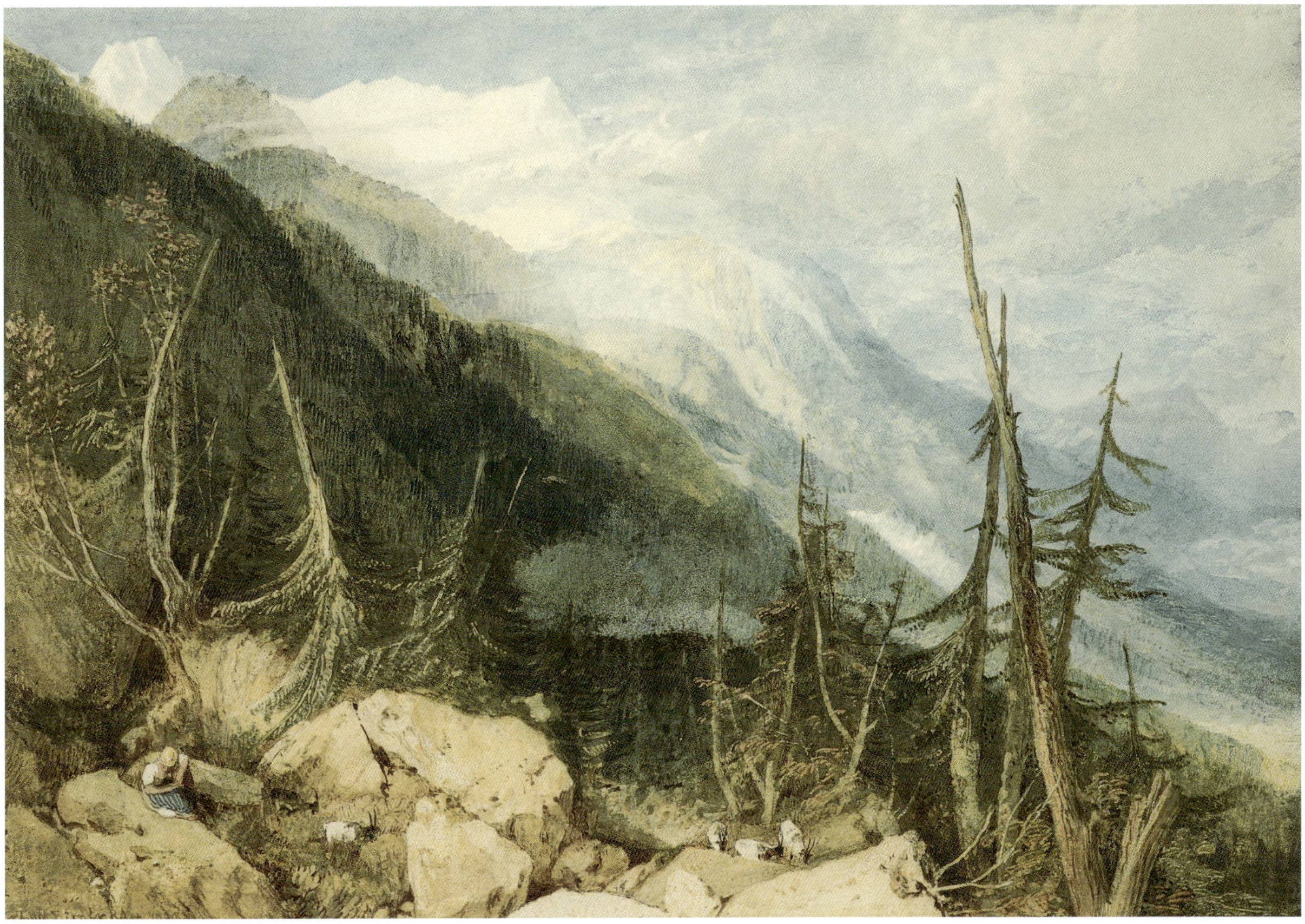

27 Inverary, Loch Fyne, Argyllshire, c. 1802-3

signed: J.M.W.Turner RA
watercolor
210 x 295 mm.
Bequeathed by James Blair in 1917
(MCAG 1917.108)

After spending most of his summers in the late 1790s sketching in England and Wales, with the new century, Turner turned his attention to Scotland. The precise dates of his tour are not known, but one of the sketchbooks he took with him records that he was in Edinburgh on July 18, 1801, and that he was back on the border, at Gretna Green, on August 5. Between these two dates he traveled across to Glasgow and then up the west coast as far as Loch Awe. It can be seen from the eight small sketchbooks he took with him that he spent more time sketching around Inverary and Loch Fyne than anywhere else on the trip. He had been commissioned by the Duke of Argyll to paint a watercolor of his castle. While he was there he took advantage of a sudden spell of fine weather to record a popular tourist spot, no doubt in the hope of gaining more commissions on his return.

One of the attractions of the area was the new town of Inverary, laid out by the architect Robert Mylne. The church tower was still under construction when Turner sketched it, as can be seen in this watercolor. The town, headquarters of the Campbell clan, held a commanding position on the peninsula of the loch with Duniquoich Hill behind. The castle Turner had been commissioned to paint is in the distance to the right of the town. It had been built between 1746 and 1761 in the "gothick" taste and added to the town's attractions.

Turner has enlivened the view with a group of fishermen in the foreground. Their herring boats were lightweight and covered, enabling them to reach the shore quickly in constantly changing weather conditions.

There are several drawings related to this watercolor in the *Scottish Lakes* sketchbook, but it most resembles *Inverary from An Otir* (T.B. LVIII 10), which belongs to a group of drawings known collectively as the *Scottish Pencils*. These are highly finished works on a large scale that Turner assembled and mounted on his return to London. All the pages have been treated with a brown wash, possibly tobacco, and are worked up laboriously in pencil and heightened with bodycolor. The tightness and austerity of this series, with its closely hatched style, informed the watercolors of the early 1800s, as can be seen in this work and in cats. 24 and 25.

The Manchester watercolor appears in its engraved state in Joseph Mawman's *An Excursion to the Highlands of Scotland and the English Lakes with Recollections, Descriptions and References to Historical Facts* published in May 1805. This commission was noted in the margin of one of the *Scottish Pencils*. Turner was to be paid seven guineas for each of four works, but in the event only three of the four were produced. The text for the illustration seems to relate quite closely to the watercolor: "We instantly had as if by enchantment, a beautiful view of the town of Inverary consisting of modern building of white stone, covered by blue slate. . . . On our landing upon the quay, the impression already received of the beauty of Inverary, situated on a small peninsula of the loch, was not diminished. Crowded with herring-busses reeling at every ebb and flow, the fore-ground diffused a lively interest over the romantic scenery in the distance."

28 Kew Palace from the Thames with Kew Bridge beyond, 1804-5

pencil and watercolor
272 x 342mm.
Bequeathed by Mary Worthington in 1904
(WAG.D.1904.14)

Formerly known as *Eton College from the Thames*, this watercolor was correctly identified in 1983 in the course of research for the *Turner Watercolours in the Whitworth Art Gallery* exhibition of 1984. It is one of a group of studies of the Thames Turner made soon after his move to Isleworth around 1804 or early 1805, when he became tenant of Sion Ferry House. Many of these studies are in the *Thames from Reading to Walton* sketchbook (T.B. XCV), including page 42, which shows a view of Kew Bridge from closer up and includes the whole span of the bridge, and page 46, which probably shows Kew Bridge seen through trees. Other studies,

on sheets of a similar size, are scattered in various collections (Wilton nos. 411-2 and 415-6), the most similar being Wilton no. 416, in an American private collection, which is almost exactly the same size. All the studies employ a very similar technique, with a dry brush loaded with color, and have the same predominantly green palette. They also share the same preoccupation with the backwaters of a busy river thoroughfare and have a mood of tranquillity, in contrast to the civilization that is rarely allowed to intrude nearer than the horizon. Turner was a keen angler and figures such as those in the foreground are not uncommon in his work.

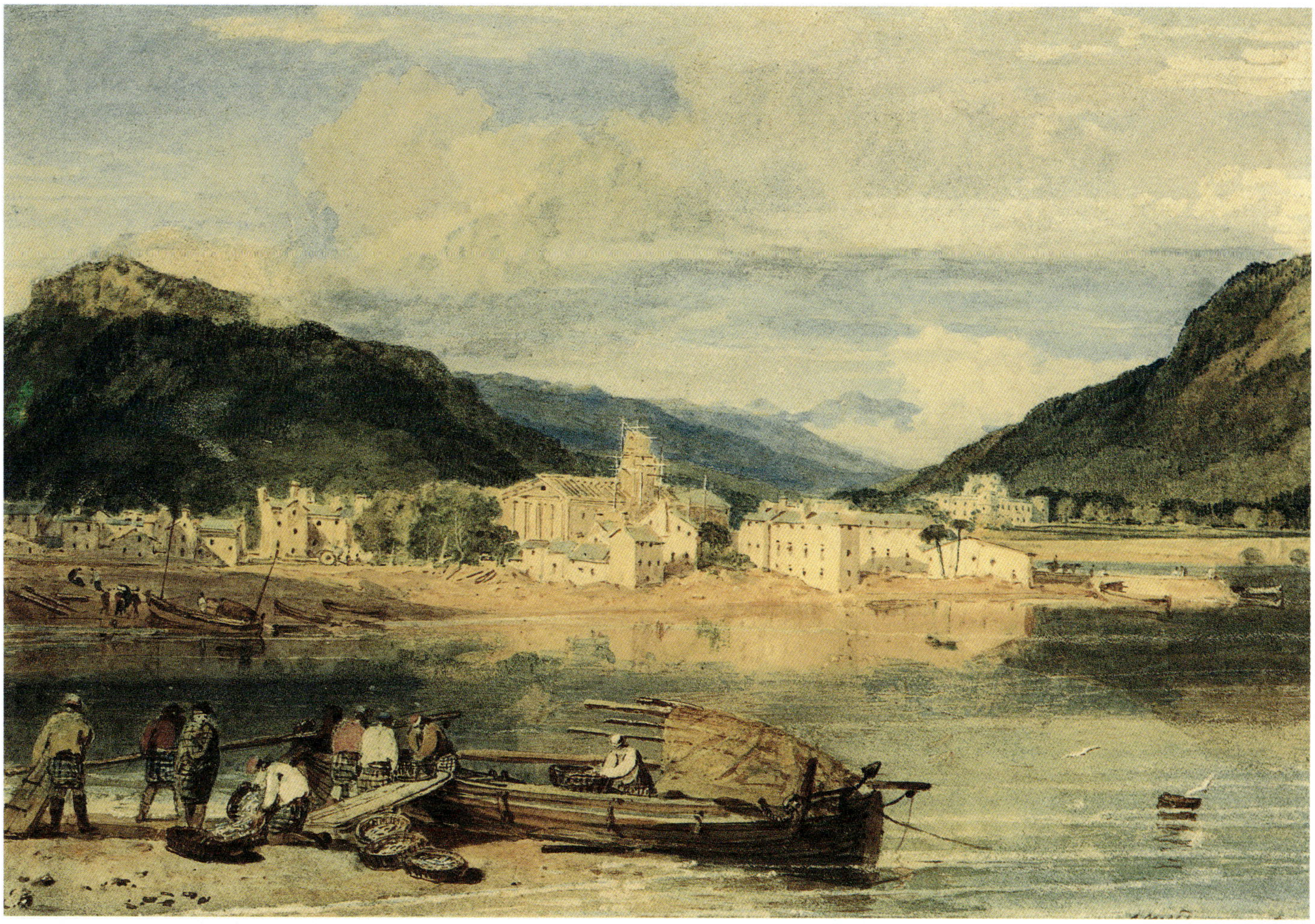

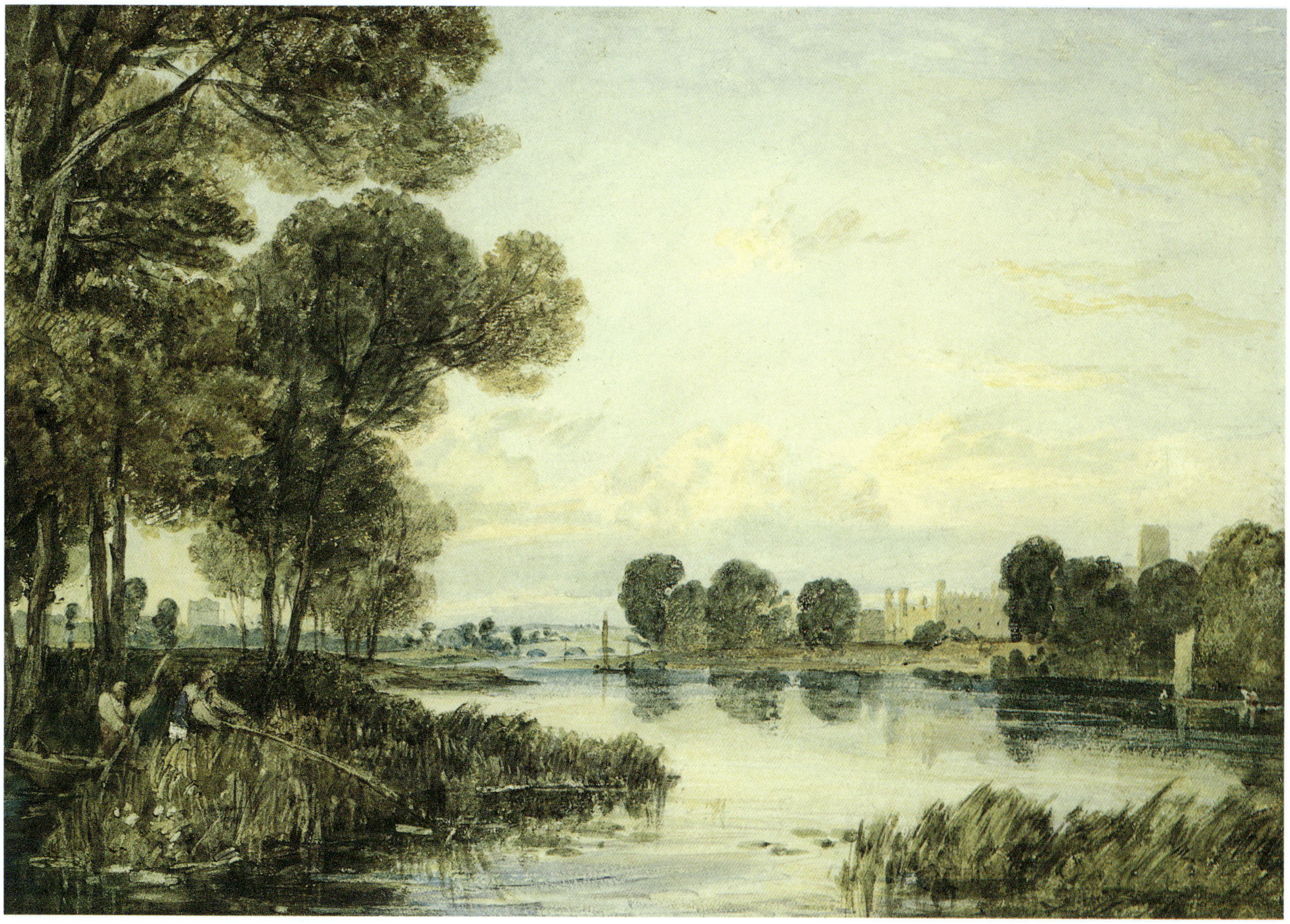

29 London from Greenwich, 1809

pen and brown ink, brown wash, on
Whatman paper dated [18]01
181 X 263mm.
Purchased from Thomas Agnew & Sons by
John Edward Taylor in 1864
Presented by John Edward Taylor in 1892
(WAG.D.1892.98)

Between 1807 and 1819, Turner executed and supervised the publication of a series of brown wash drawings; the monochrome prints that resulted were known collectively as the *Liber Studiorum*. Although conceived of in terms of Claude's *Liber Veritatis*, which was simply a record of compositions, the *Liber Studiorum* was more of a visual treatise on landscape art as seen through Turner's eyes, each plate being categorized as Pastoral, Mountainous, Marine, Architectural, Historical, or EP, by which Turner probably meant Elevated Pastoral. Using these categories, Turner was attempting to show a complete range of possibilities in landscape composition. Each part of the *Liber Studiorum* comprised five plates; fourteen of these were eventually published before the project was abandoned.

Most of the studies for the *Liber Studiorum* plates are grouped by Finberg (1909) under T.B. CXVI, CXVII, and CXVIII; the Whitworth drawing relates closely in style, medium, and size to T.B. CXVII - D, which was etched by Turner, with mezzotint engraved by Charles Turner, and published on January 1, 1811, in Part V of the *Liber*. The plate is nominally based on the large oil painting of 1809, now in the Tate Gallery (Butlin & Joll no. 97), which in turn derives from a pencil drawing in the Turner Bequest (T.B. CXX - N). In addition, conservation has recently revealed the watermark on the Whitworth drawing and shown that it and the Turner Bequest study (T.B. CXVII - D) once formed part of the same sheet, because when the original sheet was divided, the tear went right through the watermark and cut it in half. The two studies appear to be alternative compositions for the painting and for the print after it, although the argument can be made that both postdate the painting. Certainly, the direction of light and the placing of the deer is different in the Whitworth drawing from the Turner Bequest study, while both the oil painting and the final print follow the latter in those respects, suggesting that both studies precede the painting and print. The *London from Greenwich* plate appeared in the Architectural category, a category that was beginning to run dry as the project neared its end. The choice of composition may have been dictated by Turner's knowledge of John Robert Cozens' treatments of the subject in the 1790s.

30 Addingham Mill on the Wharfe, Yorkshire, c.1808-09

pencil and watercolor
276 x 387 mm.
John Edward Taylor
Bequeathed by James Blair in 1917
(MCAG 1917.98)

Addingham Mill, on the banks of the Wharfe River, close to Leeds, Yorkshire, is still standing. Nearby is Farnley Hall, once home to Turner's greatest patron and good friend Walter Fawkes. There is strong evidence to suggest that Turner's first visit to Farnley Hall, where he spent some of the happiest times of his life, took place in 1808 during his tour of Northern England and Wales. The dismembered *Wharfedale and Washburn* sketchbook can almost certainly be dated to this tour and records a trip up the Wharfe river near Fawkes's country seat. It also contains a sketch for the City Art Galleries' watercolor (T.B. CLIV - M).

Another sketchbook of the same period (T.B. CII—the *Greenwich* sketchbook) records commissions for Fawkes and payment by him for a drawing of a "mill." Stylistically the works in the *Wharfedale and Washburn* sketchbook and a series of finished watercolors produced from them relate to Turner's oils and watercolors of this period, when he was at his most naturalistic (see cat. 28). It has, however, been suggested by both Timothy Clifford (see *Turner at Manchester*) and Andrew Wilton (see Wilton no. 548) that a date of 1815-20 is more applicable.

There are two versions of this particular watercolor. It has always been assumed that the Manchester version was owned by Fawkes, as were several other works derived from the above sketchbook and recorded in the *Greenwich* sketchbook, but there is no proof of this. The second, nearly identical version belonged to the Reverend Richard Hall, a neighbor of Fawkes.

A fragment of an undated letter written to Turner by Fawkes reads ". . . everybody is delighted with your Mill - I sit a long time before it every day (T.B. CLIV - Y)." It has been suggested by David Hill, in the 1980 exhibition catalogue *Turner in Yorkshire*, page 39, that the "mill" referred to by Fawkes relates to *A View of Otley Mills* (Wilton no. 614), said to have been presented to its owner by Fawkes. It seems likely, however, that the letter refers to the Manchester picture, as Fawkes, who wrote in such glowing terms, would have hardly given away such a treasured possession. It is more probable that a second version would have been requested for a friend and neighbor after the success of the first.

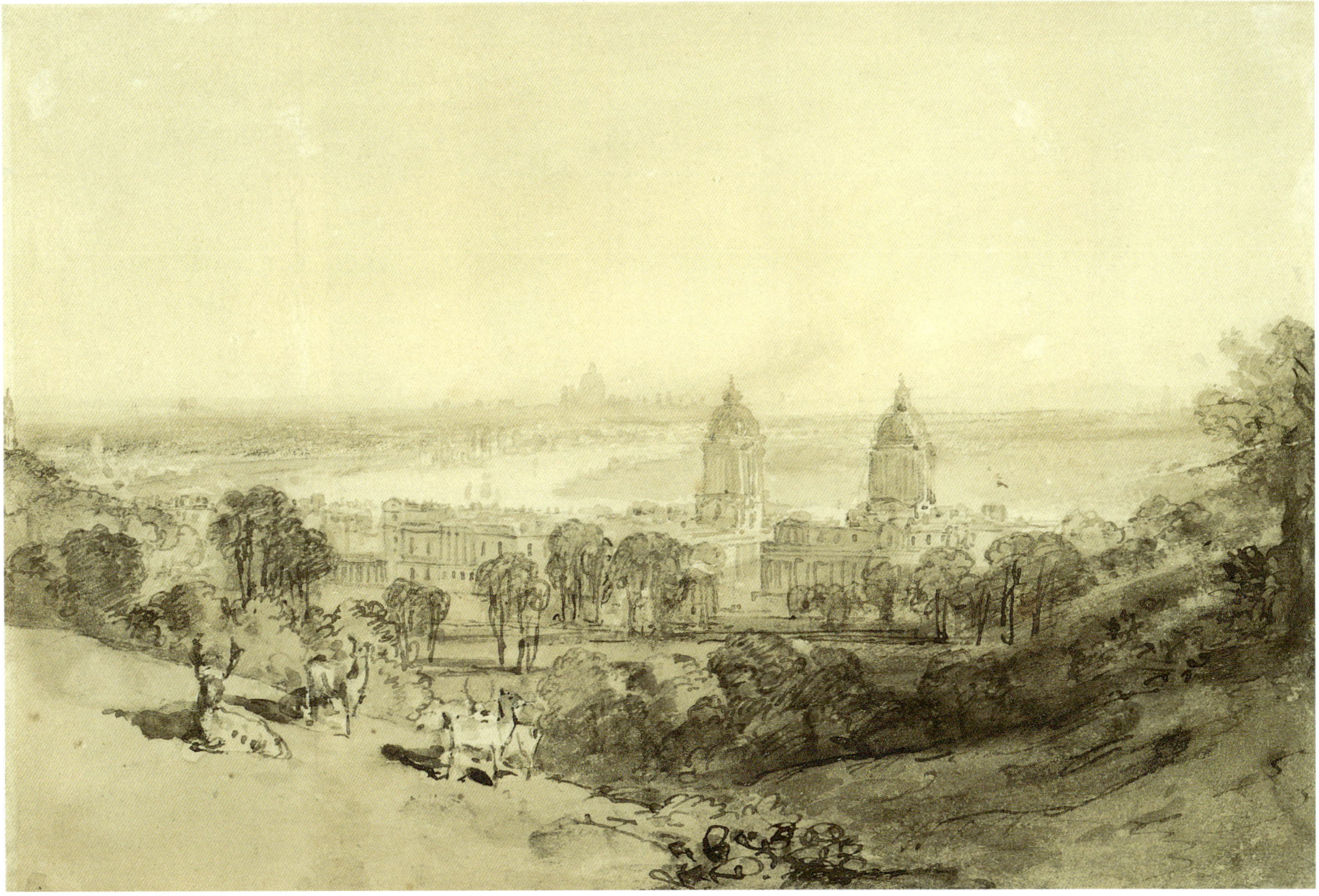

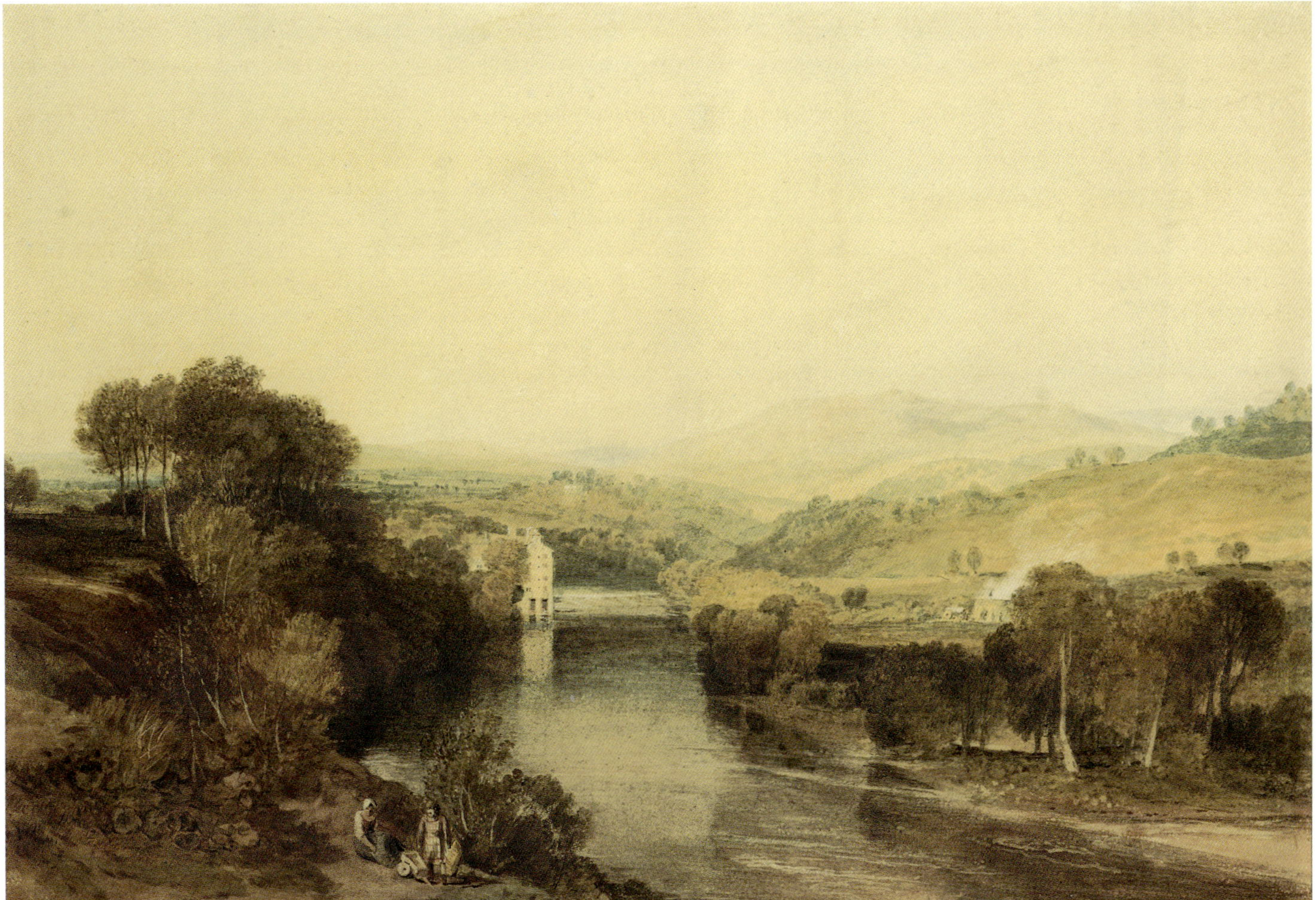

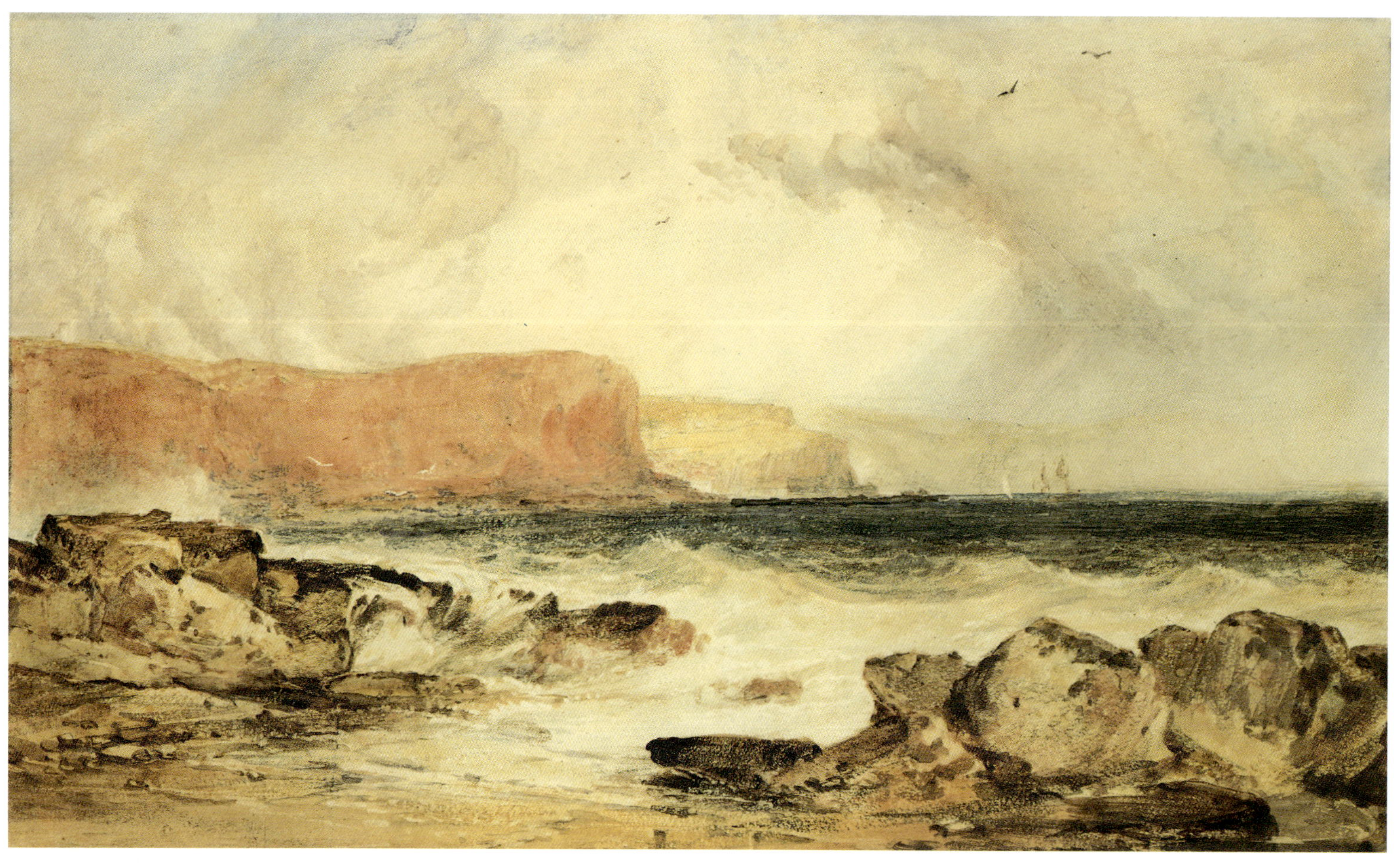

31 Whitehaven from Parton, Cumbria, 1810-15

inscribed on the reverse: "Whitehaven
from [P]arton" and "small [?ships]"
pencil and watercolor, on Whatman paper
dated 1808
218 x 353 mm.
Purchased from Thomas Agnew & Sons by
J.T. Broadhurst in 1870
By descent to Sir Edward Broadhurst
Bequeathed by Sir Edward and Lady
Broadhurst in 1924
(WAG.D.1924.52)

Previously known as *Coast of Yorkshire*, the correct title of this watercolor was discovered during the course of its conservation for the *Turner Watercolors in the Whitworth Art Gallery* exhibition of 1984, when the inscription on the reverse reading "Whitehaven from [P]arton" was revealed. A further inscription reading "small [?ships]" was also discovered. The subject of this watercolor, the port of Whitehaven on the north-west coast of Cumbria, had become during the eighteenth century one of the busiest ports in England and a thriving trading center equal to Liverpool, Bristol, and Glasgow. The port is marked on a sketch-map on the inside cover of the *Cockermouth* sketchbook (T.B. CX), which Turner used in 1809 on a trip to the Cumberland coast from Lowther Castle near Penrith, the home of his patron the Earl of Lonsdale, for whom he completed two oil paintings of the castle, exhibited at the Royal Academy in 1810 (Butlin & Joll nos. 111-112). Lord Lonsdale owed his fortune to the coalmines around Whitehaven, and indeed owned much of the town. Although he had been staying with Lord Lonsdale, Turner journeyed to the coast in connection with a com-

mission from Lord Egremont (see cat. 45) for a painting of Cockermouth Castle (Petworth House, Butlin & Joll no. 108).

The Whitworth drawing probably comes from the dismembered *Petworth* sketchbook (T.B. CIX), which was used on that trip and of which 24 leaves remain in the Turner Bequest; the watermark is identical, and the size of the sheets are very similar. The fact that this watercolor is extremely faded makes it difficult to date, although it certainly postdates 1810, which would mean that the watercolor was added later to the pencil drawing of 1809. About 1835 Turner returned to the subject of Whitehaven for a watercolor for the *England and Wales* series (Wilton no. 875, offered at Sotheby's on November 19, 1992, lot 150), possibly using a lost sketch from the Petworth sketchbook. In this watercolor, the town is viewed from much closer, and more stress is laid on its industry. But compositionally it and the Whitworth watercolor are not dissimilar. A study of Whitehaven, showing an even closer view of the port, is in a private collection (Wilton no. 893).

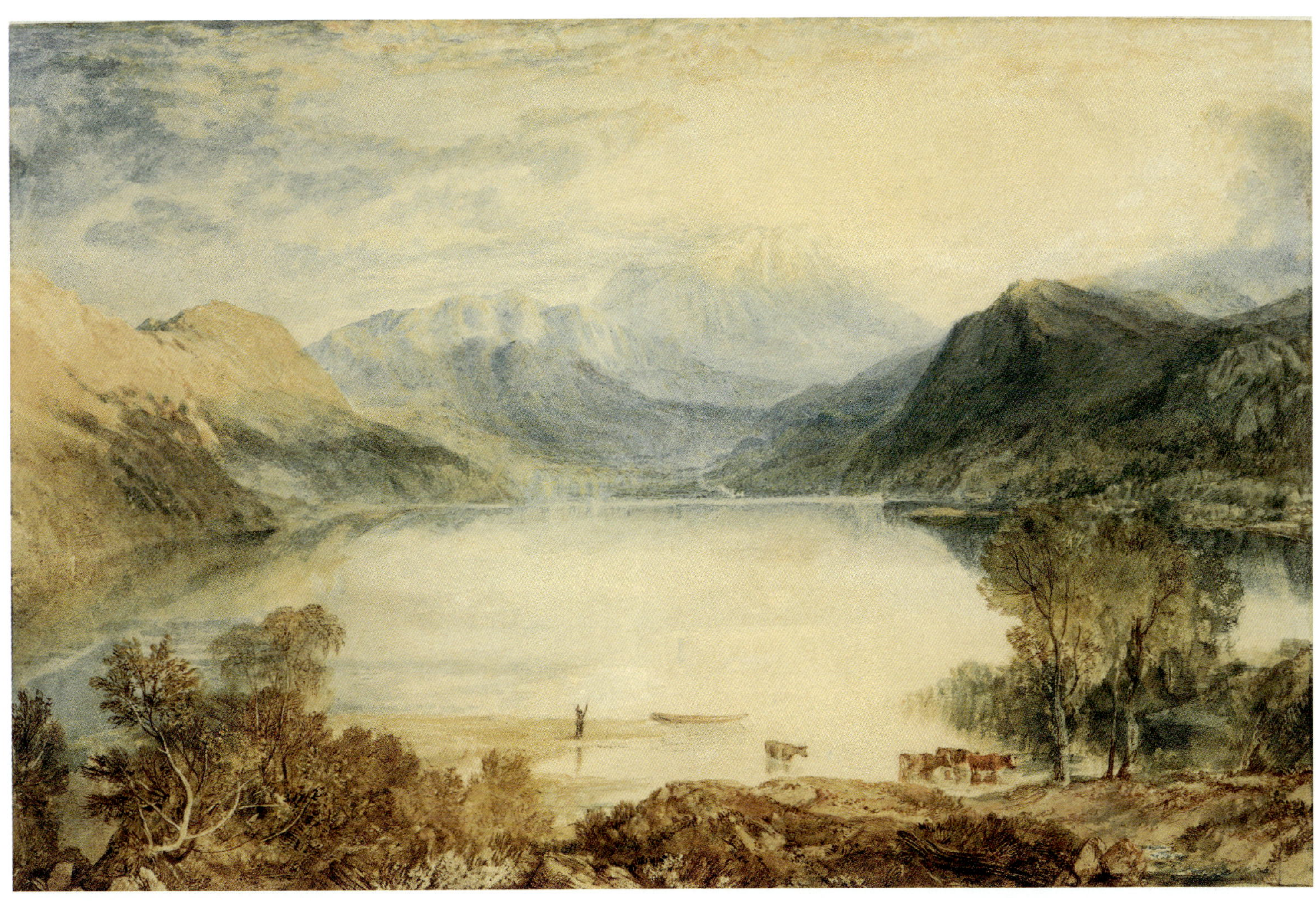

32 Ullswater from Gowbarrow Park, c. 1815

watercolor, on Whatman paper dated
1814
280 x 413 mm.
Walter Fawkes
By descent in the Fawkes family until 1890
Purchased from Thomas Agnew & Sons in
1891 with a fund presented by the
Guarantors of the 1887 Manchester Royal
Jubilee Exhibition
(WAG.D.1887.14)

It is possible that Turner visited the Lake
District in late summer of 1815, since he
wrote to the Rev. H.S. Trimmer on August 1 of
that year, "Mr. Fawkes talks of keeping me in
the north by a trip to the Lakes &c until
November." No sketches survive, however,
from the trip if it was ever made. It is more
likely that this watercolor, which is datable to
circa 1815 both stylistically and on grounds of
the watermark, was worked up from earlier
sketches of 1797 in the *Tweed and Lakes* sketchbook (T.B. XXXV). Page 43 of this sketchbook
shows approximately the same view, but taken
from lower down. In this sketch, a horse and
cart stand in the shallows, but these are

replaced in the finished watercolor by the cows
and the cowherd, as on page 40 of the sketchbook, which shows the same view, but looks
more to the right. Turner returned to the same
sketches for his watercolor of Ullswater for the
England and Wales series, which shows the same
view, but taken from the shore (private collection, Wilton no. 860). In the Whitworth
watercolor, only part of the middle reach of the
lake is shown, looking southwest, and the artist
has greatly increased the height of the mountains in the far distance, with Helvellyn in the
center, so as to give the composition a more
compressed feeling and to give the lake a more
circular appearance.

TURNER'S ILLUSTRATIONS TO THE
PROVINCIAL ANTIQUITIES OF SCOTLAND

Turner was one of several artists invited by Sir Walter Scott to illustrate the *Provincial Antiquities and Picturesque Scenery of Scotland.* The risks of publication were to be shared by some of the participants. Scott first approached friends such as the painters The Reverend John Thomson of Duddinston and Edward Blore, and the engravers George Cooke, Henry Le Keux, and William Lizar to be shareholders. It would seem that Turner was brought in to add prestige to the production as he was asked to produce more illustrations than any of the other artists and was paid twice as much. Other artists such as Augustus Wall Callcott and Alexander Nasmyth were involved to a lesser degree. The publication was issued in ten paperbound parts between 1819 and 1826 and was later also published in two volumes with additional vignettes by Turner. Sadly the venture failed and brought financial ruin to John Thomson. Turner, with his usual financial acumen, seemed to ride the storm.

It is possible that Turner and Scott first met at this time as the contract signed by them in 1818 stipulated that there were to be periodical meetings of shareholders and as Gerald Finley has pointed out in his book *Landscapes of Memory* (London 1980), there would have been a good opportunity in November of that year when at least half the shareholders were in Edinburgh. The date of this meeting may indeed have shaped Turner's research tour for the publication which began in October on the east coast of Scotland and ended in Edinburgh. At this particular time, it seems that Turner did not make a favorable impression on Scott, who wrote to his friend James Skene in the following year: "Turner's palm is as itchy as his fingers are ingenious and he will . . . do nothing without cash and anything for it." Later on, however, when Turner was employed in 1831 by the publisher Robert Cadell to illustrate other works by Scott (see cats. 60 and 61), the two men managed to resolved their differences and developed a mutual admiration.

The contract stipulated that Scott was to select the subjects for illustration and would then write the text around the illustrations as he received them. (This became increasingly difficult to coordinate as the publication proceeded.) It also stipulated that Scott was to receive "drawings and paintings which his descriptive manuscript illustrates." The four watercolors on loan to Manchester City Art Galleries are part of a set of eight which were mounted together and framed in a heavy oak frame and hung in the morning room at Abbotsford, Scott's baronial home in the Scottish borders. The frame, which Finberg described as "atrocious" (A.J. Finberg, *Turner's Sketches and Drawings,* London, 1910, p. 106), was said to have been made from an oak that had been felled in the grounds of the house.

Scott was not widely traveled in his youth—the Napoleonic wars restricted the adventures of young men of substance used to going on the Grand Tour. John Sutherland in his *Life of Sir Walter Scott,* 1995, gives some idea of the narrowness of the young Scott's perspective: Walter Scott Senior "would evidently as soon as eat human flesh, roast on Sunday, as go abroad (i.e. out of Midlothian) for his vacations; if - apart from Sabbath rest - he took vacations."

It is not surprising, therefore, that most of the views chosen by Scott could be seen on the prescribed picturesque tour of Scotland, and were mostly in close proximity to Edinburgh and the Borders where Scott was brought up and worked in his father's law firm. In general, however, Scott had little enthusiasm for painting, although he was very interested in picturesque theories, which represented common ground between himself and Turner.

33 Edinburgh from Calton Hill, c.1818

watercolor and bodycolor with
gum arabic
167 x 249 mm.
Sold by Ralph Brocklebank in 1938
On loan to Manchester City Art Galleries
from a private collection
(MCAG M10197)

The pastoral nature of Turner's 1804 water-color of Edinburgh (T.B. LX - H) has changed in this later watercolor to a more urban view. Replacing the milkmaids and cows of the ear-lier version are washerwomen conversing with soldiers and people standing on the hill admir-ing the famous view. Scott's text takes its cue from Turner's illustration: "The point which Mr. Turner has selected for the view is precisely that upon which every passenger, however much accustomed to the wonderful scene, is inclined to pause and, with eyes unsatisfied with seeing, to gaze on the mingled and almost tempestuous scene which lies before and beneath him."

At the foot of the hill on the left is the newly built Calton Jail and the round tower beyond is the monument to David Hume, designed by Robert Adam in 1777. Regent Bridge lies at the bottom of the hill, and at right angles to this the North Bridge connects the old and new town. Landmarks of the old town rising from the tangle of tenements are, from left to right, the church of St. John's, St. Giles' Cathedral, and the castle towering in the background.

Turner has taken the top of the composi-tion from a detailed double page panorama in the *Scotch Antiquities* sketchbook (T.B. CLXVII, p. 39v. -40). On the following page are sketches for some of the figures.

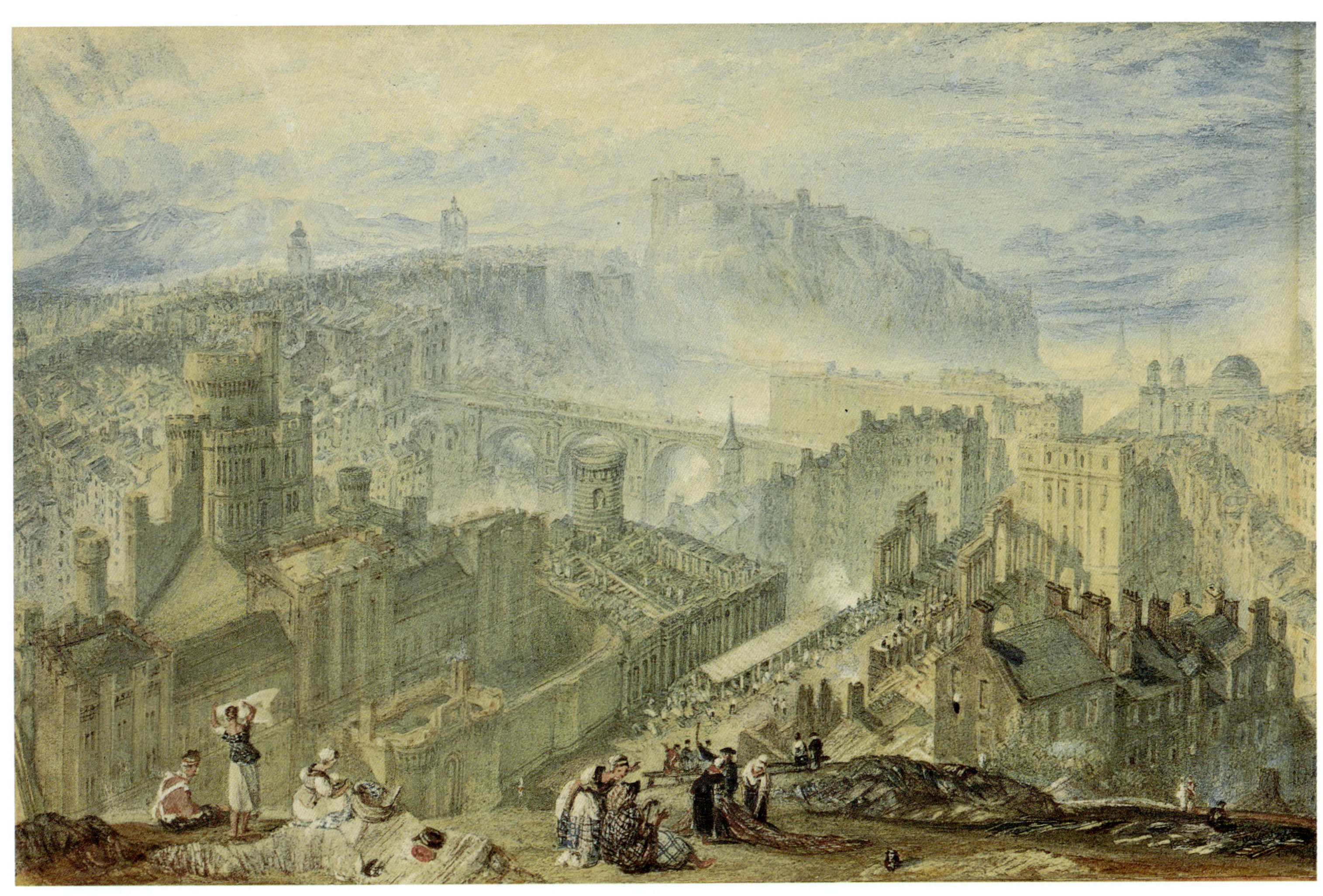

34 Heriot's Hospital, Edinburgh, 1818

signed and dated: J.M.W. Turner RA/ (?)
1816
watercolor and bodycolor
166 x 249 mm.
Sold by Ralph Brocklebank in 1938
On loan to Manchester City Art Galleries
from a private collection
(MCAG M10196)

Heriot's Hospital is the large seventeenth-century building towering over the lively scene in the West Bow, a narrow winding street leading from the High Street down to the Grassmarket, the stalls of which are just visible. There are sketches for the street scene in the *Scotch Antiquities* sketchbook (T.B. CLXVII p. 86). Turner has included a visual pun on the right-hand side by emphasizing certain letters in the "Auld Rags" sign, so that it reads "Auld R.A." Edinburgh was already being called "Auld Reekie" or "old smoky" at this time and he has added to it the words "school" and "English School." Possibly this represents a jibe at the Scots, and in particular Sir Walter Scott, who often preferred native artists such as Alexander Nasmyth to English.

In the text Scott tells us that Heriot's Hospital was founded by George Heriot (d. 1608), a wealthy goldsmith, as a charitable institution for young orphan boys. This has led Eric Shanes to comment on the old woman in the foreground, directly under the hospital building, as stretching out her arms in a charitable gesture toward the two young boys (see Picture Notes, *Turner Studies,* vol. 5 no. 2). The same old woman also appears in *Edinburgh from Calton Hill* (see cat. 33). The text also tells us that West Bow was the traditional area for metalworkers, which could be why Turner linked the two subjects together.

It is notable that 1818 was the publication date of Scott's *Heart of Midlothian* which takes charity and justice as central themes. "The steep and crooked street called the Bow" (chapter four) was the way by which the condemned were led from the notorious Tolbooth Jail to their execution in the Grassmarket.

There is some confusion as to the date of this work—the inscription on the bottom left corner appears to read 1816 but Turner did not arrive in Edinburgh for his second visit until 1818 and it was in this year that the project was first discussed.

35 Linlithgow Palace, 1821

signed and dated: JMW Turner RA/ 1821
watercolor and bodycolor with gum arabic
170 x 256 mm.
Sold by Ralph Brocklebank in 1938
On loan to Manchester City Art Galleries
from a private collection
(MCAG M10199)

Linlithgow Palace lies a few miles west of Edinburgh, close to Linlithgow town. The spire on the left is that of St. Michael's parish church. Its situation on the promontory of a large lake made it attractive as a hunting lodge for a succession of medieval sovereigns, although by Turner's day it was a burnt-out ruin. Scott writes in his text: "The sport of hunting . . . was followed with success in the neighbourhood, from which circumstance probably arises that the ancient arms of the city represent a black greyhound bitch tied to a tree."

Dogs often appear in Turner's work and can be seen in each illustration for the *Provincial Antiquities.* The dog represented here has the physique of a hunting dog and is probably a reference to the above quotation. In the *Reminiscences of C.R. Leslie* (Boston 1860), the author says Scott "liked to have a dog with him for walks, if for nothing else but to furnish a living object in the foreground of the picture."

As with several other places chosen by Scott for the *Provincial Antiquities,* such as Bothwick and Crichton Castles, Linlithgow also figures as a picturesque subject in his poem *Marmion,* which describes the castle as the home of Queen Margaret who "in Lithgow's bower, /All lonely sat, and wept the weary hour."

The Arcadian scene with bathing nymphs in Turner's earlier oil painting of Linlithgow Palace, dated 1810, (Butlin & Joll, no. 104) contrasts strongly with this version. Here the atmosphere is more bucolic and the only concession to classicism is the singular Scotsman posed as a river god. Like many of Turner's lowland Scots he is dressed in tartan, which was normally worn only by highlanders. This was a habit of Turner's deplored by Scott. Perhaps Scott was referring to the incongruity of this gentleman in the last sentence of his text: "In coming to Linlithgow by the Edinburgh road, the first view of the town is most impressive: its beautiful steeple, surmounted with a royal crown, and ruinous palace towers arising out of a canopy of trees, form a most impressive object. All that is wanting is something of more elevated dignity to the margin of the lake. But it is not easy to satisfy the inconsistent wishes of amateurs."

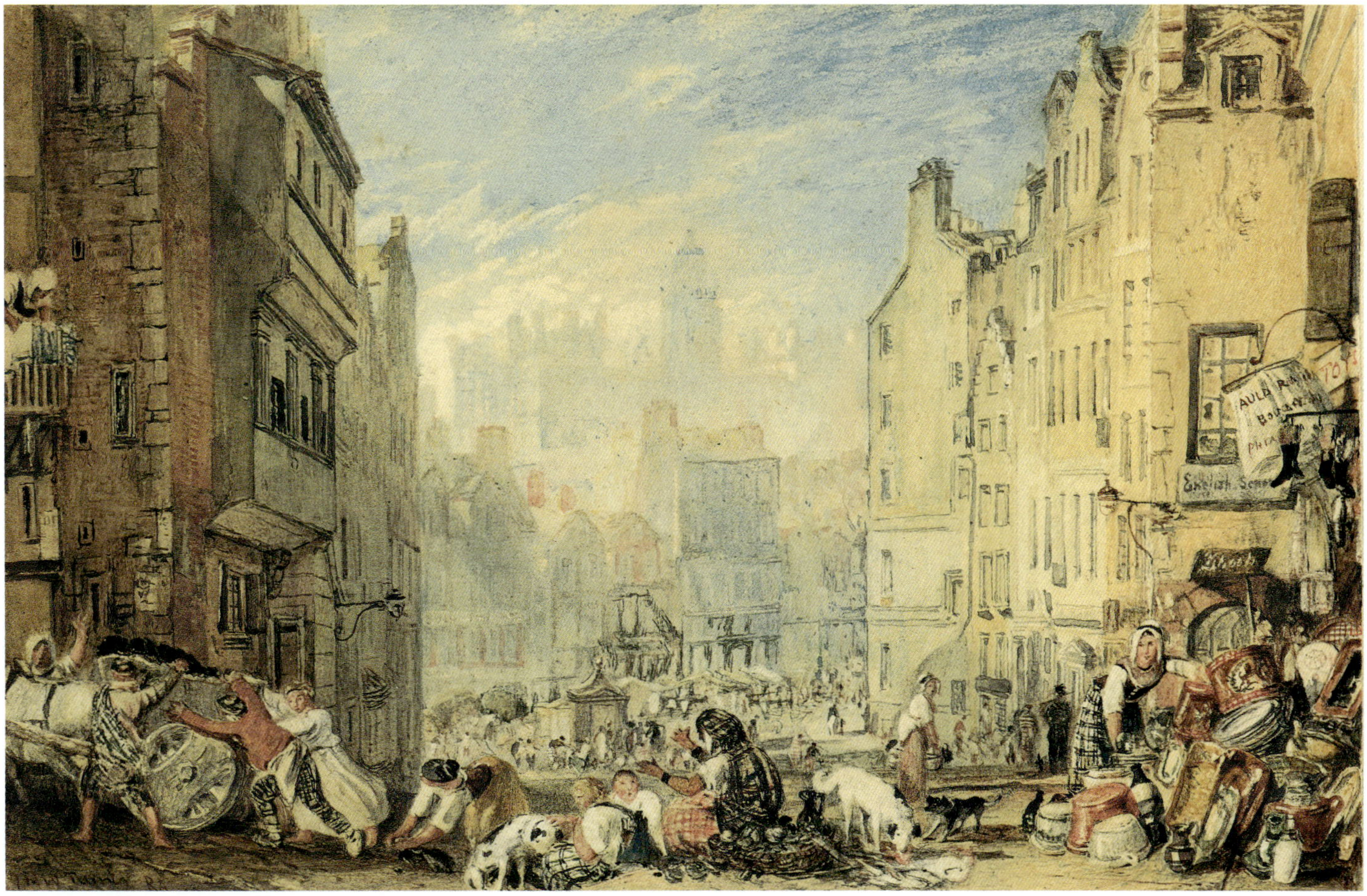

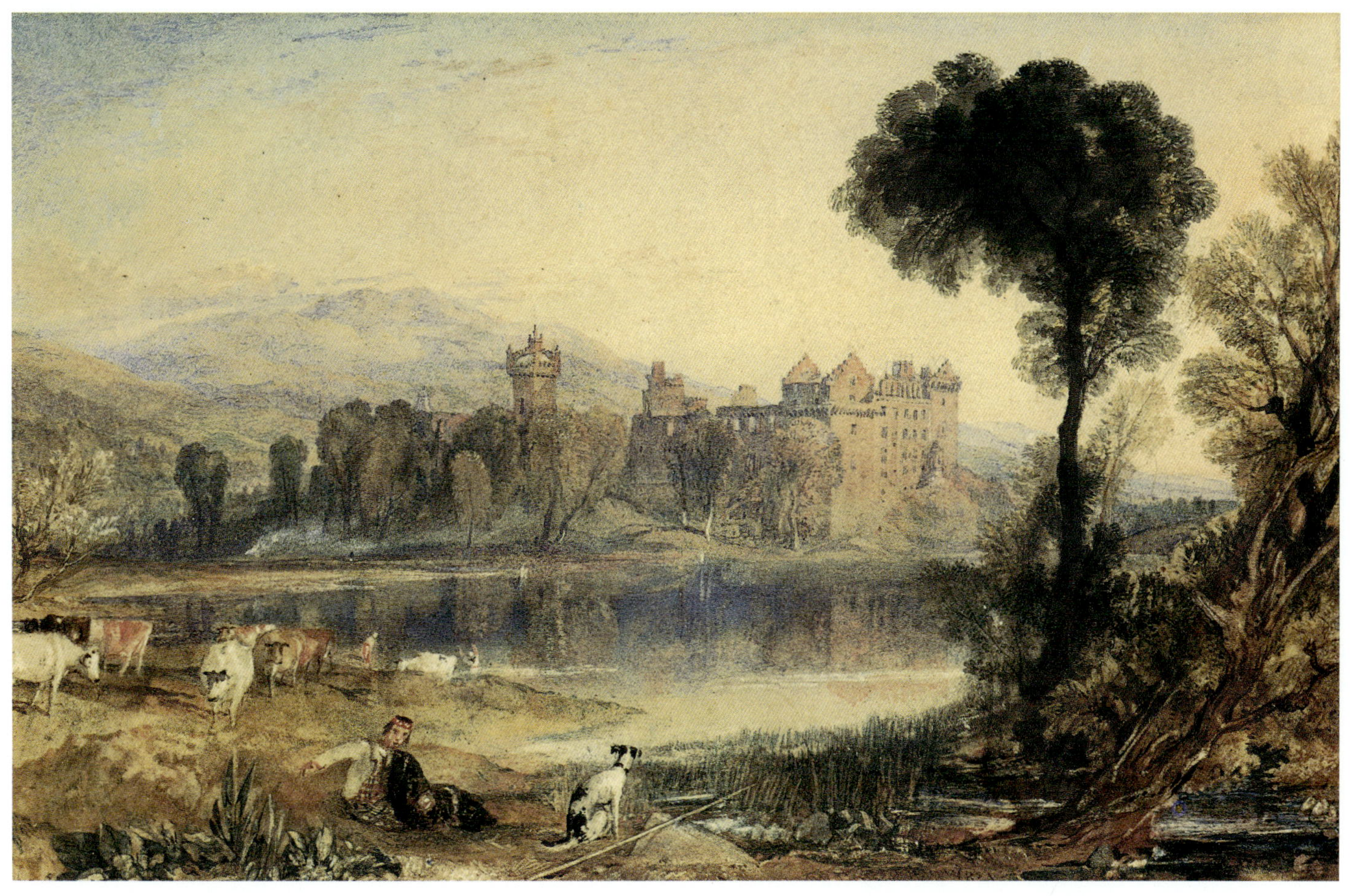

36 Tantallon Castle, 1821

signed and dated: J.M.W.Turner/1821
watercolor and bodycolor
175 x 260 mm.
Sold by Ralph Brocklebank in 1938
On loan to Manchester City Art Galleries
from a private collection
(MCAG M10198)

Tantallon Castle lies on the East Lothian coast some miles from North Berwick and the mouth of the Firth of Forth. Turner drew sketches for it in the *Scotch Antiquities* sketchbook (T.B. CLXVII p. 5v-6) on his way to Edinburgh in 1818. In the background is the Bass Rock, the subject of another illustration in the *Provincial Antiquities.*

Exposed to the sea on three sides and with its sheer fourth wall, Tantallon Castle is positioned on a rocky promontory, virtually impregnable to man but not to the massive might of the North Sea. Turner has produced one of his most effective impressions of rough sea beating against a rocky coastline, which was praised and analyzed by Ruskin in "Water as painted by Turner" in *Modern Painters* Vol. I, part II, section 35 (J. Ruskin, *Works*, p. 566).

The relationship of the two figures to their surroundings is not clear, and by the time this watercolor was produced, the links between Scott's text and the illustrations were becoming more tenuous. Perhaps Turner saw the vulnerability of the castle echoed in the vulnerability of the old woman and little boy—youth and age, the two extremes of vulnerability—who are placed directly under the castle and repeat its shape. They are somewhat protected from the gale by the natural surroundings of the rocks, just as the castle's artificial structure affords some protection, but neither natural or man-made structures can provide complete protection from the power of the sea. The futility of the boy's action in scooping up the ocean into a jar is perhaps an ironic reference to human subservience to the elements of nature.

Turner most likely would have known of Scott's references to Tantallon in *Marmion*, his romantic tale of chivalry and skullduggery published in 1808, which was well received in London. He was certainly aware of Scott by 1811 (see John Gage, *Collected Correspondence of J.M.W. Turner*, 1980, p. 46-7). The following reference appears in Canto XXXIII:

"But scant three miles the band had rode,
  when o'er a height they passed,
And sudden, close before them showed
His towers, Tantallon vast;
Broad, massive, high, and stretching far,
and held impregnable in war
On a projecting rock they rose, and round
  three sides the ocean flows."

An interesting footnote to this is provided by an observation in J.G. Lockhart's *Life of Sir Walter Scott*. Scott's friend Guthrie Wright remembers being shown an early draft of *Marmion* in 1807 and it was he who suggested that the hero's visit to Scotland should include a stay at Tantallon because of its strong dramatic possibilities: "He then asked if I had ever been there, and upon saying I had frequently, he desired me to describe it, which I did; and I verily believe it is from what I then said, that the accurate description contained in the fifth canto was given - at least I never heard him say he had afterwards gone to visit the castle," (Lockhart 2.11).

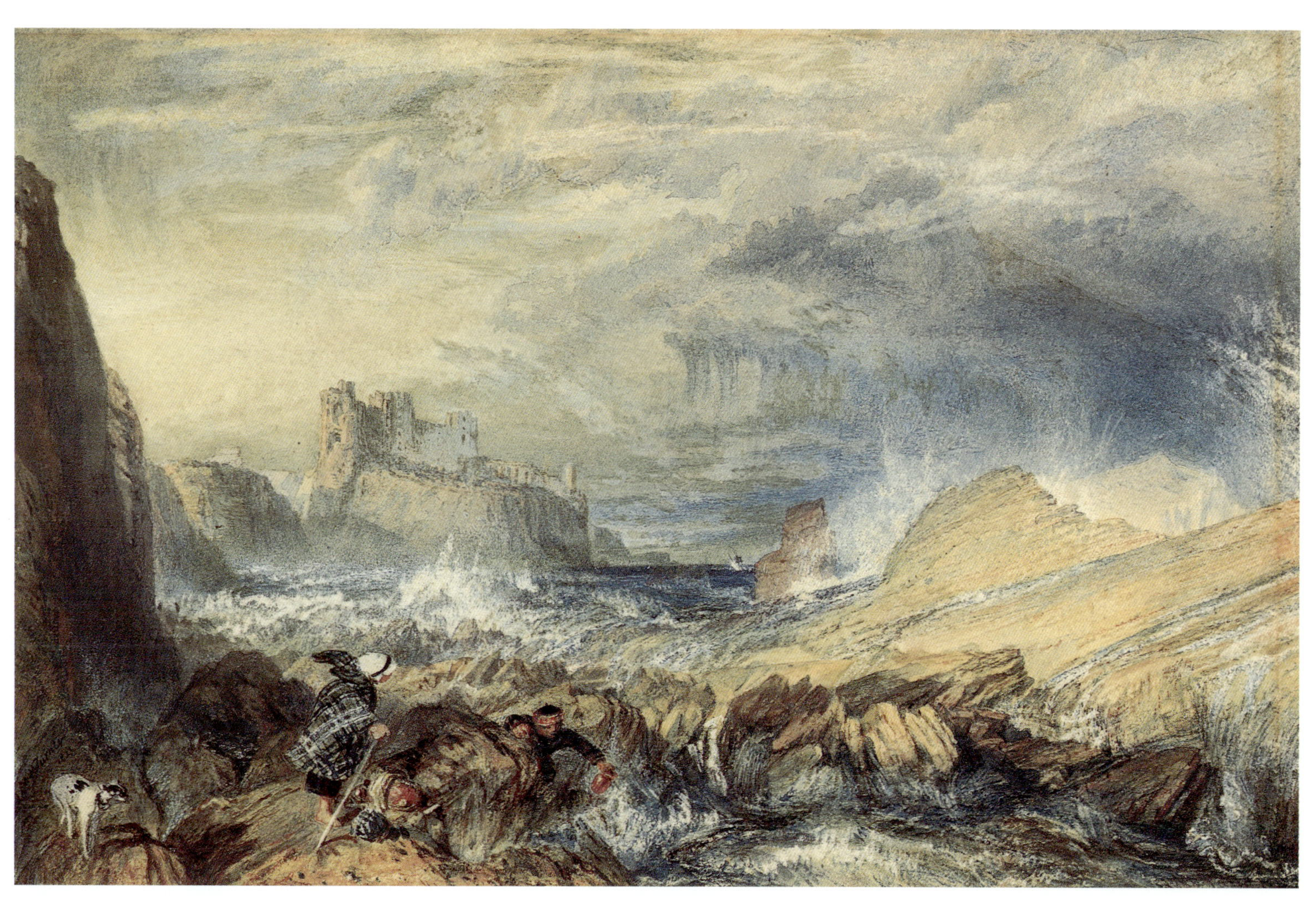

37 Eridge Castle, East Sussex, c. 1815

pencil, watercolor and bodycolor
369 x 543 mm.
Purchased from Thomas Agnew & Sons in
1891 with a fund presented by the
Guarantors of the 1887 Manchester Royal
Jubilee Exhibition
(WAG.D.1887.12)

In his Diary for April 21, 1810, Farington recorded: "Mr. Fuller, member for Suffolk [sic—Farington's mistake for Sussex], has engaged Turner to go into that County to make drawings of three or four views. He is to have 100 guineas for the use of his drawings, which are to be returned to him"; this presumably refers to some sort of engraving project. If the drawings for this project were ever executed, they are now lost, but it is more likely that the terms of the commission were altered, since Turner did complete an oil painting of John Fuller's country seat, Rosehill Park, Brightling, Sussex, for his patron in 1810 (private collection, Butlin & Joll no. 211).

This was not the end of the connection between Turner and Fuller, since about 1815 the idea of the engraving project was revived, and Turner began a series of watercolors of Sussex views, mainly for Fuller, some of which were engraved by W. B. Cooke for the Sussex landowner between 1816 and 1820. Turner was at this time closely involved with Cooke as the publisher and engraver of the *Southern Coast* series, and the latter was to undertake the same

duties here, the risk being Fuller's. Two parts, with a list of seven plates in each, were advertised as *Views in Sussex,* but only one appeared, and that with only five engravings, together with an allegorical design on the cover, drawn and etched by Turner. The project appears to have been a failure, as the second part was never published and three plates intended for it that had been commenced were left unfinished.

The Sussex watercolors, not all of which were painted for Fuller, are listed as Wilton nos. 423-439. There is no record that Fuller owned this watercolor, which is based on a pencil sketch in the *Vale of Heathfield* sketchbook (T.B. CXXXVII pp. 14a-15) of about 1810. But it is very similar in size and style to the engraved Fuller watercolors and may have been drawn for the owner of Eridge Castle, the 2nd Earl of Abergavenny, who was a friend and neighbor of Fuller. Abergavenny had rebuilt Eridge Castle in 1787 transforming it into a Gothic Revival castle; it was demolished in 1938-9.

38 Study of a dead Pheasant, 1815-20

pencil and watercolor
282 x 377 mm.
Walter Fawkes
John Ruskin
Purchased from John Ruskin by Thomas
Agnew & Sons in 1869
Purchased from Thomas Agnew & Sons by
John Edward Taylor in 1869
Presented by John Edward Taylor in 1892
(WAG.D.1892.94)

Turner created this watercolor at Farnley Hall, where shooting was a regular pastime. As well as shooting, Walter Fawkes numbered natural history and ornithology among his many amateur enthusiasms. In 1823 he published a four-volume *Synopsis of Natural History*, which was a broad survey of the animal kingdom, ranging from animals and birds to amphibia, fish, insects, and shells. The book was illustrated by Samuel Howitt. Running concurrently with this project was the compilation of five albums, giving a complete survey of British birds, called the *Ornithological Collection*. The family was involved in the compilation of these albums from 1815 onward. They were illustrated with 55 watercolors, twenty of which were by Turner. These were subsequently removed from the albums and mounted in a separate book,

known as the *Farnley Book of Birds*, which remained in the library at Farnley until being acquired by Leeds City Art Gallery in 1985.

This study is datable to 1815-20, since one of the watercolors in the *Farnley Book of Birds* is based on a sketch of 1815 and two similar studies of pheasants in the Turner Bequest are on paper watermarked 1818 (T.B. CCLXIII - 358 and 359). Although not produced for the *Ornithological Collection*, the Whitworth watercolor is clearly related to it, and is one of several studies of birds Ruskin acquired from members of the Fawkes family. Ruskin, who visited Farnley twice, said that Turner painted birds: "Nowhere but at Farnley. He could only do them joyfully there." He too painted watercolors of dead pheasants, which are obviously influenced by Turner.

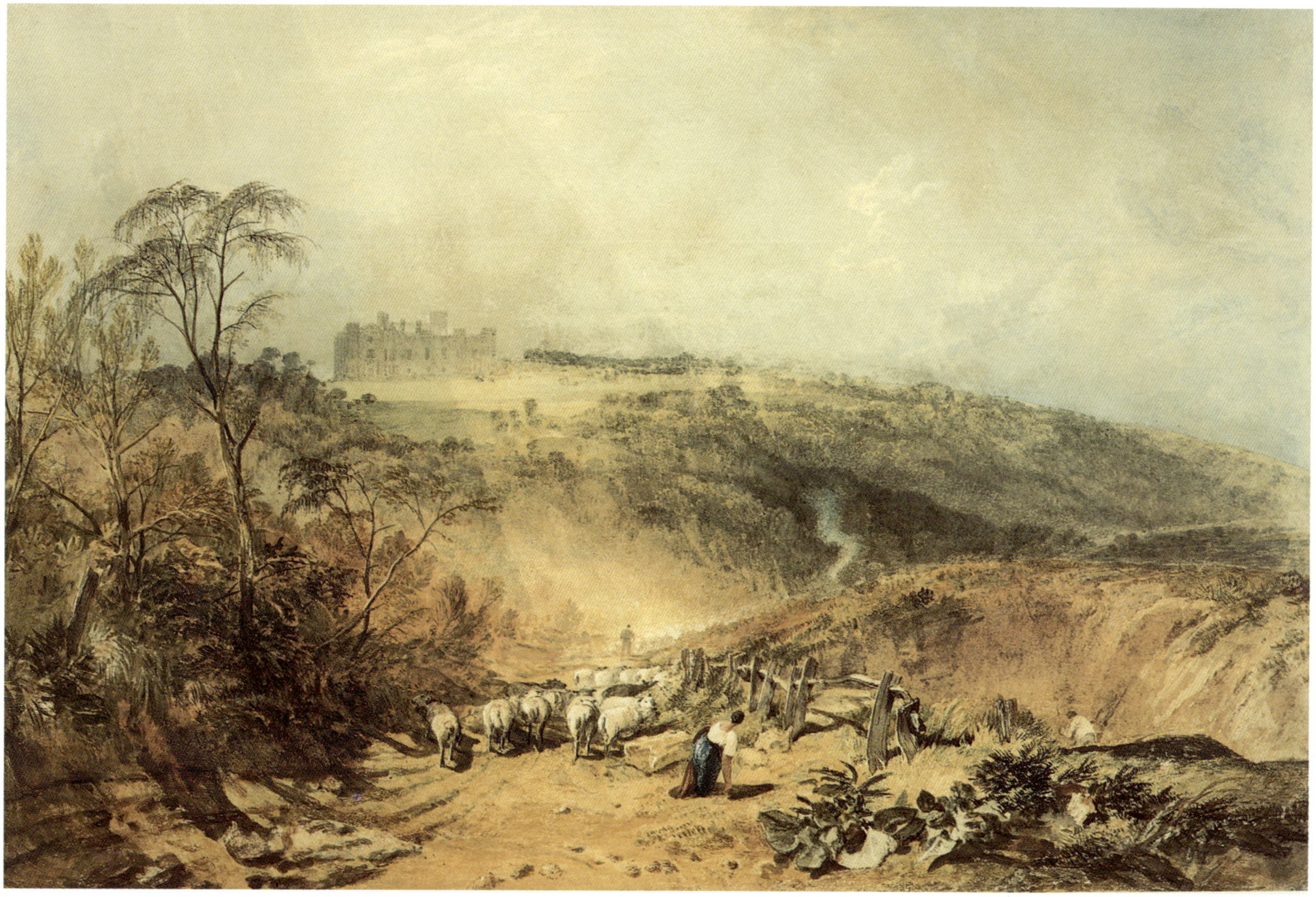

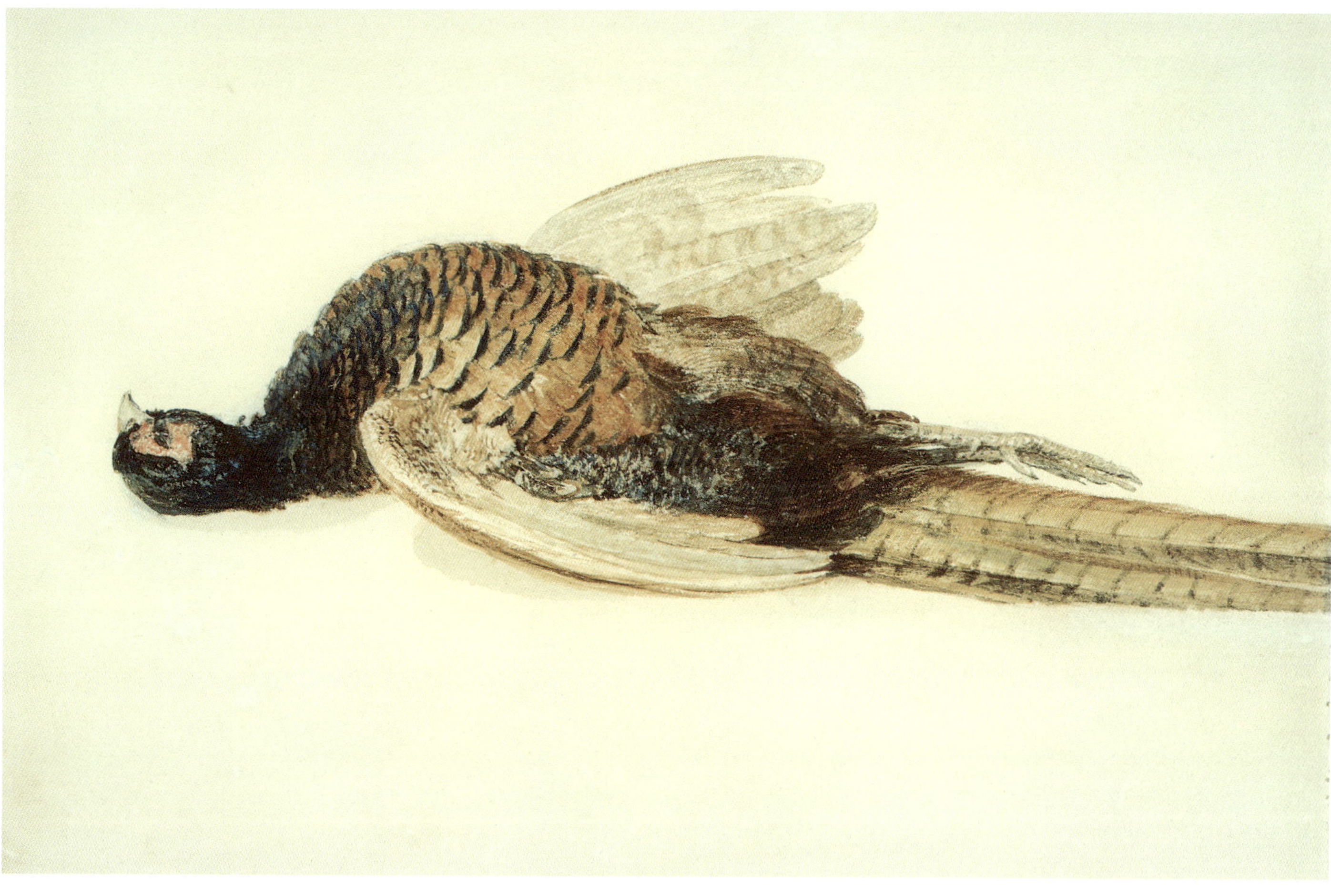

THE RHINE SERIES OF 1817

Napoleon's final defeat at Waterloo in June 1815 unleashed a flood of visitors to the Continent. A further catalyst was provided by the publication in November 1816 of Canto III of Byron's *Childe Harold's Pilgrimage*, which contained moving and powerful descriptions of the Field of Waterloo and the Rhineland. In setting out for these two destinations in the summer of 1817, Turner was thus doing nothing out of the ordinary. What was different about this journey was that it was his first on the Continent since 1802 and his first alone and unaccompanied. As was to be the pattern for later Continental tours, Turner did a lot of homework before departure, relying on recently published guidebooks, and also on an older book, *Views Taken on and near the River Rhine* by the Rev. John Gardnor, first published between 1788 and 1791, and reissued in a smaller format in 1792. This book contained descriptions of all the main sights and also suggested the best viewpoints, recommendations that Turner often followed.

The Rhine tour of 1817 is one of the best documented of his entire career, since he kept a timetable of it in the *Itinerary Rhine Tour* sketchbook (T.B. CLIX), which records his departure from London on August 10 through his arrival in The Hague on September 6. The precise itinerary of the tour has been discussed in some detail by Cecilia Powell in *Turner in Germany* (1995). The most important work in watercolor to derive from this tour is the series of 50 watercolors that Turner completed on his return and sold almost immediately to Walter Fawkes in the autumn of 1817. According to Turner's biographer Thornbury, the artist produced the drawings out of the breast-pocket of his great-coat "rolled up slovenly and anyhow" and sold them to Fawkes "for about £500." The collection remained in the possession of Fawkes's descendants largely unknown except to connoisseurs and friends, until they began to be sold off in 1890; they are now widely scattered around the world.

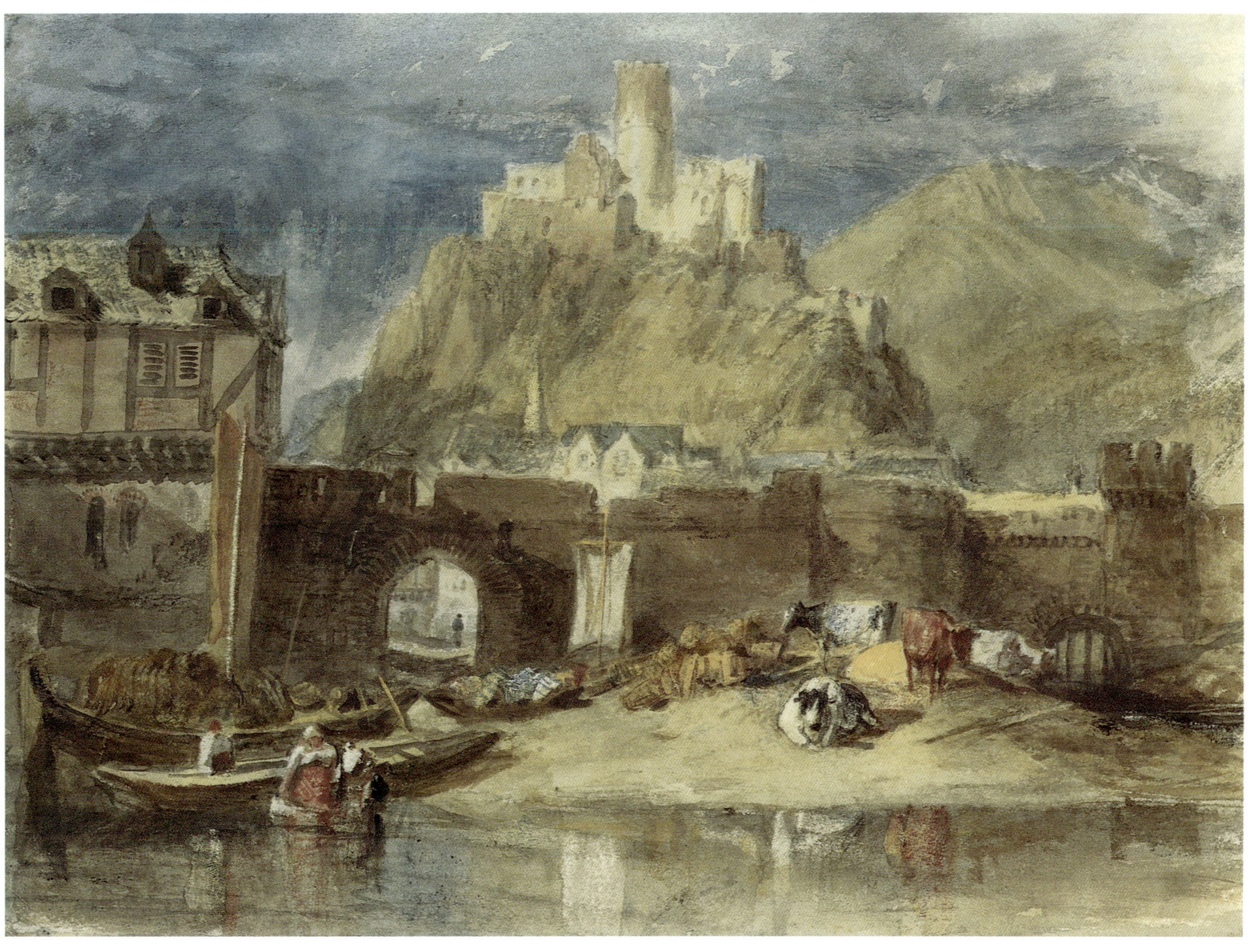

39 Fürstenburg, 1817

watercolor and bodycolor with gum arabic, on prepared gray paper
235 x 311 mm.
Walter Fawkes
By descent in the Fawkes family until 1890
Bequeathed by James Blair in 1917
(MCAG 1917.118)

The 1817 Rhine tour was mostly accomplished on foot, traveling light with only a "wallet" (rather like a haversack). After visiting the battlefield of Waterloo he traveled through Belgium and arrived in Cologne on August 18. For the rest of the month he toured the area between Cologne and Mainz, walking down the west bank of the Rhine along the recently completed Route Napoleon until he reached Mainz. He returned to Cologne by boat. Some days were spent only walking, occasionally stopping to make quick sketches, while on other days he spent more time in villages or towns that interested him.

He took with him several notebooks. The *Rhine* sketchbook was a large horizontal book for detailed sketches. The *Waterloo and Rhine* sketchbook was for small sketches with sometimes as many as six horizontal views on a double page. The sketch for Fürstenburg is in the latter (T.B. CLX p. 64r). It is the middle of three sketches on that page. The finished watercolor follows it closely although the peo-

ple and boats are a later addition. As the view taken is from the water itself, it is possible that it was made on his return up the Rhine by boat.

The ruins of Burg Fürstenburg tower over the little walled village of Rheindibach. Like most of the castles in this area it was built to safeguard the natural border of the Rhine and to protect the lands of the Archbishop of Cologne from the marauding French, who eventually destroyed it in 1689. Turner must have been attracted to the quaint, medieval, half-timbered houses with their walls parallel to the shore as seen from the river. Like many of his works he shows normal life going on in the shadow of ruins and contrasts it with the reminders of past greatness. He uses the rectangle of the castle tower, echoed in the shape of the sail below, as a strong vertical in the middle of the picture to counteract the unusual device of placing the village wall nearly parallel to the picture plane.

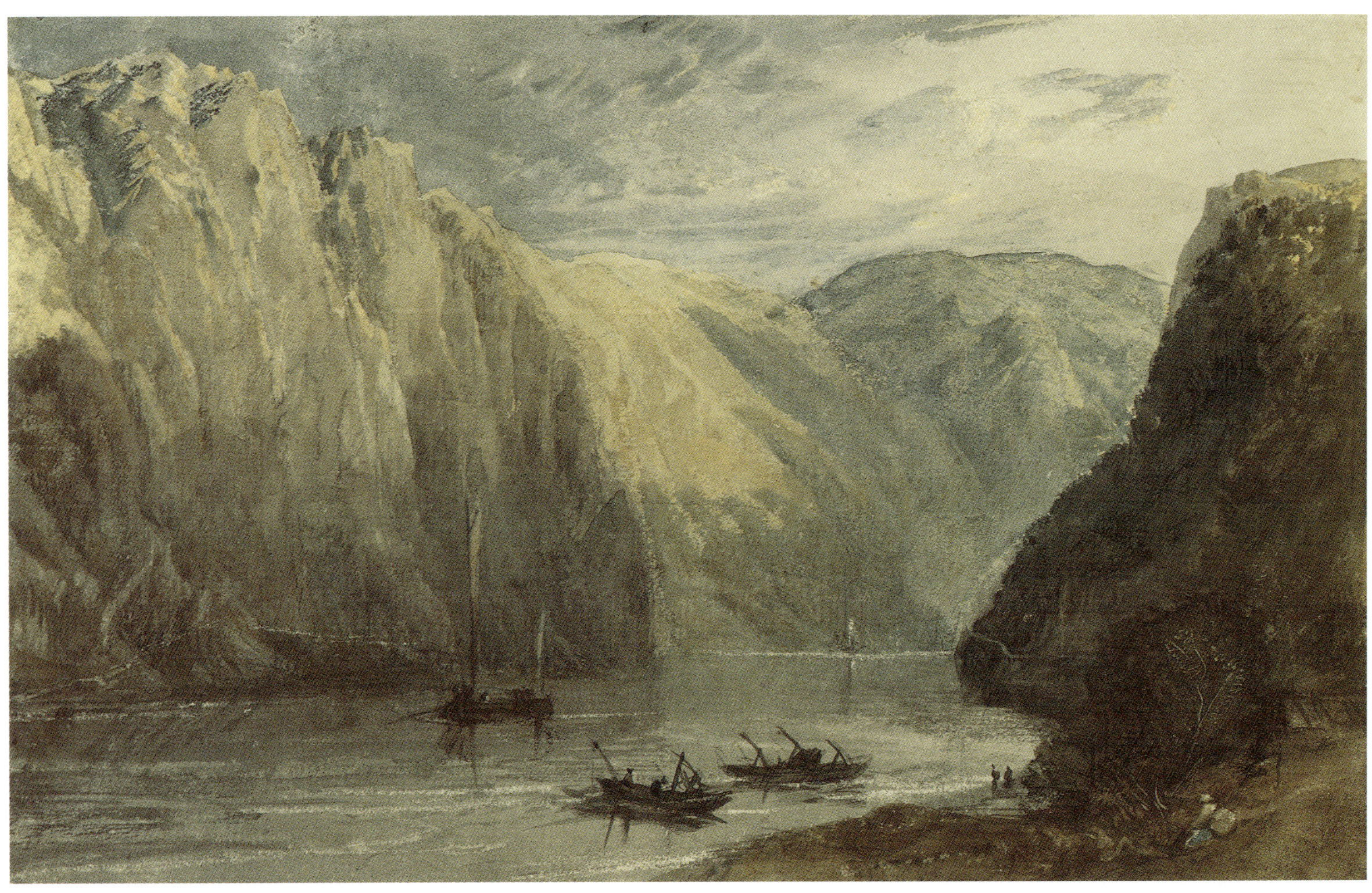

40   The Lorelei, 1817

watercolor and bodycolor, on prepared
gray paper
197 x 305 mm.
Walter Fawkes
By descent in the Fawkes family until 1890
Purchased from Thomas Agnew & Sons in
1925
(WAG.D.1925.57)

Like cat. 39, this watercolor is one of the Rhine series of 50 watercolors. All of the drawings are executed on paper prepared with a gray wash, in a manner similar to the Alpine sketches of 1802. For this reason and others, it used to be thought that the series was painted on the spot, a view first put forward by Ruskin and reinforced by the technique and fluid handling of the works. However, this has now been established not to be the case, and virtually all of the watercolors in the Rhine series derive from tiny pencil sketches in the *Waterloo and Rhine* sketchbook (T.B. CLX). The Whitworth drawing is closest to the lowest of four sketches of the Lorelei on the reverse of page one of the sketchbook.

The Lorelei, a massive cliff on the east bank of the Rhine halfway between Coblenz and Bingen, was the subject of seven watercolors in the Rhine series, easily the largest number devoted to one subject. At this point, the river gorge is particularly narrow with several bends, and the combination of the fast current and hidden rocks made the spot of particular danger to shipping. From this arose the legend of the siren who lured sailors to their deaths at the base of the rock. But, as this legend was invented by Clemens von Brentano in 1802, it seems unlikely that Turner would have known of it. He was probably attracted to the subject by the sublime scenery alone. This drawing, along with two others, shows a view of the Lorelei from downstream on the west bank with the cliff on the left of the composition.

THE HAKEWILL SERIES OF ITALIAN DRAWINGS OF 1818

In 1818 Turner was approached by an acquaintance, James Hakewill, with the idea of producing watercolors copied from Hakewill's own drawings for publication as engravings in a proposed book *A Picturesque Tour of Italy*. Turner completed twenty watercolors for this publication, which was published in parts between 1818 and 1820, and issued as a book in the latter year. All the watercolors are based on pencil drawings made by Hakewill with the aid of a *camera obscura* in Italy between the spring of 1816 and the summer of 1817. The majority of the Hakewill drawings are now in the British School at Rome.

It is not known how Turner met Hakewill. But since the latter came from a family of architects, exhibited architectural designs at the Royal Academy, and was nearly the same age as Turner, it is not surprising that they knew each other in London's artistic circles. Hakewill returned from Italy with the idea of producing several books on the country, although in the end only one was published. He approached eight artists, including Turner, and commissioned them to work up finished watercolors from his drawings—the practice of a professional working up the sketches of others for engraving purposes was quite usual at this date. Indeed, Turner was to continue such activities well into the 1830s, providing views of places he never visited as far afield as Greece and the Himalayas. After Hakewill approached the artists, the publisher John Murray, who was working with Hakewill, felt that he had overstepped himself, and canceled the commissions to three of them, so that in the end the book only had engravings after Turner, John Varley, Copley Fielding, Frederick Nash, and J. A. Atkinson. The original idea was for 60 engravings to accompany the book, but in the end only 36 were published, eighteen of which were after Turner drawings (two of Turner's drawings were not used).

Fortunately, because the records of the publishers John Murray's survive, our knowledge of the Hakewill commission is unusually full. An entry in the Ledger Book records a payment of 200 guineas to Turner on June 15, 1818, for ten watercolors, which can only be part of the Hakewill series, and, although there is no record of a further payment to the artist, Turner's notes of expected income - "Murray 400" - on page 58 of the *Liber Notes (2)* sketchbook (T.B. CLIVa) make it clear that there were twenty drawings originally commissioned. A further entry in the Murray Ledger Book records the sale in 1824 of twenty unspecified watercolors, which can only be the Turner Hakewill series; they were sold for £315, i.e. fifteen guineas each, which shows that by this date Murray was prepared to take a hundred guinea loss on the *Picturesque Tour of Italy* project. Although Turner was well versed in Italian topography from his study of the Cozens sketchbooks in the Monro Academy, because of the Napoleonic Wars he did not visit Italy until 1819. His only previous trip abroad was during the brief Peace of Amiens of 1802 (see cats. 24 and 25). The Hakewill drawings therefore also predate the first journey to Italy, and it is undoubtedly true that the commission stimulated Turner to visit Italy himself, since the notes that fill most of the *Route to Rome* sketchbook (T.B. CLXXI) of 1819 are written by Hakewill, and are in effect a manuscript guidebook to Italy.

41 Florence from the Ponte alla Carraia, 1818

signed: Turner RA
watercolor and bodycolor
139 x 216 mm.
Purchased from Thomas Agnew & Sons in
1891 with a fund presented by the
Guarantors of the 1887 Manchester Royal
Jubilee Exhibition
(WAG.D.1887.13)

As is to be expected with *camera obscura* drawings, the prototypes from which Turner had to work are wooden and lifeless, which can be seen in the sketch for this watercolor in the British School at Rome. This wooden quality is to a certain extent reflected in the finished watercolor. By adding figures and details on the right of the composition, Turner strengthened the effects of light and reflection on the bridge and river. The title used here is the one given to the engraving in the book. However, it is misleading as the view is not taken from the Ponte alla Carraia but from the upper window of Schneider's Hotel on the Lungarno Guicciardini, showing the Ponte della Trinità with the Ponte Vecchio behind it.

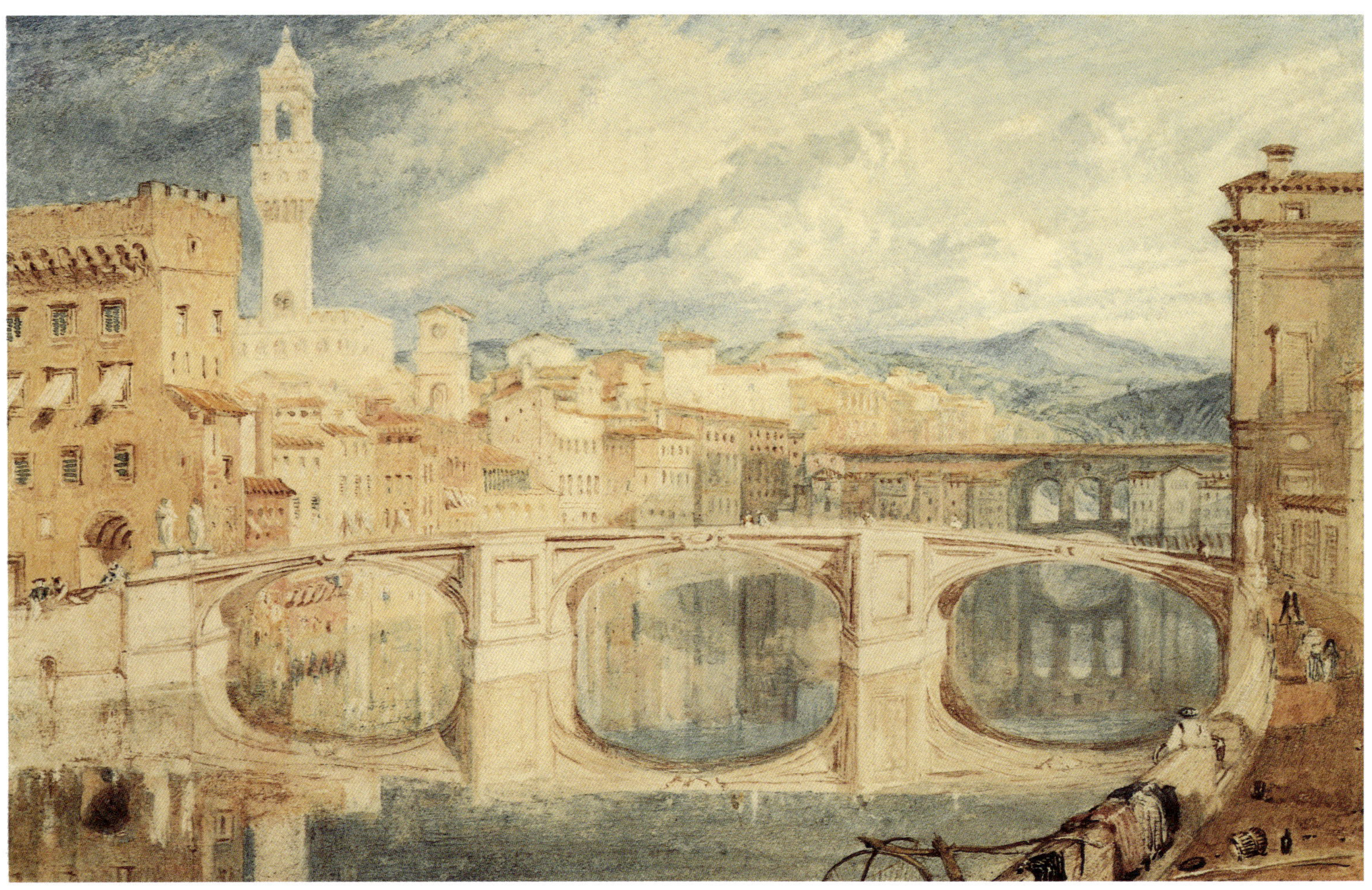

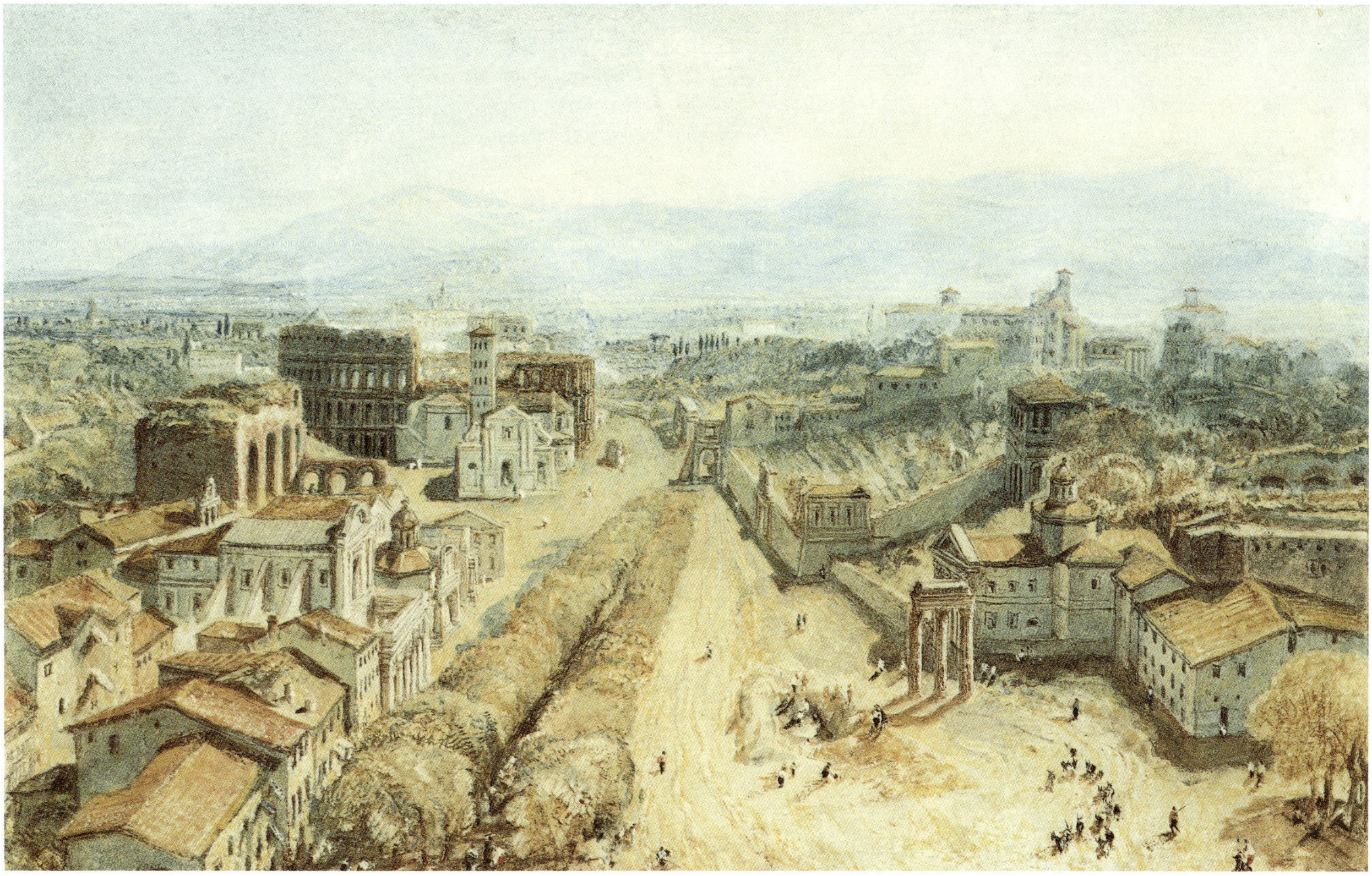

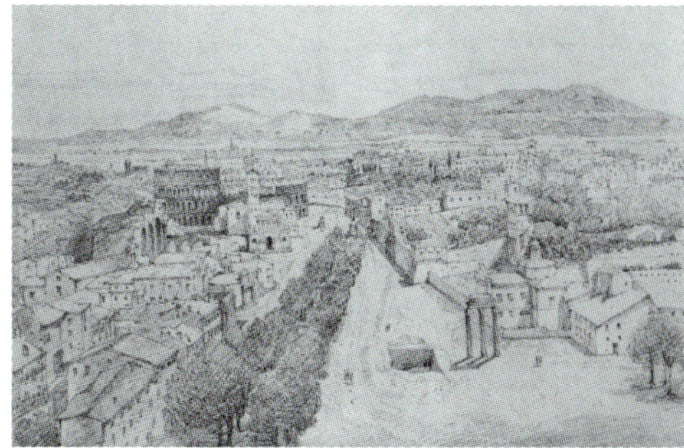

42 The Roman Forum from the Tower of the Capitol, 1818

pencil and watercolor
139 x 216 mm.
By descent in the Haworth family
On loan from a private collection
(WAG.L.1995.3)

The original for this Hakewill drawing is one of the few not in the British School at Rome, but is instead in an American private collection (see fig. 16). One of the problems that delayed and added unexpected expense to the Hakewill project was the engraver's slowness in producing the plates. Hakewill sent John Murray a "Memorandum of the State of the Italian Work" on July 17, 1818, and noted that the work on engraving the plate after this watercolor was "nearly done." However, George Cooke, the engraver who had been entrusted with the task, wrote to Murray the following day: "As to Mr. Hakewill's Plate, the great quantity of Labour and attention requisite to do it justice cannot possibly enable me to get it ready by the first of the Month." The delay in producing the plate in the end held up publication of Part II of *A Picturesque Tour of Italy* until November 1818. This watercolor, on loan to the Whitworth from a private collection, is one of the more lively and successful in the Hakewill series, with goats and animated figures being added in the forum and particularly in the open excavation, elements that are not present in the original drawing. Turner again adopted a high viewpoint to render the city in his sketch of Rome from the Vatican (T.B. CLXXXIX - 41), which was developed into the famous large oil painting of the subject exhibited at the Royal Academy in 1820 (Tate Gallery, Butlin & Joll no. 228).

Figure 16. James Hakewill, *The Roman Forum from the Tower of the Capitol,* pencil, private collection

43 Sidmouth, 1827-8

watercolor
184 x 263 mm.
Presented by Frederick John Nettlefold
in 1948
(WAG.D.1948.8)

On his return from Italy in 1820, Turner resumed work on a number of engraving projects and started afresh with others.

One that was in its final stages was *Picturesque Views on the Southern Coast of England*, which Turner was working on for the publisher William Cooke (1778-1855). Cooke was also involved with the *Rivers of England* series, which began to appear in 1823 and was intended to be a companion to the *Southern Coast* series. The sixteen watercolors that Turner produced for the later project are among his most beautiful. In spite of the success of the *Rivers of England* project, Turner and Cooke found working closely together too much of a strain and quarreled at the end of 1826, bringing their relationship to an end.

At this point, Turner began working with Thomas Lupton, who had been one of the engravers on the *Rivers of England* project. Together they planned to publish as mezzotints 24 watercolors in twelve parts, of two engravings each, for a series to be called *The Ports of England*. The Whitworth drawing was intended to form a part of this series. The engravings began to appear in 1826, but only three parts had appeared by 1828, when the project was abandoned. The Whitworth drawing was eventually published after Turner's death, when Lupton collaborated with Ruskin to produce a set of twelve plates (the six already published and six more) entitled *The Harbours of England*. The Whitworth watercolor is based on two sketches in the *Devonshire No. I* sketchbook (T.B. CXXIII), made in 1811, and is a conflation of pages 203a and 205. As Hartley (1984) points out, there is no evidence to support the view that the prominent phallic-looking rock in the foreground is a reference to the marriage of the 65-year-old Lord Sidmouth to a much younger woman in 1823. Indeed, the watercolor probably dates from four or five years later.

44 Study of Boats, 1827-30

signed with initials: JMWT
pen and brown ink and brown wash
heightened with white, on blue paper
130 x 182 mm.
Presented by John Edward Taylor in 1892
(WAG.D.1892.92)

This is one of a number of studies of shipping on blue paper that appear to have been executed on the south coast around 1827-30. It compares closely to a number of drawings in the Turner Bequest, in particular T.B. CCLXIX - 21, and to a study of shipping in the Yale Center for British Art (Wilton no. 915). The latter and the Whitworth drawing are similarly signed with initials at the lower right, as were two comparable drawings in the J.P. Heseltine sale at Sotheby's on March 25, 1920, lots 182 and 183, entitled *View of a Seaport* and *Fishing Boats at Sea - boarding a Steamer.* The technique of pen and ink and wash on blue paper relates these drawings to the Petworth series (see cat. 45 in this exhibition) and to drawings executed at East Cowes in the summer of 1827, including several listed under T.B. CCXXVII(a) and T.B. CCXXVIII. There are two pencil drawings of shipping in a private collection; these are similarly signed with initials for presentation to a friend who was staying at East Cowes at the same time as Turner and can thus be securely dated to 1827. Similar signatures can be seen on two further undated finished pencil drawings of shipping in the Vaughan Bequests at the National Galleries of Scotland and the National Gallery of Ireland; these and the Yale and Whitworth drawings were presumably signed for presentation or sale.

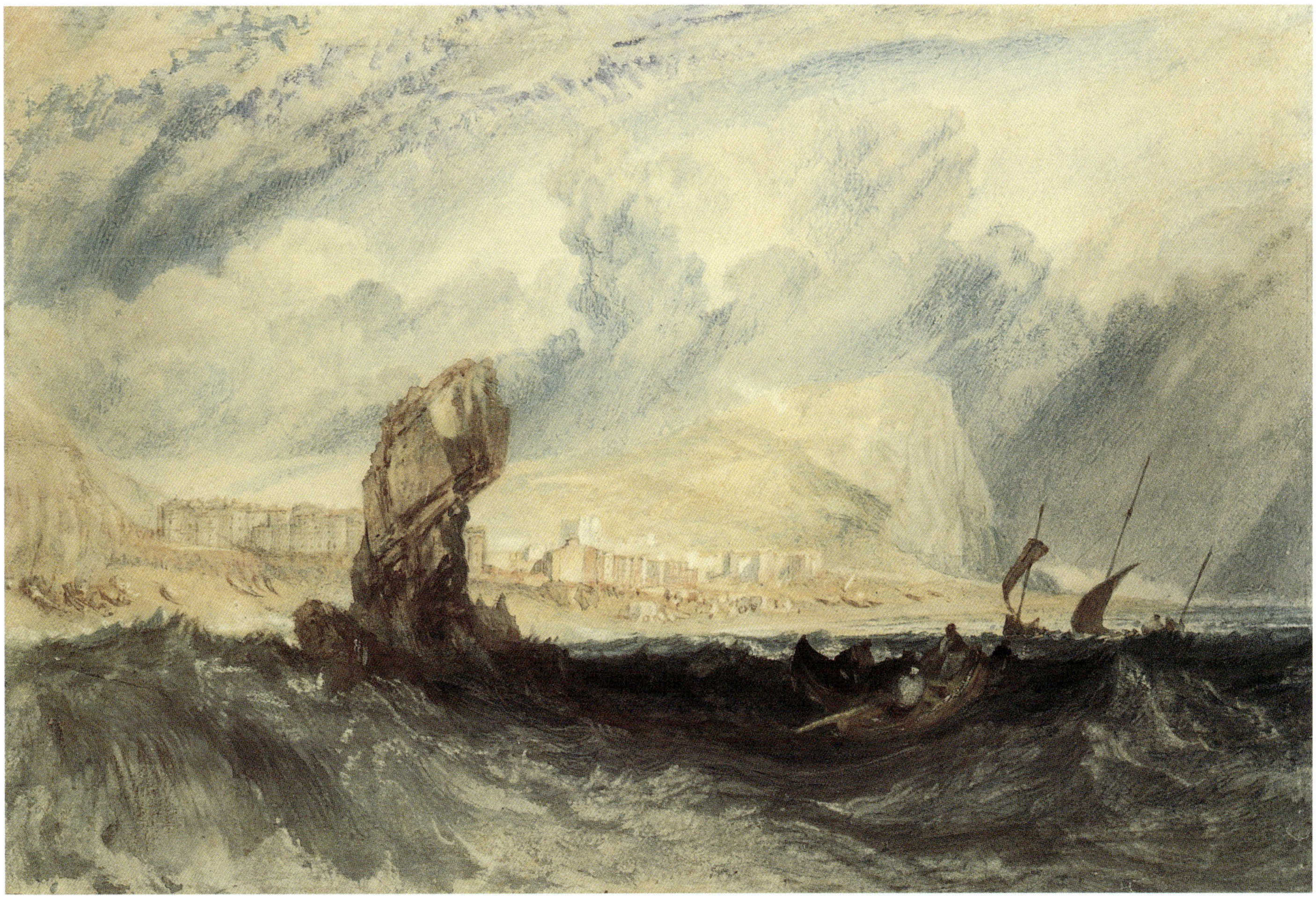

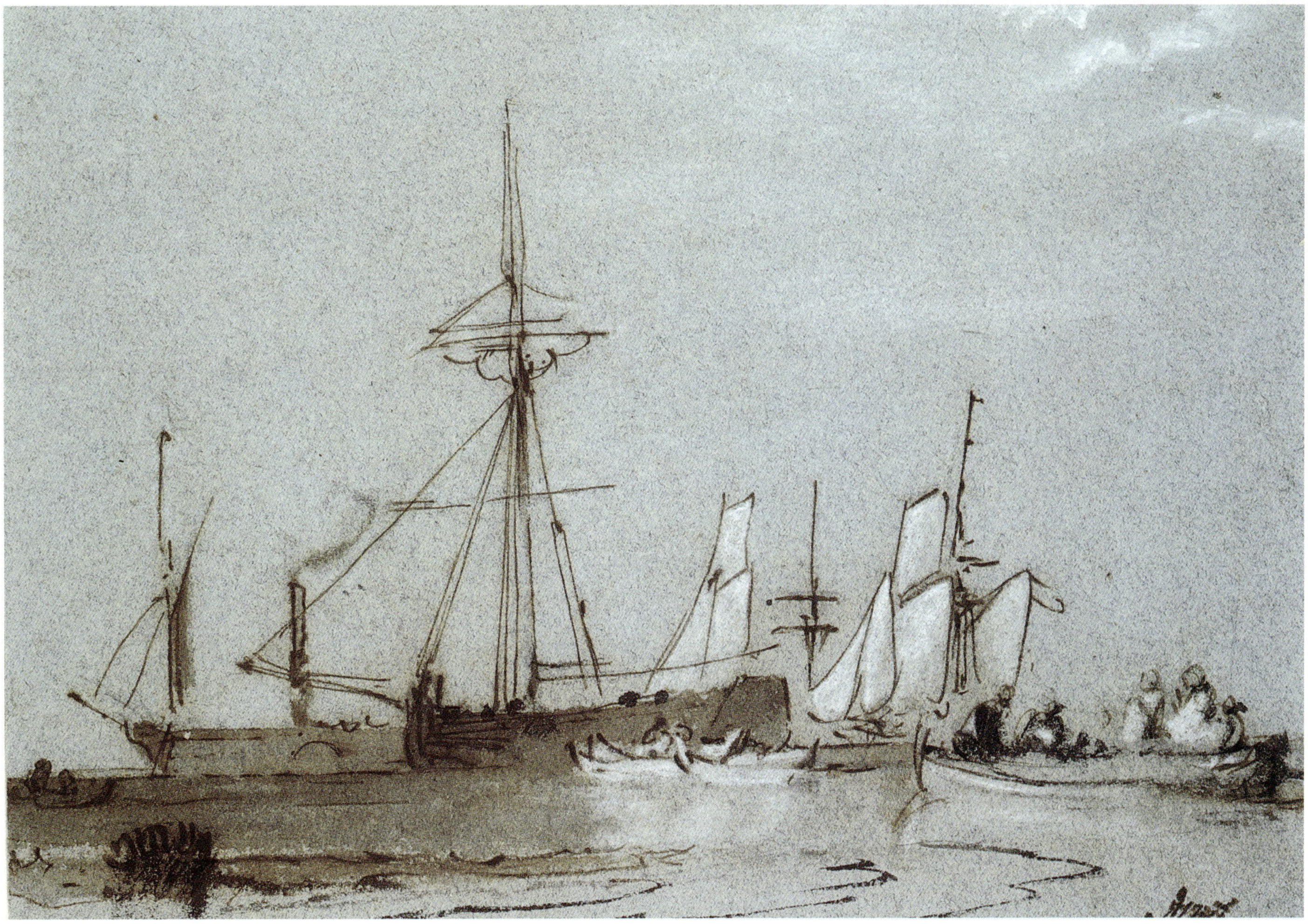

45 Deer in Petworth Park, West Sussex, 1827

watercolor and bodycolor, on blue paper
140 x 194 mm.
Presented by John Edward Taylor in 1892
(WAG.D.1892.91)

This drawing is one of a large group—all of nearly the same size and executed with the same technique of watercolor and bodycolor on blue paper—that are associated with one of Turner's many visits to Petworth Park, the country seat of the 3rd Earl of Egremont. Lord Egremont was a leading collector of British contemporary art in the first half of the nineteenth century, and assembled what is now the largest collection of Turner oil paintings outside the Tate Gallery. He had also inherited a fine collection of Old Master paintings, with excellent examples by Rembrandt, Van Dyck, and Claude, which exercised a profound influence on Turner. Because the first public gallery at Dulwich did not open until 1811 and the National Gallery did not open until 1824, one of the few opportunities young artists had to see Old Master pictures at this date was in the collections of their aristocratic patrons. Lord Egremont, along with Sir John Leicester, later Lord de Tabley, the Duke of Bridgewater and others, helped to establish Turner's reputation in the early years of the nineteenth century, purchasing works between 1802 and 1812. There seems to have been a cooling of the relationship with Lord Egremont after 1814 when Turner exhibited at the British Institution *Appullia in Search of Appullus* (Tate Gallery, Butlin & Joll no. 128), which some considered to be a slavish copy of Egremont's painting by Claude, *Jacob with Laban and his Daughters*.

Turner again began to visit Petworth regularly in the mid-1820s. Egremont had commissioned two paintings from Turner before 1810 during the first period of his patronage, *Dewy Morning, Petworth* (Butlin & Joll no. 113) and *Cockermouth Castle* (Butlin & Joll no. 108), both still at Petworth, and in the late 1820s he commissioned four long landscapes (Butlin & Joll nos. 288-291) to hang in the Carved Room at Petworth, where they still hang; these were executed between 1827 and 1829. Lord Egremont kept an open and somewhat disorderly house for artists and whoever happened to be visiting. It is clear that, after the death of his close friend and patron Walter Fawkes in 1825 and of his father in 1829, Turner came to regard Petworth as his second home. Certainly, its combination of grandeur and informality provided a stimulus for him and prompted him to produce the remarkable series of Petworth drawings, of which this is one.

Some 120 of this series remain in the Turner Bequest (T.B. CCXLIV), while only a handful (listed as Wilton nos. 906-12) are in other collections. What is unique about the Petworth drawings is that, unlike any other series of drawings by Turner, they were not the result of a commission (Lord Egremont did not collect drawings) and are not preparatory to anything else. They were drawn entirely for the artist's own pleasure, which is why the majority remain in the Turner Bequest. Recent research into the architectural history of Petworth Church, the interior of which appears in some of the drawings, suggests the whole set was executed on one visit to Petworth in the late summer of 1827. The Whitworth drawing is in a minority in the group, because the majority of the drawings are of interiors, some with figures, which brilliantly recapture the atmosphere of the great house and the activities of its inhabitants.

The whole Petworth group was somewhat neglected in the nineteenth century, Ruskin describing a large number of the sheets as "rubbish," "inferior," or "worse," but they have escalated hugely in popularity in this century, the most recent book on the series, *Turner at Petworth* (1988), commenting: "The burst of activity during the visit of 1827 is almost a song of joy at rediscovering a friendly environment to which he could escape after the loss of Farnley. Apart from their intrinsic merits and beauty as works of art, Turner's drawings provide the most privileged of insights into the remarkable and slightly eccentric behaviour of Petworth life (p. 69)."

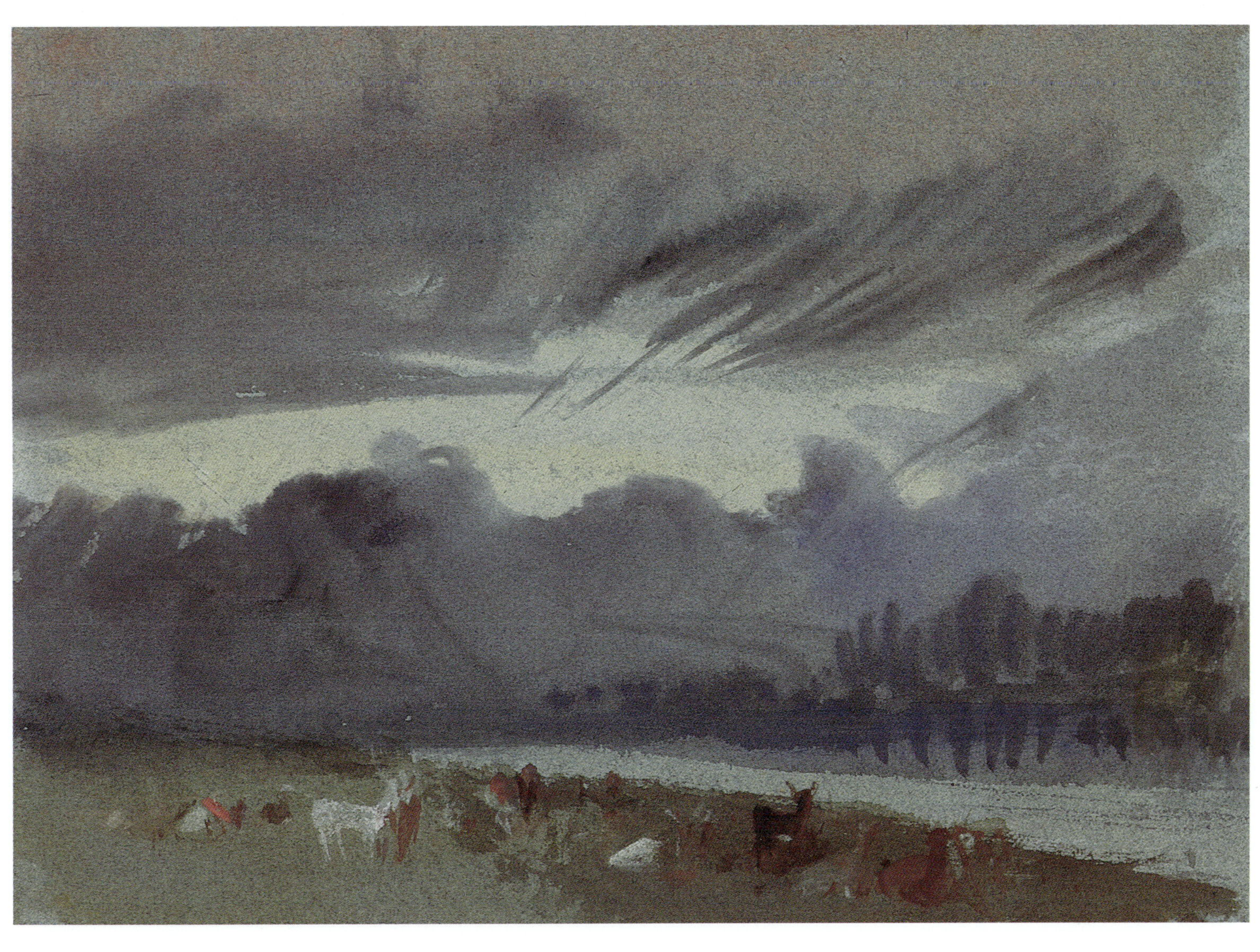

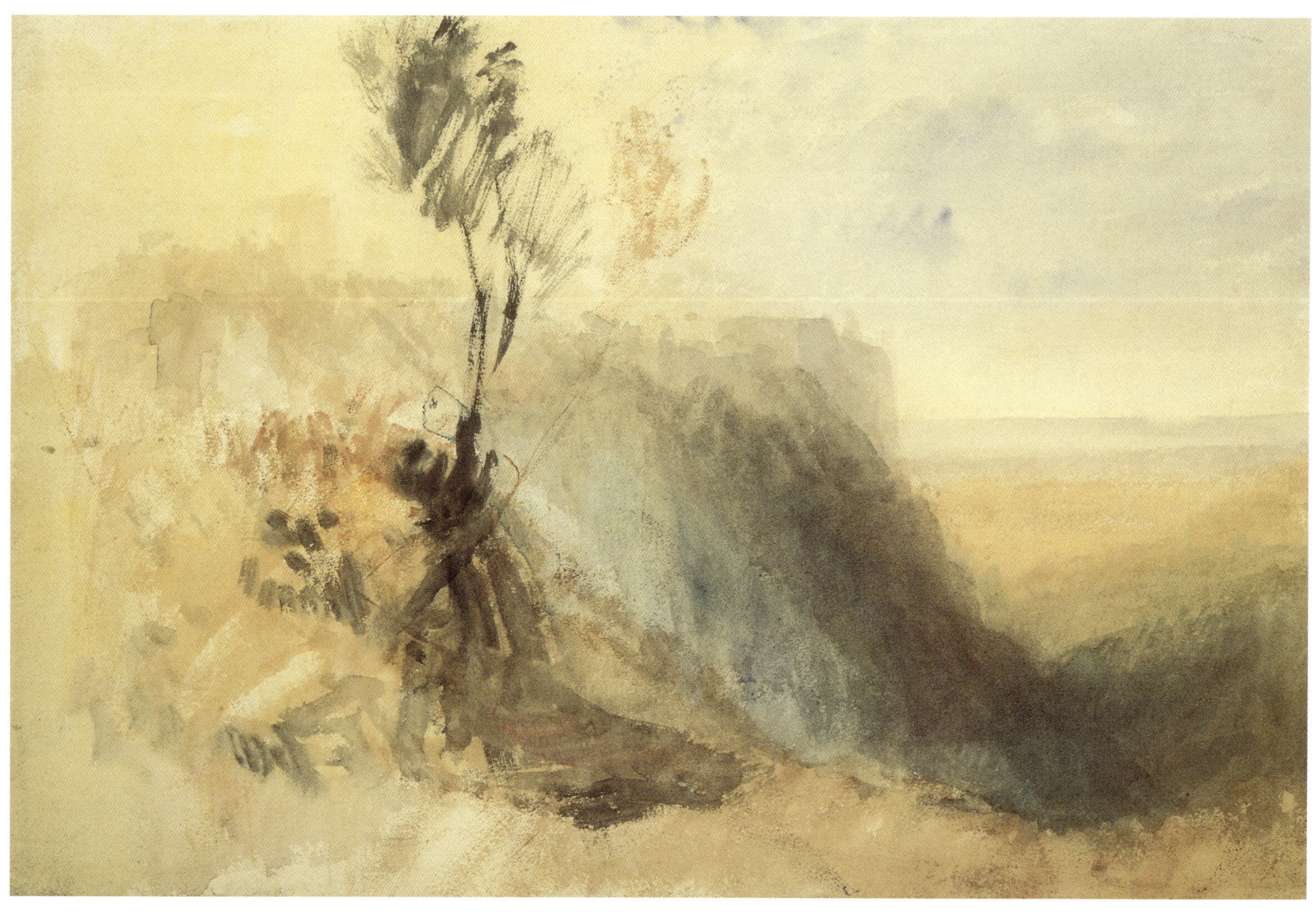

46 Tivoli, c. 1828

watercolor
303 x 436 mm.
Purchased from the Cotswold Gallery
in 1922
(WAG.D.1922.31)

Previously, this "color beginning" was thought to relate to the large watercolor *Landscape: Composition of Tivoli*, exhibited at the Royal Academy in 1818 and now in a private collection. It was also compared to a "color beginning" of circa 1820 of La Bastiaz near Martigny (T.B. CXCVI - Q), which has a tree executed with a similarly dry brush. The first of these suggestions must be false, because the Whitworth drawing has to postdate the Italian trip of 1819, as it is loosely based on a sketch made on that journey in the *Tivoli* sketchbook (T.B. CLXXXIII - p.2). Other sketches of Tivoli appear in this book and in the *Tivoli and Rome* sketchbook (T.B. CLXXIX), while watercolors showing a similar view of Tivoli are *Tivoli, with the Cascades* and *General View of Tivoli*, both in the *Naples, Rome Color Studies* sketchbook (T.B. CLXXXVII - pp. 32 and 38).

Unlike these views, the Whitworth watercolor appears to be preparatory to something else. It may, therefore, date from rather later in the decade and be a study for the projected series *Picturesque Views in Italy,* on which Turner started work before returning to Italy in 1828. The project was abandoned very early and only three finished watercolors are known to be connected with it, *Florence from San Miniato*, *Lake Albano*, and *Arona, Lago Maggiore* (Wilton nos. 728, 730, and 731). The first of these has a "color beginning" (T.B. CCLXIII - 16), similar in coloring and handling to the Whitworth watercolor, which may therefore date from circa 1828 and be preparatory to an unexecuted watercolor for the *Picturesque Views in Italy* series.

47 "Loch Katrine," c. 1828

pencil and watercolor
303 x 457 mm.
Cotswold Gallery
Presented by A.E. Anderson through the
National Art Collections Fund in 1922
(WAG.D.1922.45)

The title by which this drawing is known is erroneous, as there is no evidence to support it. It is not remotely connected to any of Turner's renderings of the subject, the finished watercolor for Scott's *Poetical Works* (Wilton no. 1084, now in the British Museum), nor the sketches in the *Stirling and the West* sketchbook (T.B. CCLXX). Given that "Loch Katrine" has the same provenance as the Tivoli "color beginning" (cat. 46)—the donor purchased it from the same dealer at the same time—it is possible that it is of the same date. Stylistically,

it may be compared to *Tivoli* and to *A Bridge between Trees* (Wilton no. 694). All three may, therefore, date from circa 1828. Indeed, *A Bridge between Trees* and *"Loch Katrine"* are compositionally and stylistically similar to a group of oil paintings of Italian subjects datable to 1828 in the Turner Bequest, such as *Southern Landscape* (Butlin & Joll no. 299), *Ariccia(?): Sunset* (Butlin & Joll no. 305), and *Italian Landscape with Tower, Trees and Figures* (Butlin & Joll no. 307).

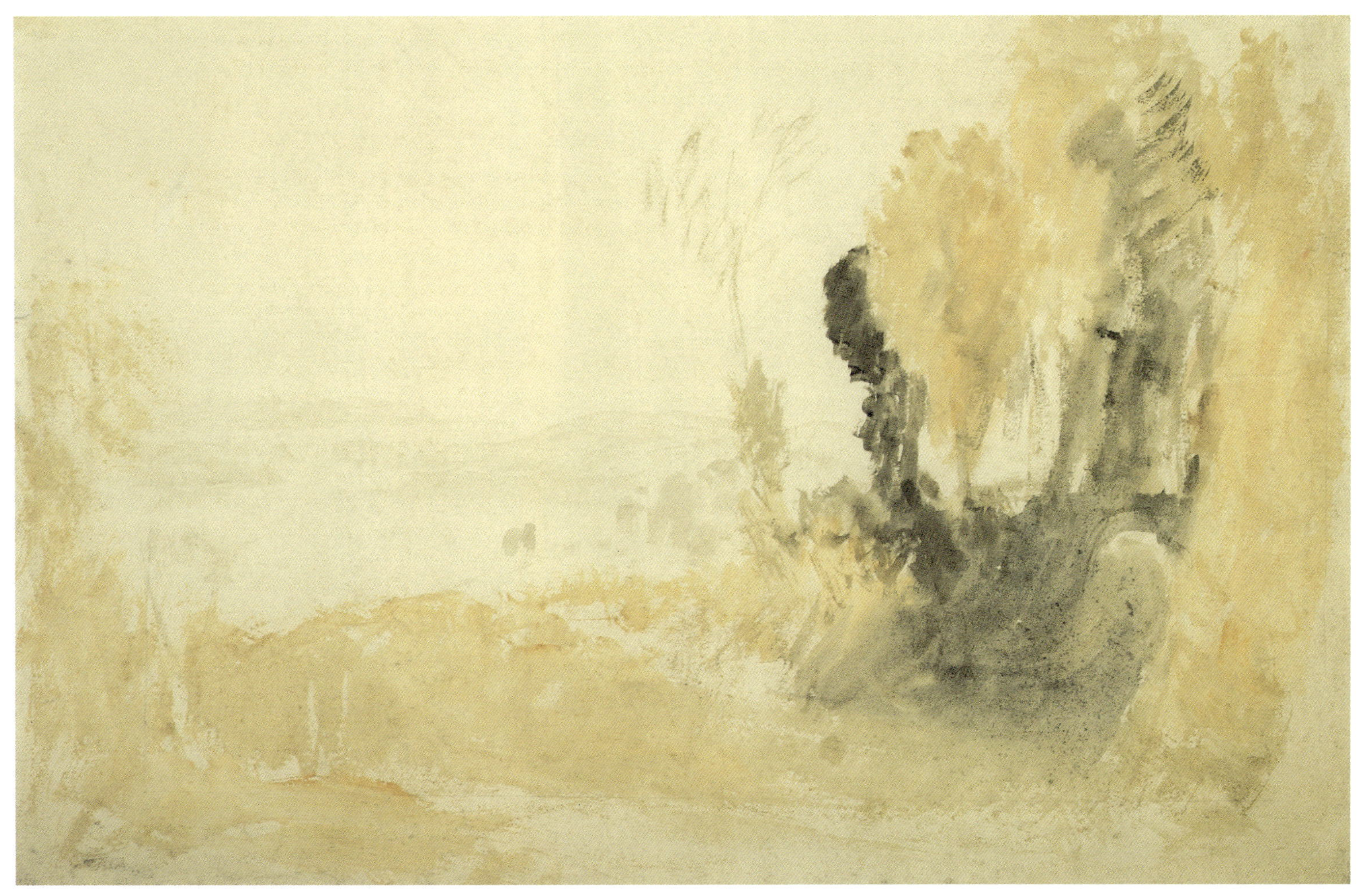

The England and Wales Series of 1825-1838

In 1825 Turner entered into an agreement with the engraver and publisher Charles Heath to produce over a number of years a large quantity of watercolors, from which Heath would choose 120 to be line-engraved and published under the title *Picturesque Views in England and Wales.* It is not known for certain how much Turner was paid for this commission, although it was probably 25 guineas per watercolor. The first three parts were published in 1827, each consisting of four engravings accompanied by a letterpress. Although executed solely with engraving in mind, some of the watercolors were exhibited as part of Charles Heath's attempts to promote the sale of the engravings. The first exhibition of 35 watercolors and some of the completed engravings took place at the Egyptian Hall, Piccadilly, in 1829. Among the works displayed were *Exeter* (cat. 48) and *Dunstanburgh* (cat. 49).

These were also included, along with *Malvern Priory, Warwick Castle, Upnor Castle* and *Carew Castle* (cats. 50-53), in a second and larger exhibition, which took place in June and July 1833 at the Moon, Boys and Graves Gallery, Pall Mall, London. The gallery was by this date a part owner of the project. The exhibition included 66 of the watercolors, the largest number ever assembled. The show was a critical success, the *Athenaeum* reviewer saying of it (June 15, 1833): ". . . these drawings are of a beauty for which we can find no parallels," but failed to promote the sale of the engravings, which by this date were only appearing in two parts a year. By 1838, Turner had produced more than 100 watercolors, of which 96 had been engraved. Also, Charles Heath was by this date a virtual bankrupt so that the operation of producing the prints had been taken over by the publishers Longmans, who decided to cut their losses and terminate the series. The 96 plates were published in two volumes of 48 plates in 1838. The watercolors in the *England and Wales* series show Turner at the height of his powers and were much admired then and ever since.

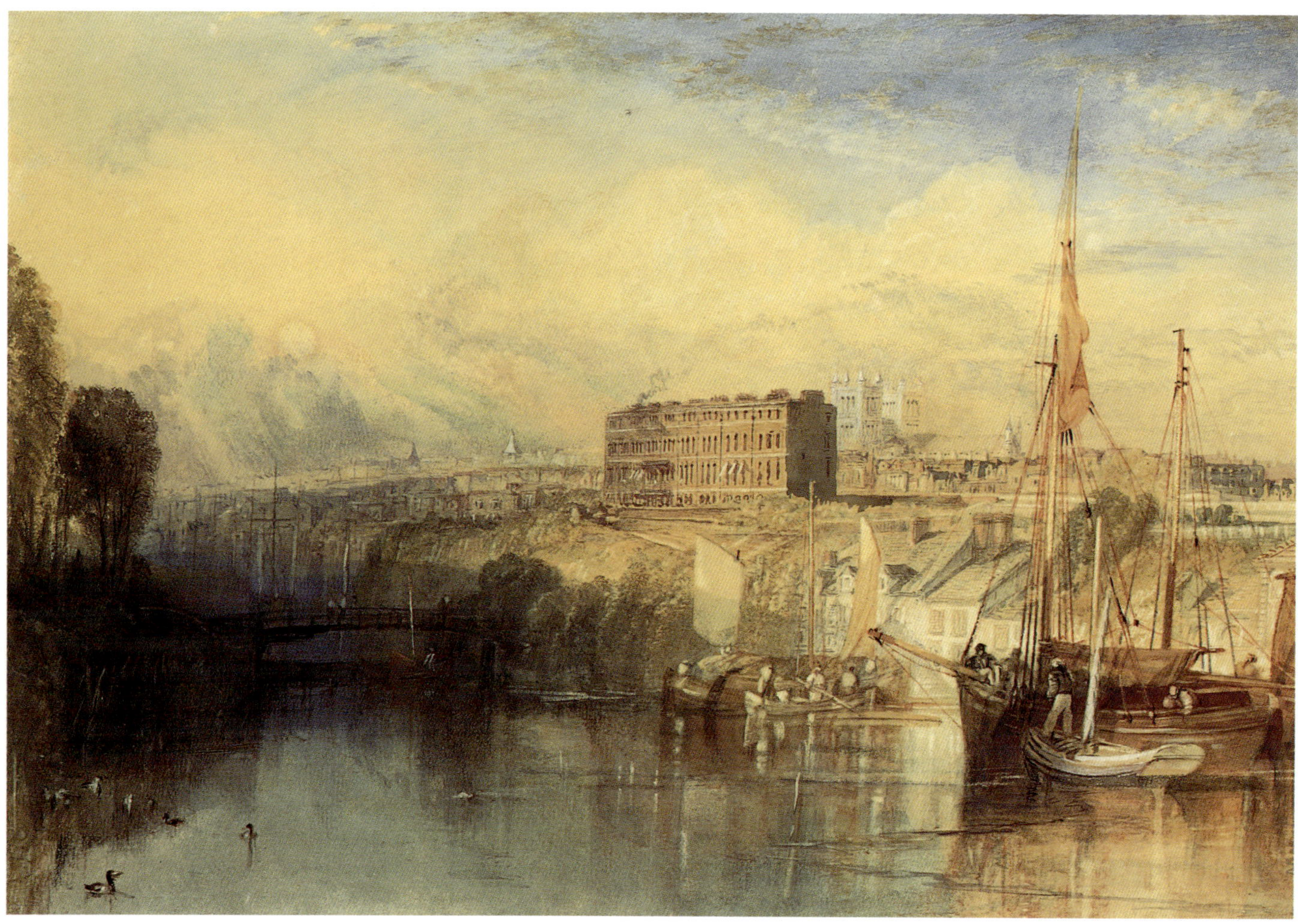

48

48 Exeter, c. 1827

watercolor with gum arabic
298 x 425 mm.
Bequeathed by James Blair in 1917
(MCAG 1917.107)

Turner's links with Devon, of which Exeter is the county town, were strong. While the theory that he was born there can be safely discarded, both his father and grandfather hailed from South Molton, north of Exeter, and during his extensive tours of Devon in 1811 and 1813, the artist contacted relatives in Exeter and elsewhere. His depiction of the city is here shaped by his attraction to maritime activity and contemporary architecture. These features take precedence over Exeter's most outstanding topographical feature, its cathedral, which is included as a rather subdued landmark in the middle distance. The artist's composition reflects both the increasing nineteenth century eclipse of ecclesiastical and historical architecture by secular buildings and activities, and his own predilection for new advances.

Turner's vantage point is a v-shaped piece of land, ahead of which two waterways meet. The Exe River stretches before the viewer, while behind and to the left lies the Exeter Canal. The dividing promontory, just forward of the canal floodgates, is suggested by a ripple beneath the foreground boats moored at St. Leonard's Quay. The artist's long-standing affection for water and sailing has here been fired by the clusters of sea-going vessels that were essential to Exeter's position as a center of trade and commerce, based largely on the export of woolen textiles. The swing-bridge that lies between St. Leonard's Quay and the main quay has long since been replaced by a manual ferry.

Of equal interest to Turner would have been the system of locks, weirs, and flumes by which great use was made of the once dysfunctional river. Indeed, it is the canal, begun in the sixteenth century, that would have been the means by which the craft shown would have traveled. The river itself has never been navigable beyond Topsham, some five miles out on the estuary. In the suggested year for this watercolor, the canal was improved by the eminent engineer James Green, and shortly afterward it was extended to incorporate a deep basin situated on the western bank where Turner placed a group of trees.

The central feature of Turner's drawing is Matthew Nosworthy's Colleton Crescent, begun in 1802. Fashionable architecture would have been especially prominent in the artist's thoughts at this time, as in 1827 he spent an extended period as a guest of John Nash, the King's favorite architect, who was now turning his attention to the rebuilding of Buckingham Palace. The motif of the house overlooking a river would have particularly appealed to Turner, reminding him of his own home on the Thames at Twickenham and of his recent commissions in oils depicting the house of William Moffat, also on the Thames.

It is perhaps Turner's attraction to recent building, particularly domestic riverside architecture, that has led to the Crescent appearing more imposing than it actually is, even though the viewer today sees a bank far more built upon and wooded. The view has certainly been generalized in favor of an overall effect which, although largely successful, fails in the area where the foreground houses appear to sink below the waterline. The whole account is typically based on atmospheric coloring rather than precise delineation.

It is worth noting how the artist has used gum with his watercolor to achieve the distant blue of the left part of the river and a stopping -out mixture (i.e. a mixture of turpentine and beeswax which forms a resist on the paper) to give a sharp definition to the mast of the boat in the foreground. Much of the sunset effect, however, is the result of a happy coincidence, as the drawing was stained before it entered the Manchester collection.

**49 Dunstanborough Castle,
Northumberland, c. 1828**

watercolor and bodycolor
291 x 421 mm.
Purchased from the H.A.J. Munro of Novar
sale at Christie's by John Heugh in 1874
Bequeathed by James Blair in 1917
(MCAG 1917.110)

In 1798 Turner exhibited *Dunstanborough Castle, N.E. Coast of Northumberland. Sun-Rise after a Squally Night* at the annual Royal Academy exhibition. Based on drawings of the previous year in the *North of England* sketchbook (T.B. XXXIV), it was to be translated some thirty years later into this watercolor for inclusion in the *Picturesque Views in England and Wales* series.

Dunstanborough is Northumberland's largest and most impressive castle, covering an area of over ten acres. Evelyn Joll in his essay "Turner in Dunstanborough, 1797 - 1834" for the *Turner* exhibition (Canberra, 1996), suggested that the artist might have been initially attracted to the motif by his friend and rival Thomas Girtin who had visited it the year before. It was at this time that both young men developed the subject of the ruined castle from an interesting topographical subject into a vehicle for haunting melancholy (see also *Kilgarran Castle*, cat. 15). Several versions were to follow in both oil and watercolor. Most show the little cottages below the castle without duly emphasizing them, and in the earlier versions the rugged rocks in the foreground are used to convey the wildness of the spot. There is also a version which was produced for Turner's *Liber Studiorum* (part III, 1808) that can perhaps be seen as a transitional image, coming between the original oil painting and the *England and Wales* version.

All three versions show the morning after a stormy night. The earlier version was augmented by lines from Thomson's *The Seasons* to convey the contrast between the black horror of the night and the gentle dawn of another day. In the later versions he refines the silhouette of the castle against the sky. In the Manchester watercolor Turner is able to dispense with rugged rocks and accompanying verses and uses his virtuosity in watercolor to convey a particular mood—the wetness of sand, the relentless sea, with some of its power abated, and the dawn light playing on the stonework of the castle heralding a new day. Economical brushwork depicts the castle windows and their shadows in a few strokes, and his expertise at floating washes of color on wet paper achieves the feeling of a watery sky.

The broken mast of the wrecked ship points to the ruins of the castle, both now rendered impotent and useless. At a time when excise duty was high, smuggling and wrecking were rife in coastal areas of Britain. Mounted customs officers, known as Riding Officers, were appointed to patrol the coast. Their salaries were low and bribery was inevitable. Here the Riding Officer oversees the wreckers as they salvage what they can from the vessel. He has to protect the interests of the Crown against those who are probably his friends and neighbors. Wreckers had a claim to half the cargo as did the owners of the stretch of coastline where the vessel sank; this was known as Royalty of Wrecks and was often disputed by both sides.

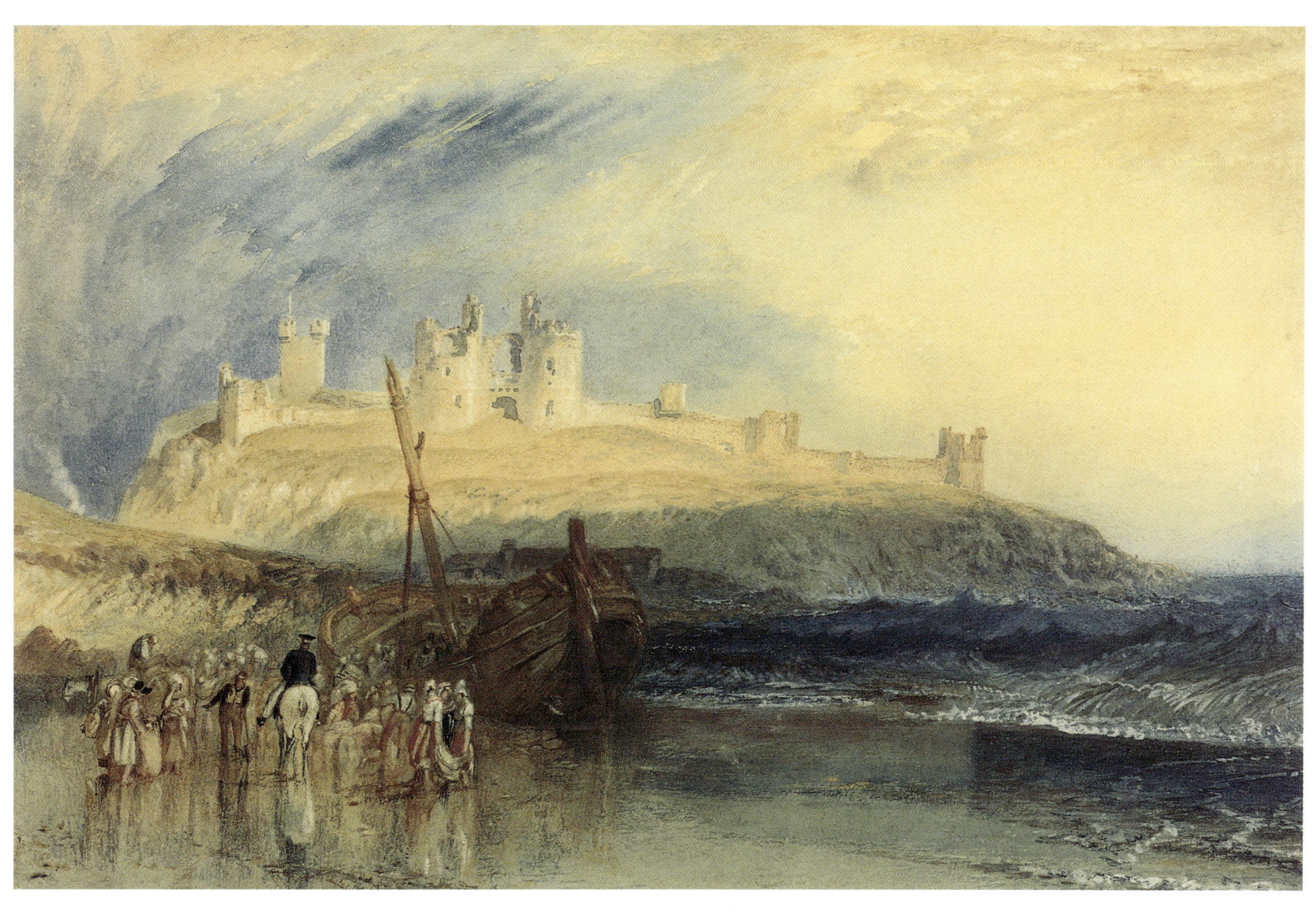

50 Great Malvern Priory and Gatehouse, Worcestershire, from the North-west, c.1830

watercolor
296 x 422 mm.
Bought by John Heugh from the B.G.
Windus sale
Purchased by John Pender and sold by him
in 1873
Bequeathed by James Blair in 1917
(MCAG 1917.104)

Great Malvern in Worcestershire became well known as a spa resort in the eighteenth and nineteenth centuries and was later patronized by Queen Victoria. In the twentieth century it has become a popular location for retirement as well as being part of the commuter belt serving Worcester and Birmingham.

The abbey was originally a Benedictine priory, built mainly between circa 1420 and 1460 in the Perpendicular style. Following the dissolution of the monasteries by Henry VIII, it was bought by local people to be used as a parish church. When A.W.N. Pugin saw it in 1833 he noted that it was in grave need of repair.

Turner made several sketches of the abbey on his 1793 visit there. One of them forms the basis for the Whitworth Art Gallery's *Great Malvern Priory and Gatehouse* (cat. 5). Other drawings now untraced are presumed to be the source of *Malvern Abbey*, exhibited at the Royal Academy in 1794 (Wilton 50—one of two versions owned by the Manchester collector Thomas Ashton and bought by him from Agnew's). When commissioned to reproduce an image of Malvern for the *Picturesque Views in England and Wales,* Turner must have turned to records of his 1793 tour as the viewpoint is nearly identical. In both versions, there are carpenters in the foreground, and again Turner associates events or people with certain views (see, for example, cats. 55 and 60). By 1830, however, the topographical approach of the 1790s, with its careful delineation and mellow colors, has long since been abandoned for a style where color is used to depict light and shade. Ruskin describes the atmosphere as "Afternoon, great heat, thunder gathering," (*Modern Painters,* vol. I, in J. Ruskin, *Works,* vol. III, p. 422). The sultry blue-gray of the storm clouds provides a rich contrast to the cold yellow of the stone gatehouse, with its shadows picked out in mauve as sunlight flickers delicately over the stonework. The ghostly tower of the abbey catches the last of the sun before the storm breaks. The workmen run for shelter as the first drops of rain fall. In the engraved version a flash of lightening conveys the impending storm, but in the watercolor Turner is able to express this simply by the use of color.

51 Warwick Castle, 1830-1

watercolor and bodycolor
297 x 451 mm.
John Ruskin
Purchased from Colnaghi's by John
Edward Taylor in 1865
Purchased from John Edward Taylor by
Thomas Agnew & Sons in 1868
Purchased from Thomas Agnew & Sons by
Abraham Haworth before 1887
Bequeathed by Jesse Haworth in 1937
(WAG.D.1937.22)

This watercolor for the *England and Wales* series dates from 1830-1 and belonged to Ruskin in the 1860s. It is based on sketches in the *Kenilworth* sketchbook (T.B. CCXXXVIII), used by Turner on his tour of the Midlands in 1830, which he made to gather material for the series. The sketch on page 38 gives details of the fenestration of the castle, while that on page 38a-39 shows this view with a little more on the left, with the balustrade of the bridge lightly sketched in on the right. The church of St. Mary's on the right is taken from another more distant view on page 40. The engraving deriving from the watercolor, along with seven others, is dated 1832. Of the eight engravings dated 1832, four derive from sketches in the *Kenilworth* sketchbook (*Ashby de la Zouche, Warwick, Kenilworth,* and *Tamworth*). This watercolor is very typical of the series generally, with its emphasis on light and the inclusion of figures; the building repairs on the bridge seem to be Turner's invention, as no major works are known to have been carried out on the bridge at this date.

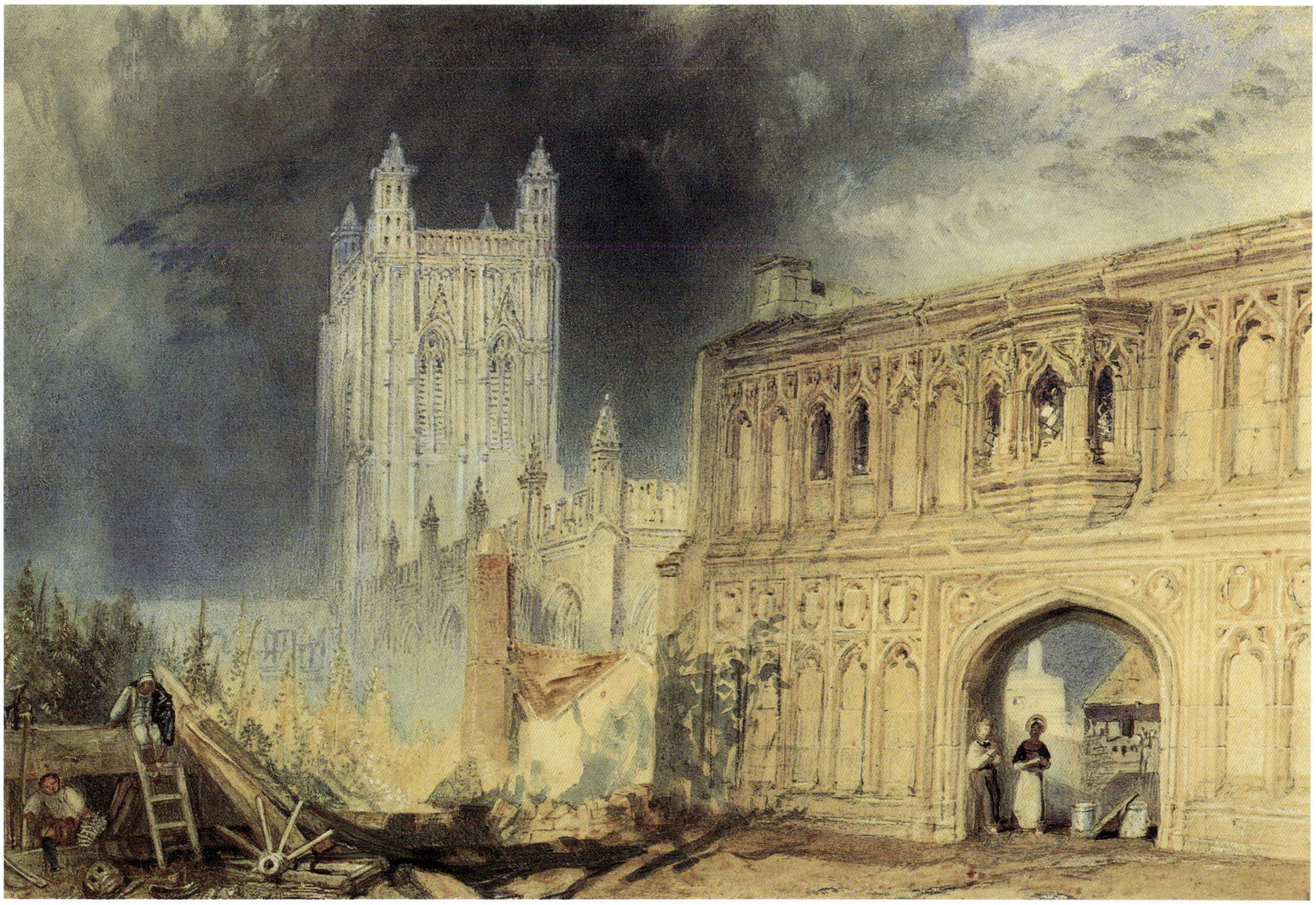

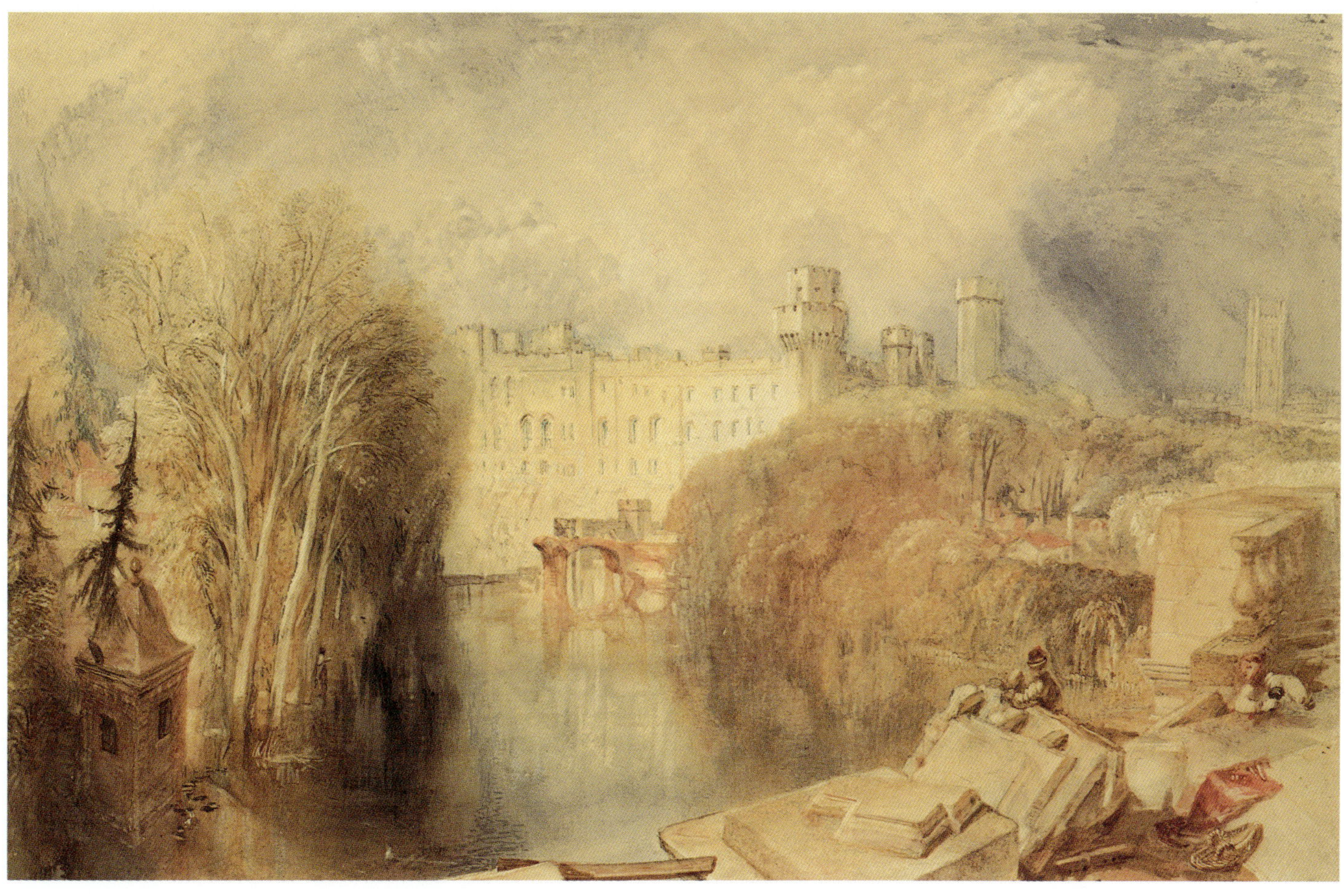

52   Upnor Castle, Kent, 1831-2

watercolor and bodycolor
290 x 437 mm.
Purchased from Thomas Agnew & Sons by
Miss Ashton in 1862
Mrs. Ashton
Bequeathed by Sir Edward and Lady
Broadhurst in 1924
(WAG.D.1924.41)

Upnor Castle was one of six engravings published in 1833, and must therefore only slightly post-date *Warwick Castle*. For the *England and Wales* series, Turner frequently returned to sketches of a much earlier date. This drawing of Upnor Castle is one such, being based on sketches probably made around 1821 in the *Medway* sketchbook (T.B. CXCIX pp. 87 verso and 88 [sketchbook inverted] show the whole composition, while one of the sketches on p. 86 verso is for the right hand end of the castle). The *Medway* sketchbook contains many studies of ships and details of rigging and the sketch on page 43 seems to be the basis for the man-o-war on the left in this watercolor. As in the sketch, she is shown without topmasts, which would have been normal for warships prior to their servicing in Chatham Dockyard, seen to the far left.

The letterpress accompanying the engraving makes reference to the defense of the castle against the Dutch raid down the Medway in June 1667, the only occasion in which the castle saw action. Although extensive damage was caused by the Dutch further down the Medway, and the occasion was described by the diarist John Evelyn as "a Dreadful Spectacle as ever any English men saw, & a dishonor never to be wiped off," the firepower from Upnor Castle caused the Dutch Admiral Van Ghent to retreat and not to attack Chatham and Rochester. By Turner's day, the castle was being used as a powder magazine, a function to which the musket in the foreground may refer. As in many of the *England and Wales* watercolors, the light effects are at their most brilliant; the view looks west and is clearly a sunset, although Ruskin thought that it was a sunrise. Ruskin also thought that the reflections in the water one of the best examples of "perfect truth," (*Modern Painters*, Vol. I, in J. Ruskin, *Works*, Vol. III, pp. 542).

53   Carew Castle, Pembrokeshire, c. 1832

watercolor and bodycolor
305 x 457 mm.
Bequeathed by James Blair in 1917
(MCAG 1917.99)

Turner sketched Carew Castle on his 1795 tour of South Wales (see *South Wales* sketchbook T.B. XXVI p. 25). He drew the castle from the north-west showing its two drum towers with their prominent spur buttresses built around 1300 for Sir Nicholas de Carew. The artist never returned to this part of Wales and some thirty years later, when planning a watercolor for engraving in the *England and Wales* series, he referred back to his pencil drawing of the castle and part of the landscape. He changed very little, save that the castle walls in the watercolor are slightly steeper in perspective, giving the building a more imposing appearance, and the sheep in the drawing have been replaced by cows in the watercolor.

The seventeenth century pack-bridge at Carew on the left of the composition was part of the original sketch but the children are a later addition. They are engrossed in their game, unaware of the natural beauty around them. The ruined castle resurrected momentarily as the morning sun streams through the windows refers poignantly to the fleeting nature of their lives.

In *Turner's England* Eric Shanes has noted that the tower of Carew Cheriton, seen here on the right, is actually over a mile away and would not be visible from this spot. Turner has also applied some artistic license in bringing the water closer to the castle.

This is one of the later watercolors for the *England and Wales* series and was engraved in 1834, dating it to the early thirties. It is not Turner's most successful work as there are difficulties with perspective. The relative size of the two groups of cows are problematic and the Carew river is not clearly defined, appearing to be flowing upward, but Turner is able to unify the composition with his strong sense of light and color. This overall impact prompted Ruskin to praise the work, describing the sky as "descending sunbeams through soft clouds, after rain," (*Modern Painters,* vol. I, in J. Ruskin *Works*, vol. III, p. 422).

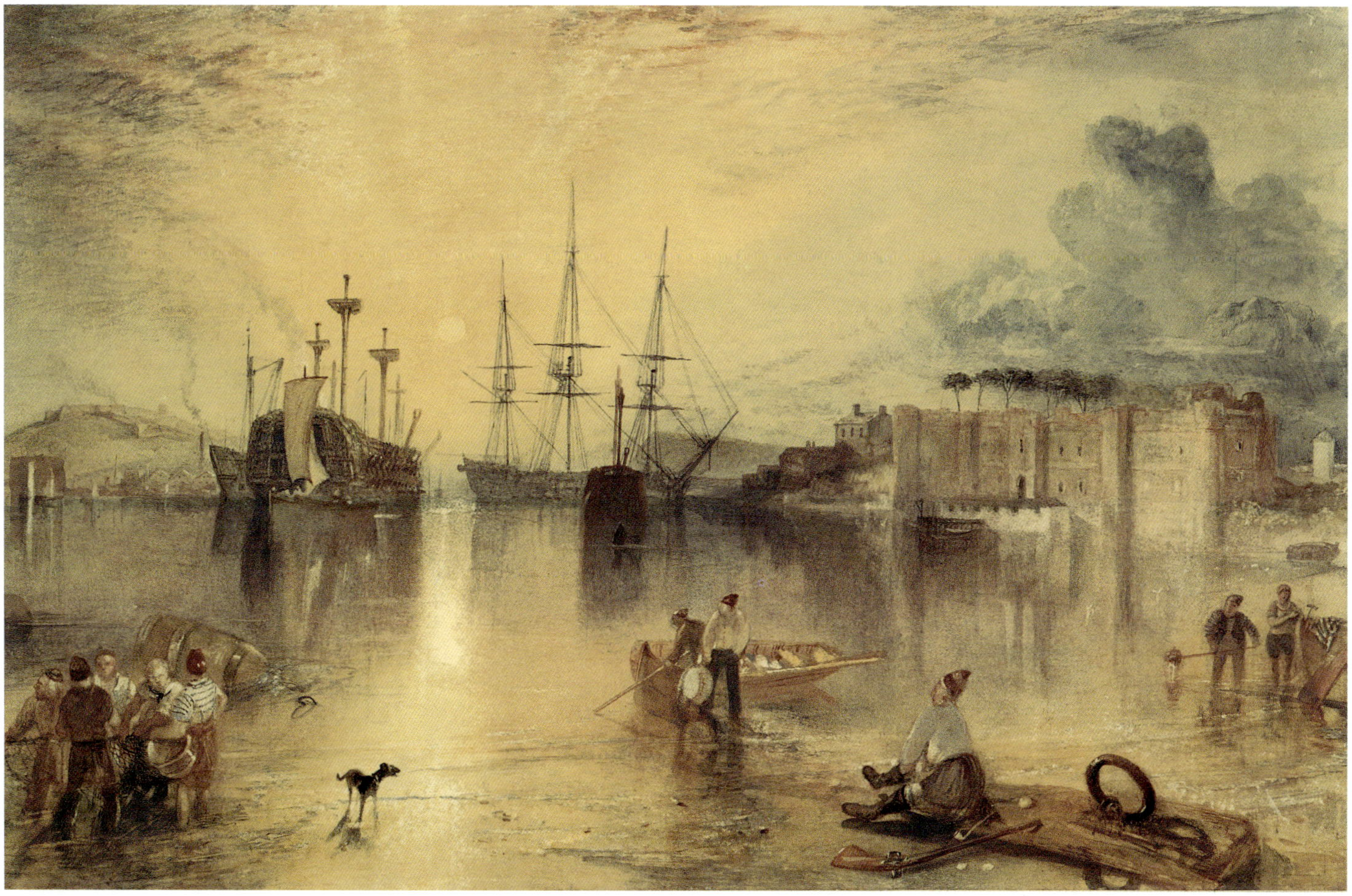

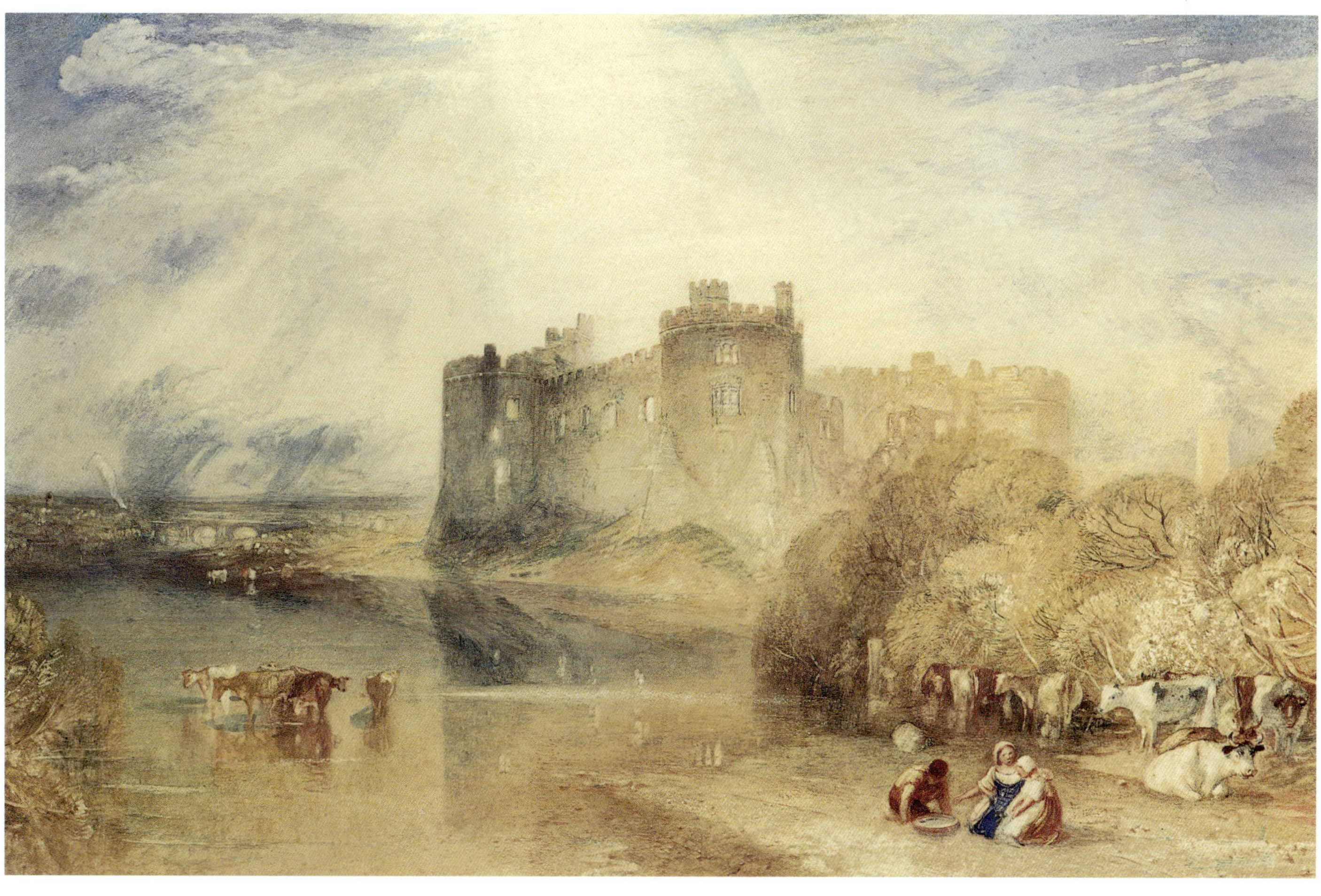

54 Chain Bridge over the Tees, c. 1836

watercolor
278 x 426 mm.
Abraham Haworth, by 1887
On loan from a private collection
(WAG.L.1991.1)

Formerly the property of Munro of Novar and included in his sale at Christie's in 1878, this watercolor is one of the latest in the *England and Wales* series. Certainly, it was among the last to be engraved, and the engraving is one of only four dated 1838, the others being *Rochester, Stroud and Chatham, Richmond Terrace*, and *St. Michael's Mount*. The watercolor dates from circa 1836, although the pencil drawing from which it derives, as with many of the *England and Wales* watercolors, dates from many years earlier. The sketch is in the *Yorkshire No. 5* sketchbook (T.B. CXLVIII-p. 6 verso) of about 1816. The highly dramatic scene is Caldron Snout Falls on the Tees river, one of the highest waterfalls in the British Isles. There is a strong emphasis on diagonals in the composition, with the armed man at the top left ominously approaching the covey of grouse in the bottom right with a chasm yawning between them. These diagonals are emphasized in the engraving by shafts of light that fall across the water-

fall and clearly have been added by the engraver W. R. Smith following Turner's instructions.

Ruskin was particularly impressed with this watercolor, praising it for the truthfulness both of the water and the foliage: "Turner was the only painter who had ever represented . . . the force of agitated water . . . nature gives more than foam, she shows beneath it, and through it, a peculiar character of exquisitely studied form bestowed on every wave and line of fall; and it is this variety of definite character which Turner always aims at . . . in the *Chain Bridge over the Tees*, this passiveness and swinging of the water to and fro are yet more remarkable. . . . The piece of thicket on the right . . . is peculiarly expressive of the aerial relations and play of light among complex boughs," (*Modern Painters*, Vol. I, in J. Ruskin, *Works*, Vol. III, pp. 552-4). Along with cats. 51, 77, and 78, this watercolor was exhibited at the Manchester Royal Jubilee Exhibition of 1887. All were lent by members of the Haworth family.

55 Oxford from North Hinksey, c. 1836-38

watercolor and bodycolor
370 x 515 mm.
Bequeathed by James Blair in 1917
(MCAG 1917.102)

Turner knew Oxford well. He had sketched it as a young boy and some of his earliest known drawings are of the city (see, for example, his copy of a page from the *Oxford Almanack* for 1780, Wilton no. 5, and several panoramic views from North Hinksey between 1789 and 1791, see also cat. 7).

This particular watercolor was produced in response to a commission by James Ryman, a print seller of High Street, Oxford. It was engraved by Edward Goodall and published in 1841. Goodall's son Frederick, also an artist, recorded his memories of Turner and the commission in his *Reminiscences* published in 1902: "One of the Dons of a College accompanied Turner to the spot from which they wanted the drawing made. . . . When they got up to the hill on the third day, a thunderstorm was coming on, with dark purple clouds over the city bringing out all the fine buildings into light against it. 'This will do,' said Turner, 'I don't want to make a sketch' . . . the publishers asked my father to go down to the spot and look at the view . . . to make the drawings of the distant buildings, and put them in their proper place, for Turner was a little careless about that . . . but I thought when I looked at the city it was not as beautiful as Turner had made it."

There are several panoramic sketches of Oxford in the *Oxford and Moselle* sketchbook (T.B. CCLXXXIX), which were drawn by Turner when staying with Ryman in July 1834. Pencil studies on pages 25 - 25a show detailed topographical views from North Hinksey to the west of the city.

In contrast to Goodall's account, W.G. Rawlinson (entry for no. 651) said that two dons accompanied Turner to watch him paint and so he included them in the work. It would, however, seem that the two dons were included as a visual association of Oxford. Indeed, they appear in several depictions of the subject (for example Wilton nos. 306 and 853).

There does not seem to be a logical connection between the view of the city, the dons, and the happy scene of harvesting in the foreground, but several suggestions could be made. Turner may be contrasting the theoretical work of the dons and the manual labor of the harvesters. (Manchester City Art Galleries also holds Ford Madox Brown's masterpiece *Work*, which expands this theme.) He might also have seen the activities of the harvesting and gleaning as metaphors for academic activities. The scene appears to depict the end of harvesting when the men have gone and left the women to glean. Gleaning was a contentious issue in this period; it was encouraged as an act of charity but could be open to abuse. Turner with his usual dry humor has seen the women in their groups as the same shapes as the sheaves.

Oxfordshire was a center of great agricultural unrest at this time, not apparent in this idyllic watercolor. Enclosures of land had meant hardship and loss of freedom for the farm laborers. This area of Hinksey Hill had been enclosed since 1777, but Turner and many other artists preferred to show open farming either for aesthetic reasons or perhaps for reasons of nostalgia.

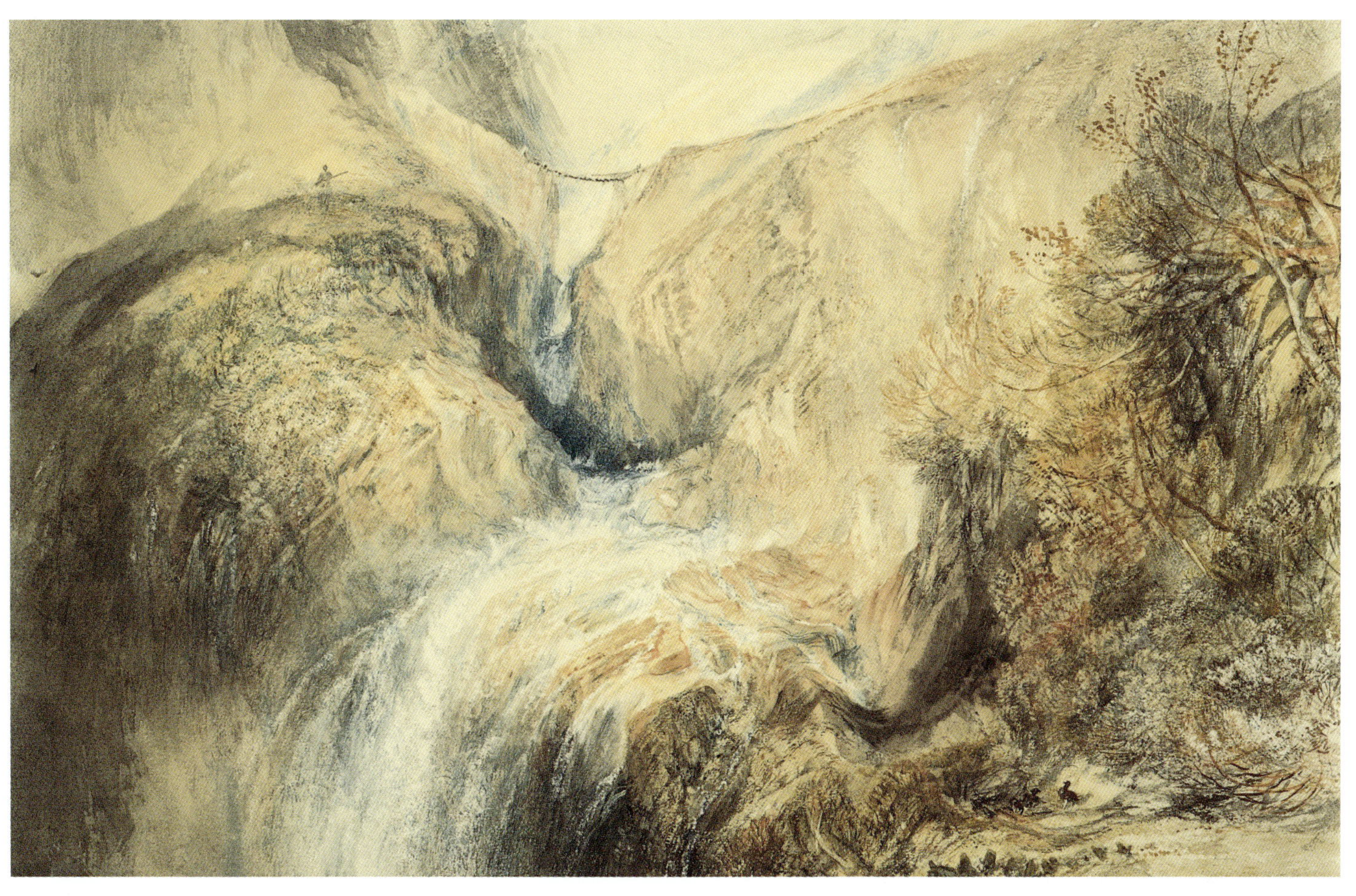

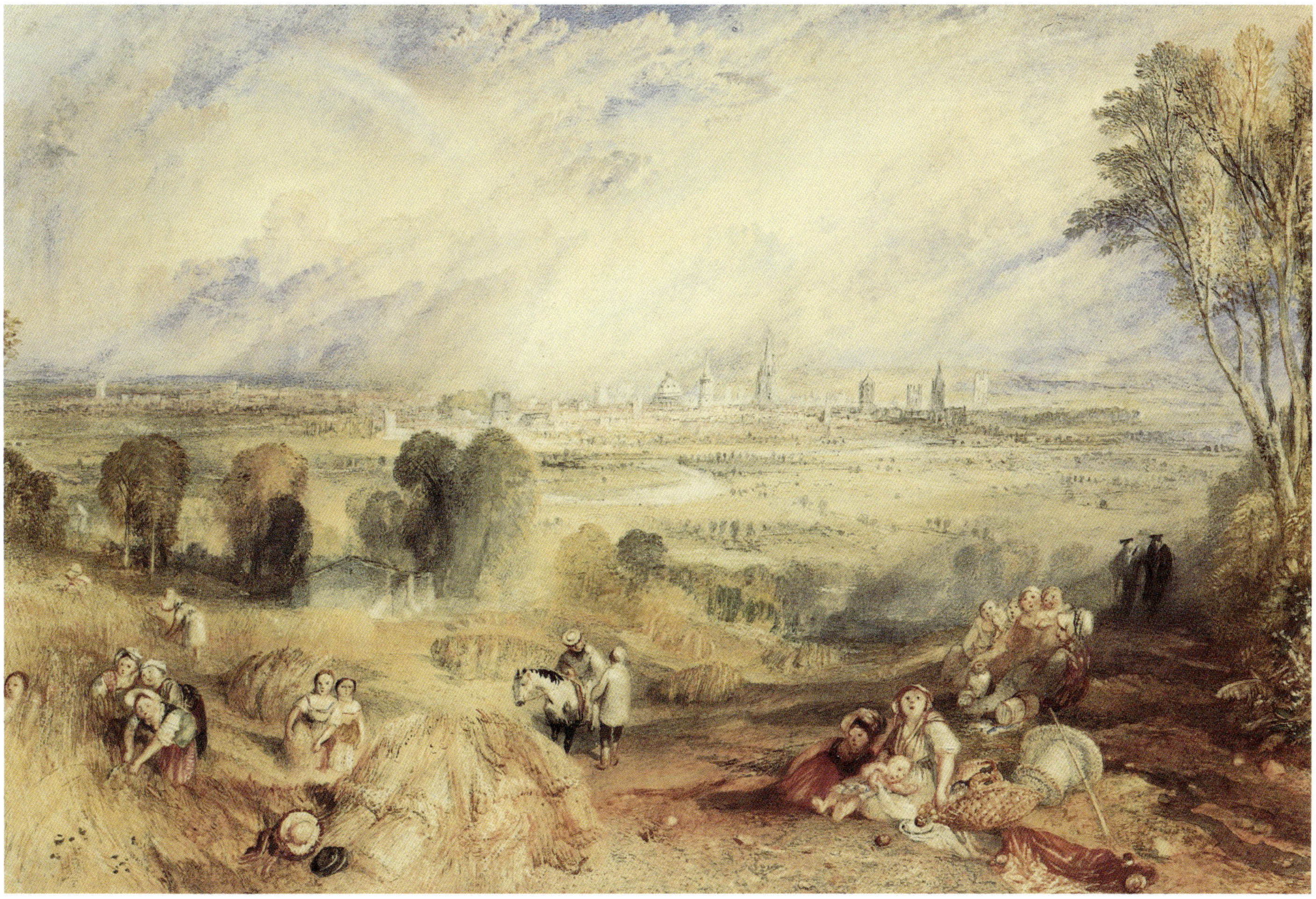

Dunwich, Suffolk, c. 1827

watercolor and bodycolor, on blue paper
172 x 256 mm.
Owned by Sir Joseph Heron
(Manchester's Town Clerk and subscriber
to the Art Treasures Exhibition) and sold
by him in 1890
Bequeathed by James Blair in 1917
(MCAG 1917.94)

In the second decade of the nineteenth century Turner was involved in a project to record the south coast of Britain. The recording of the British coastline was a novelty at a time when inland views had become very popular and publishers were looking for different subjects. Turner collaborated with two brothers, William Bernard and George Cooke who both produced and engraved the series; other artists involved included Peter de Wint and Richard Westall. Part I appeared in 1814. After the success of the *Southern Coast* series the idea was to record the rest of the coastline; by this time, however, Turner had quarreled with the Cookes and decided to publish a project for the *Picturesque Views on the East Coast of England* on his own in collaboration with the line-engraver J.C. Allen. The project did not materialize but Turner produced six gouache drawings and four vignettes, all on blue paper. Three of the vignettes and three rectangular illustrations (including Dunwich) were eventually engraved.

At a time when much of Britain's wealth was tied up with the sea, the perils of fishermen and sailors were the subject of much morbid curiosity. The east coast of Britain is particularly prone to gales, and its busy passage to the Continent meant that rich cargoes and their crews were always vulnerable to shipwreck. Smugglers and wreckers were rife (see also cat. 49). Turner saw the fortunes of sailors as yet another example of fallacious hope as they put their trust in beacons and lighthouses to guide them safely ashore. His views of the east coast reflect the poems of the Suffolk poet George Crabbe, who wrote about the harsh life of fisher-folk around Aldeburgh and Dunwich. A copy of his poems was found in Turner's house after his death.

The villagers of Dunwich launch their pitifully small lifeboat pointing toward the shipwreck just faintly visible on the horizon. They are no match for the power of the sea, which has already claimed its victim for the night, debris of which can be seen in the foreground. Its constant battering has eroded the coastline and has turned the once prosperous port into a poor fishing village. The church of All Saints is also in a perilous position and was eventually swallowed up by the sea in 1912. Turner may well have been referring to the waning influence of the church in an age of growing materialism. Eric Shanes has pointed out in *Turner's England*, 1990, that Turner has rotated the angle of the church so that the spire is near to the sea.

The choice of blue paper and the prominent use of white increase the dramatic impact of these works so that the east coast works have a more threatening nature than the earlier, more optimistic south coast scenes. The contrast in the engraving is even greater, and the dramatic impact is increased by a bolt of lightening aimed at the church.

There are sketches of Dunwich and other east coast subjects in the *Norfolk, Suffolk and Essex* sketchbook (T.B. CCIX p. 41a) used by Turner around 1824. This particular work was engraved by J.C. Allen between 1827-30.

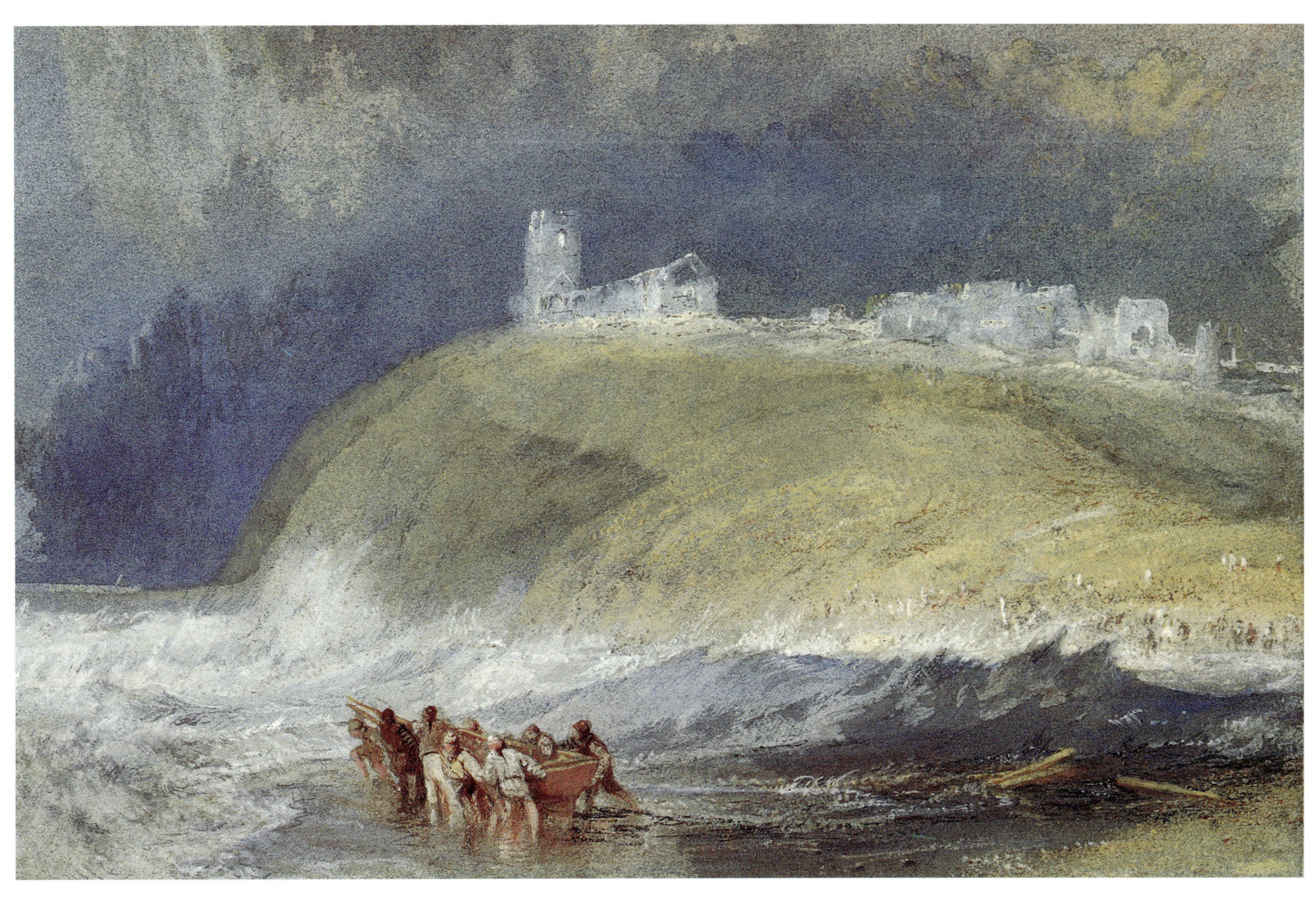

57 Vignette Study of a Lighthouse, c. 1834

pencil and watercolor, on card embossed
with a crown stamp and EXTRA
SUPERFINE DRAWING BOARD
198 x 155 mm.
John Edward Taylor, by 1870
Presented by John Edward Taylor in 1892
(WAG.D.1892.101)

Although Turner's first published vignette was
W.B. Cooke's engraving of *Martello Towers at
Bexhill* in Volume I of *Picturesque Views of the
Southern Coast of England*, published in 1814-
1816, he did not become generally known to
the public for this distinctive form of book
illustration until 1830, when he contributed 25
vignettes to illustrate Samuel Rogers's poem
Italy. These are the most famous of all Turner's
vignettes and were the first examples of his
work to be seen by the ten-year-old Ruskin,
marking the beginning of a lifelong enthusiasm.
In the years that followed, Turner produced a
number of vignettes for various poetic, literary,
and topographical publications. Finberg
grouped some 209 drawings together under
T.B. CCLXXX as *Studies for Vignettes*; many of
these are stylistically similar and drawn on thin
card similar to the Whitworth drawing. T.B.
CCLXXX - 85 has the same crown stamp and
T.B. CCLXXX - 205 is on IMPROVED
SUPERFINE LONDON BOARD.

This drawing has been thought to relate to
one of the title-pages of an annual known as
Turner's Annual Tour, published in 1833, 1834,
and 1835. Confusingly, the book has several
titles: it is also known as *Wanderings by the Loire*
(1833) and *Wanderings by the Seine* (1834 and
1835), although the spines of each volume and
the title pages each read "Turner's Annual
Tour." The volumes were later collected and
republished in 1837 as *Rivers of France*. The
watercolor that has been thought to relate to
the Whitworth drawing was engraved as the
frontispiece of the 1834 volume, entitled *Light
Towers of the Heve*, and is in the Turner Bequest
(T.B. CCLIX - 136). However, the identification of the Whitworth watercolor is far from
certain. It is certainly close to a vignette in the
Lady Lever Art Gallery, Port Sunlight (Wilton
no. 1004), which is inscribed "Mar" and has
been traditionally identified as Margate. Both
the Whitworth and the Port Sunlight watercolors may relate to a more finished vignette,
which was not engraved, in a private collection
(Wilton no. 1002), or may be unused studies
for another vignette, which got no further than
this stage.

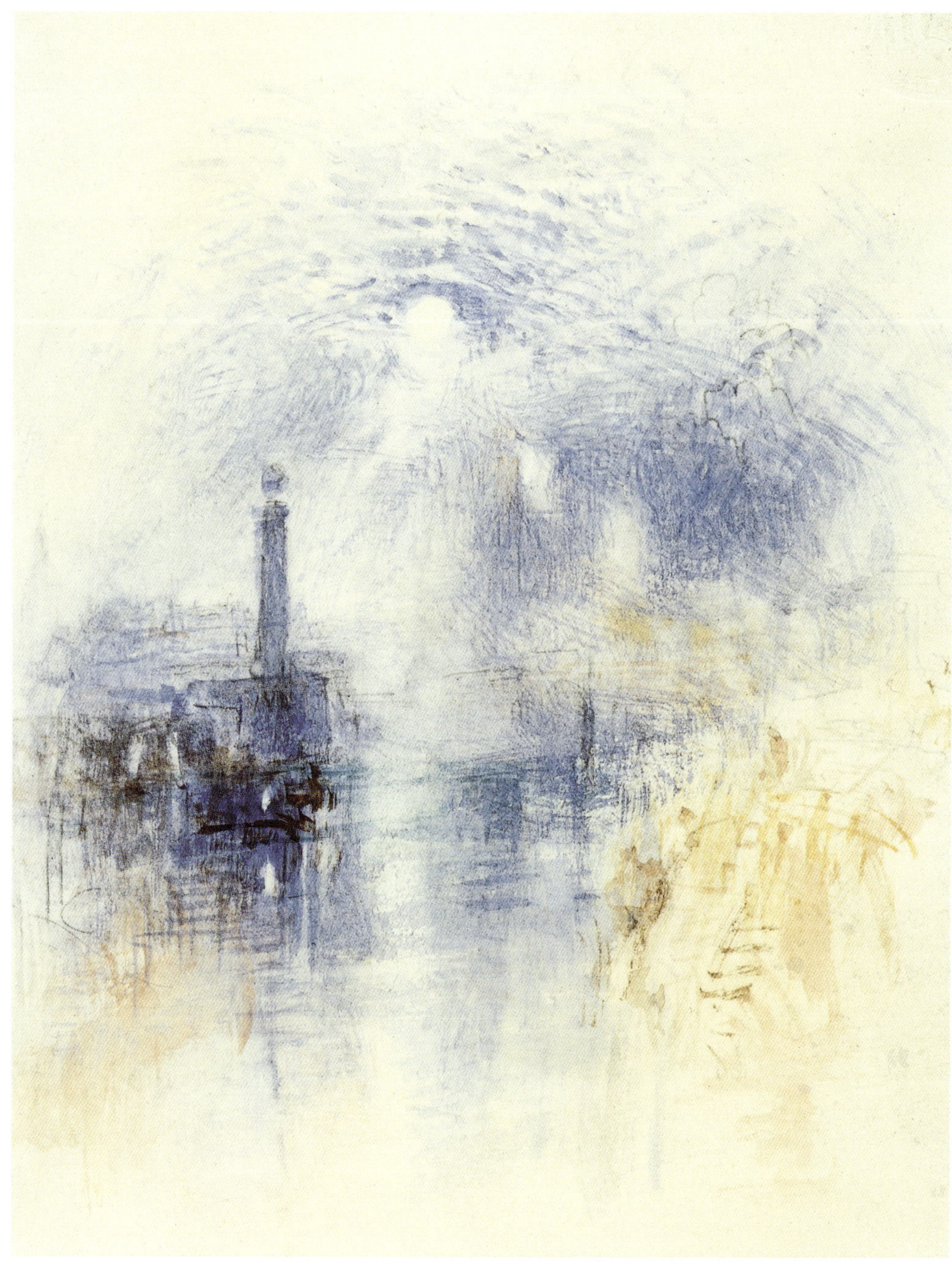

58 A Mountain Pass in Moonlight, 1840s

pencil and watercolor,
watermark Ruse and Turner 1840
177 x 127 mm.
John Edward Taylor
Bequeathed by Dr. David Lloyd Roberts
in 1920
(MCAG 1920.583)

A vignette is a small illustration often used for
the title page of a book. It is derived from the
words "little vine" and was originally an ornamental printer's device of grapes and vine
leaves. By Turner's time it had largely lost its
ornamental purpose and had come to mean a
small delicate illustration with irregular edges,
often fading away at the edges, and frequently
used as a contrast to a rectangular frontispiece.

The subject of this rough sketch for a
vignette has not been positively identified. (See
previous entry, cat. 57, for information on
Turner's use of the vignette.) It has the compact serpentine motif with a light source as a
key element that characterizes some of his later
designs, for example the illustrations for
Moore's *The Epicurean*, published in 1839.
Although previously thought to be a design of
the mid 1830s (see Wilton no. 1145), recent
conservation has revealed an 1840 watermark.
This post-dates all the illustrative work published in Turner's lifetime and places it with a
group of unspecified vignette sketches of continental subjects executed in the 1840s.

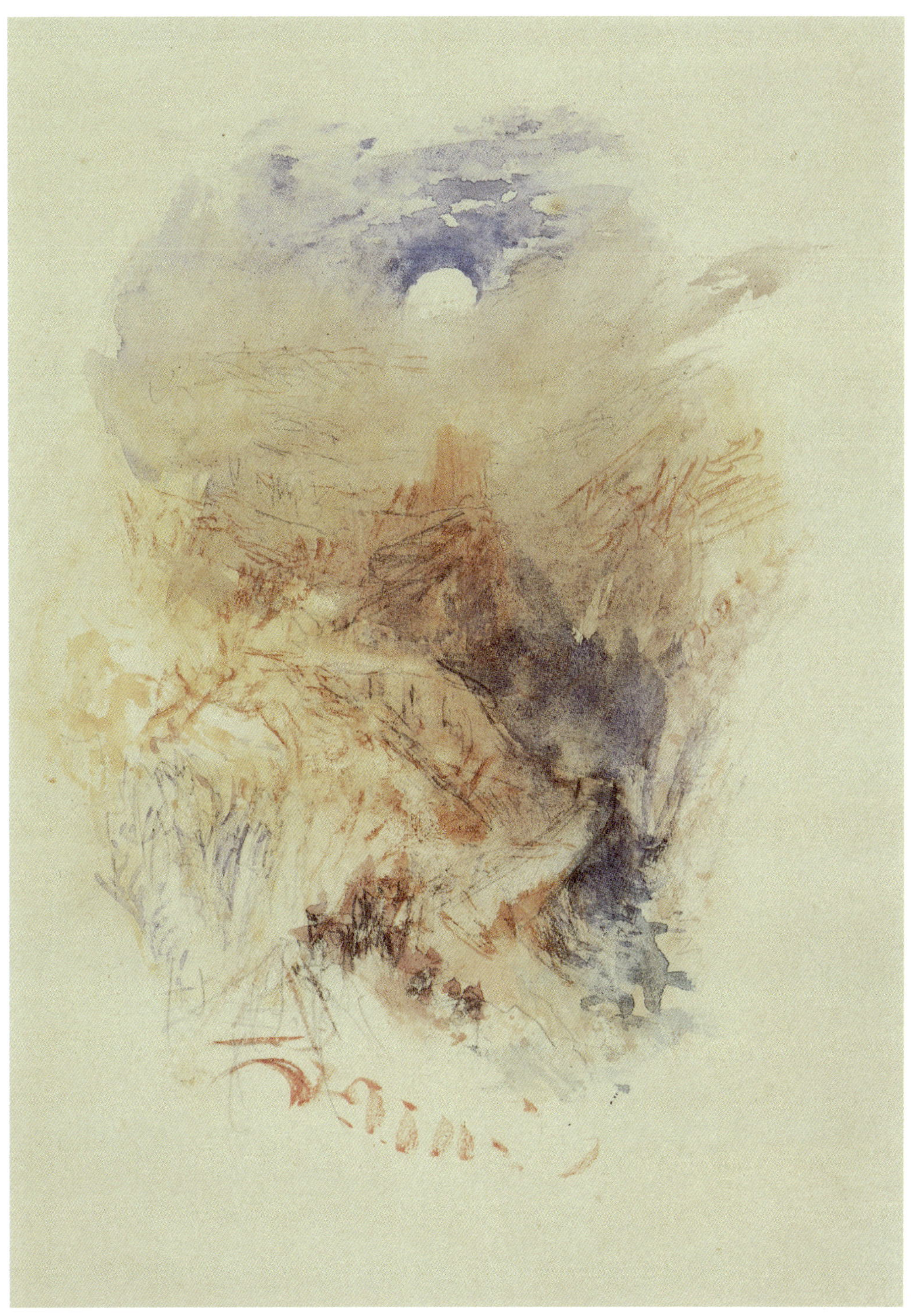

59   The Drachenfels, Germany, c. 1832

pencil, watercolor and bodycolor
126 x 203 mm.
Bequeathed by James Blair in 1917
(MCAG 1917.113)

The Drachenfels, or Dragon Rock, is one of the Siebengebirge, or seven hills, that dominate the banks of the Rhine just below Bonn. It is seen on the right hand side of this watercolor with Rolandseck to the left and the former convent or Nonnenworth on the island to the far right. Turner painted several versions of this famous view; this one was to be included in Finden's *Landscape Illustrations to Byron*. As its title shows, this publication was not intended to illustrate specific incidents in Byron's poems but to produce evocative landscape illustrations of places mentioned in them with a written commentary.

The Drachenfels was to illustrate *Childe Harold*, which was published in four cantos between 1812-18 and describes a journey through Europe. In his preface Byron states that it "was written, for the most part, amidst the scenes which it attempts to describe." Turner shared with Byron (and Sir Walter Scott, see cat. 60) a strong sense of place, and it was this that was to make his illustrations so appealing to a nineteenth-century audience hungry for information about travel to far-away places. He would also have appreciated Byron's comments spoken through Harold in Canto III, "I live not in myself but I became/Portion of that around me." Byron introduced a fictitious character to connect the poem. His young knight Harold cast a melancholy eye over wartorn Europe and remembers its past glories. There is a romantic sense of alienation that focuses on his yearnings for his lost love.

The third canto was published in 1816, nine months before Turner's first visit to Germany. Like Byron's imaginary knight, Turner visited the field of Waterloo before continuing on into Germany and the Rhineland. When he came to illustrate the Drachenfels in the 1830s, he referred back to the work from this 1817 tour (see Wilton nos. 666 and 667). This watercolor illustrates the lines from Canto III:

> "The castled crag of Drachenfels
> Frowns o'er the wide and winding Rhine,
> Whose breast of waters broadly swells
> Between the banks which bear the vine"

This is the beginning of a small section in rhyming couplets in the manner of a German folk song that is interpolated between verses about the romantic legends of robber knights in their castles in verse LV and the description of the fertile Rhineland in chapter LVI. The song goes on to talk of the blue-eyed maidens who remind Harold of his love.

Byron's idealistic view of the Rhine can be contrasted with that of another traveler at the time. Leitch Ritchie in his *Travelling Sketches in the Rhine, and in Belgium and Holland*, 1833, writes, and the quotations are from the continuation of the above rhyming couplets: "We have scarcely any where seen human nature in such a state of greater degradation. . . . The 'deep blue eyes' of the peasant girls glare upon you with the scowl of famine, from between the ridges that are heavy with corn and wine; and the hands 'that offer early flowers' grasp a rope - fit token of their bondage - the loop of which is yoked round their waist, as they drag their barges against the stubborn stream."

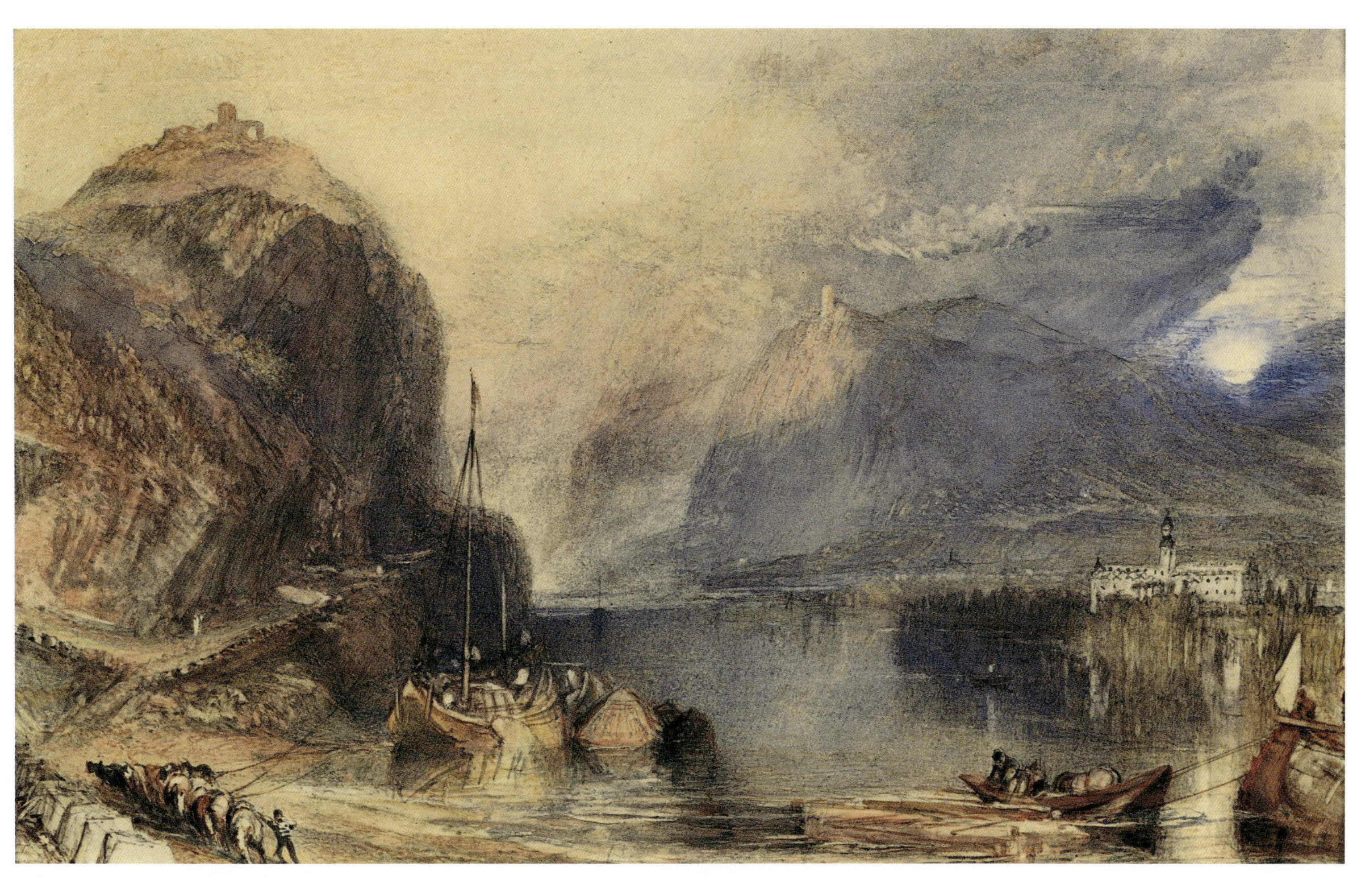

60 Rouen: A distant View, c. 1834

pencil and watercolor
82 x 142 mm.
Bought by John Ruskin in 1878
Bequeathed by James Blair in 1917
(MCAG 1917.95)

The city of Rouen is situated on the Seine northwest of Paris. This view is taken from St. Catherine's Hill. The Cathedral of Notre Dame is clearly visible, with the rather squat church tower of St. Maclou to its left. Turner has shown the old central spire of the cathedral, which was destroyed by fire in 1822, and so was probably relying on sketches he made in the *Dieppe, Rouen and Paris* sketchbook (T.B. CCLVIII), which he used on his tour of 1821. He did, however, return to France in 1832 to make sketches for his illustrations to Sir Walter Scott's *Prose Works,* of which this is part, and at the same time to glean material for his *Rivers of France* series.

The *Prose Works* was to complete the publisher Robert Cadell's edition of Scott, eventually published in 1836. Turner's main task on his 1832 trip was to obtain material for the *Life of Napoleon,* but he also had to produce illustrations for the two French volumes of *Tales of a Grandfather;* this consisted of five volumes of Scottish history and two of French, and was dedicated to Scott's grandson, John Hugh Lockhart who lived in London. *Rouen* was the frontispiece for volume 27 and is paired with a vignette of *Calais* on the title page. As with the Byron series, these engravings were meant merely to give a sense of place rather than to illustrate specific incidents. Most of these two volumes deal with the struggles between the English and the French over Normandy. Rouen figures in both volumes 27 and 28. It is particularly significant in volume 27, however, as the headquarters of Rollo, the son of the King of Denmark, who in A.D. 911 became a Christian and whose line a century later produced a dynasty of English kings (pp. 96-100).

This watercolor was first owned by the great Turner collector, Munro of Novar who was particularly interested in Turner's watercolors for illustrations of the 1830s. After the dispersal of his works in 1877, it passed into the hands of Ruskin, who also owned another watercolor of the same subject as part of the *Rivers of France* series. The Manchester example, he said, was "One of the most exquisitely finished of the Scott series but forced in effect to suit the purpose of engraving" whereas the other version was "a record of a real impression, carried out for its own sake." He also noticed that Turner "always signs a locality with some incident; the diligence coming up the hill and passengers walking therefore occur in both the views of Rouen," (J. Ruskin, *Works*, vol. XIII, pp. 446 and 451).

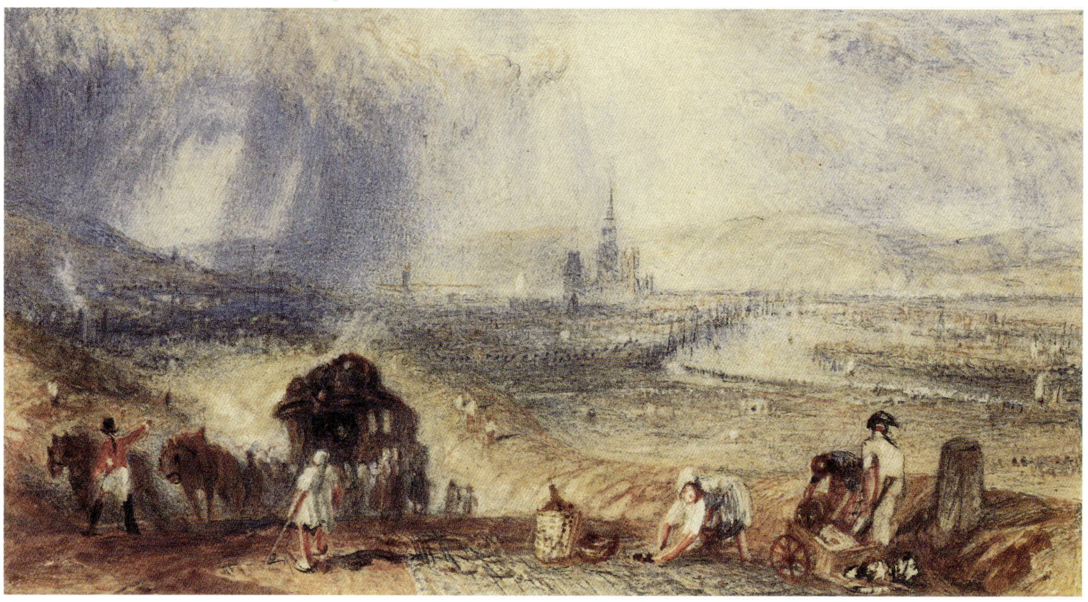

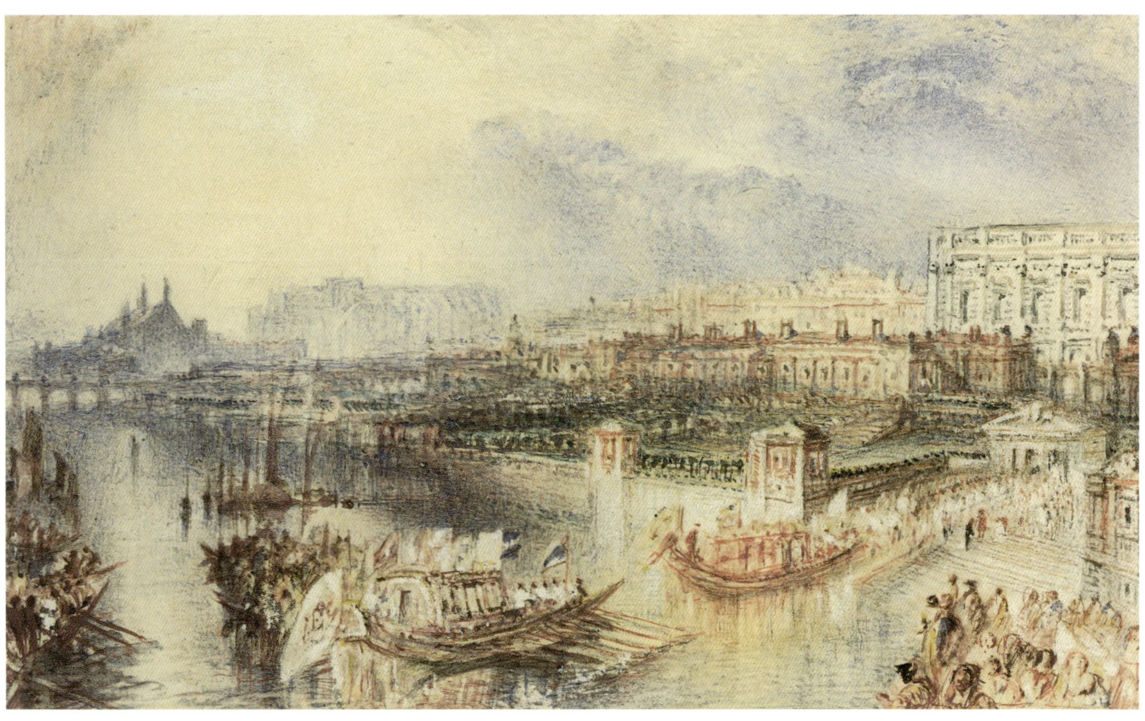

61 Whitehall, c. 1835

pencil, watercolor and bodycolor
91 x 149 mm.
Bequeathed by James Blair in 1917
(MCAG 1917.114)

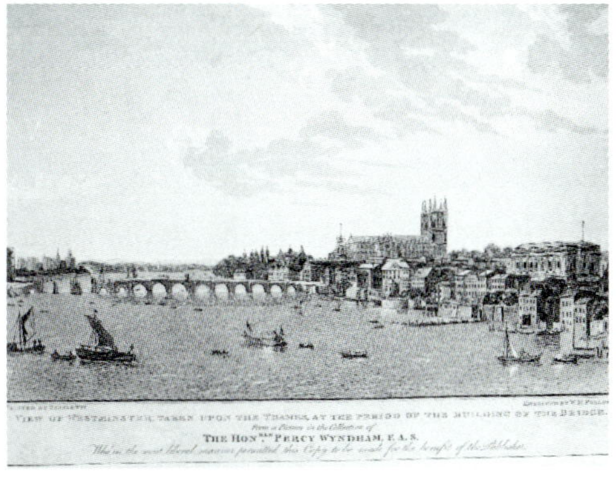

Figure 17. *View of Westminster, taken upon the Building of the Bridge* from *Antiquities of Westminster*, 1807, Manchester Public Libraries

This is most probably a design for an illustration made for Henry Fisher's two-volume *Landscape-Historical Illustrations of Scotland and the Waverley Novels* published in 1836-7. It was previously thought to be an illustration for *Woodstock* (set in the seventeenth century) as the watercolor shows Inigo Jones' Banqueting Hall of 1625, but Dr. Jan Piggott has now advanced a more convincing theory soon to be published in the *Turner News Letter* and I am grateful to him for allowing me to read his article before its publication. Piggott suggests that this is an illustration for another Walter Scott novel, *Kenilworth*, showing the Embarkation of Queen Elizabeth at Greenwich (vol. I, chapter XV). The design was never engraved, probably because Turner painted the sovereign departing from Whitehall instead of Greenwich. Turner and Fisher quarreled around this time and this may well have been a reason. (See Finley, *Landscapes of Memory*, p. 258, n. 52).

Turner's source for this watercolor was an engraving, *View of Westminster, taken upon the Thames at the Building of the Bridge* based on a painting by Canaletto. It was published by John Thomas Smith in 1809 as part of a series of additional plates to his *Antiquities of Westminster*, 1807 (fig. 17). Smith was also the Keeper of Prints and Drawings at the British Museum from 1816 to 1833 and was an acquaintance of Turner. (It was he who painted the watercolor of Turner examining a print in the British Museum, now in the Indianapolis Museum of Art.)

The view shows the Palace of Whitehall on the north bank of the Thames. Turner has included Westminster Bridge, built 1738-49, to the far left and above it the pitched roof of Westminster Hall (The Houses of Parliament), which was destroyed by fire in 1834. For Turner's watercolors of this event, see Evelyn Joll in the catalogue of the recent *Turner* exhibition, (Canberra, 1996, pp. 87-99).

Westminster Abbey can be seen next to it without Hawksmoor's west towers of 1734-45. The extension of the banqueting hall in the foreground and the addition of garden pavilions are Turner's, but he has copied Canaletto's barge on which he has added the letter E. Queen Elizabeth can be seen descending the stairs of the palace with Sir Walter Raleigh spreading his cloak for her to walk on. The identical moment was shown in the engraving that was published after a design by Henry Melville.

62 A Conflagration, Lausanne, 1836

watercolor and bodycolor
240 x 305 mm.
Presented in memory of John Edward
Taylor by his nephews in 1912
(WAG.D.1912.6)

Like *Sunset at Sea with Gurnets* and *Sunset on wet Sand* (cats. 69 and 80), this watercolor did not form part of the Taylor Gift to the Whitworth in 1892, but was purchased by his nephews at his posthumous sale at Christie's in 1912 and presented to the Whitworth in Taylor's memory. This drawing and cats. 63 and 64 derive from Turner's 1836 tour of Switzerland, made in the company of his friend and patron Munro of Novar. For much of the trip they retraced the route taken by Turner on his first visit to the Alps in 1802. After traveling through France to Geneva and making a circuit of the lake embracing Lausanne, Vevey, and Chillon, they traveled south through Bonneville and Cluse to Chamonix and then through the *Val d'Aosta* to Turin. The route of the tour can be followed in the *Val d'Aosta* and *Fort Bard* sketchbooks (T.B. CCXCIII and CCXCIV), albeit in a muddled way since Ruskin removed some of the pages and confused the order of both books.

Like no. 63, this sheet also comes from a roll-sketchbook used on the tour and since

broken up. The group of drawings traditionally associated with the 1836 tour are scattered among the Turner Bequest and various public and private collections (Wilton nos. 1430-56). As Wilton (1979) points out, they are often of a rather square format, and share a rich and dark coloring. The Whitworth drawing may be particularly compared with *A Scene in the Val d'Aosta* and *Couvent de Bonhomme, Chamonix*, both in the Fitzwilliam Museum (Wilton nos. 1430 and 1449). Other drawings possibly from the same roll-sketchbook—since the sheets are almost exactly the same size—are in the Vaughan Bequest at the National Gallery of Ireland, *An Alpine Pas in the Val d'Aosta* (Wilton no. 1443) and *Chatel Argent near Villeneuve* (Wilton no. 1442). Another view of Chatel Argent, from a different angle and probably from the same roll-sketchbook, is in the Vaughan Bequest at the National Galleries of Scotland (Wilton no. 1434).

63 Chillon Castle from Villeneuve, 1836

pencil and watercolor
236 x 325 mm.
Purchased from Thomas Agnew & Sons in 1891 with a fund presented by the Guarantors of the 1887 Manchester Royal Jubilee Exhibition (WAG.D.1887.17)

This drawing was bought in the very early days of the Whitworth Art Gallery in the mistaken belief that it was an early work. In fact, it is probably a sheet from a roll-sketchbook (i.e., a sketchbook without hard covers) that Turner used on his 1836 tour of Switzerland and subsequently broke up. No finished watercolor resulted from this tour, but the Whitworth drawing is one of a large group of colored studies of mountain scenery now scattered among various public and private collections (these are listed as Wilton nos. 1430-56), which have long been associated with the journey. Many others from the group, as well as other drawings from other tours, are in the Turner Bequest, unbound and listed under T.B. CCLXIII, CCCXLIV, and CCCLXIV.

Turner first visited Chillon in 1802 on his first Alpine tour, and sketches from this tour formed the basis for two watercolors of circa

1809 showing the castle from the other side (British Museum, Wilton no. 390, and Untraced, Wilton no. 395). In the meantime, in 1817, Byron published his celebrated romantic poem *The Prisoner of Chillon*. Turner was well versed in Byron's works, having exhibited four paintings with Byronic themes or with quotations from the poet at the Royal Academy between 1818 and 1836, as well as having worked on a series of watercolor illustrations to Byron's poetry for the publisher John Murray in 1823-4 and 1830-1832. The choice of Chillon as a subject may well have been influenced, therefore, by his knowledge of the Byron poem, although there is no hint of its dark subject matter. Pencil sketches of the castle drawn on the 1836 tour appear in the *Val d'Aosta* sketchbook (T.B. CCXCIII), including similar views from Villeneuve on pp. 42-3.

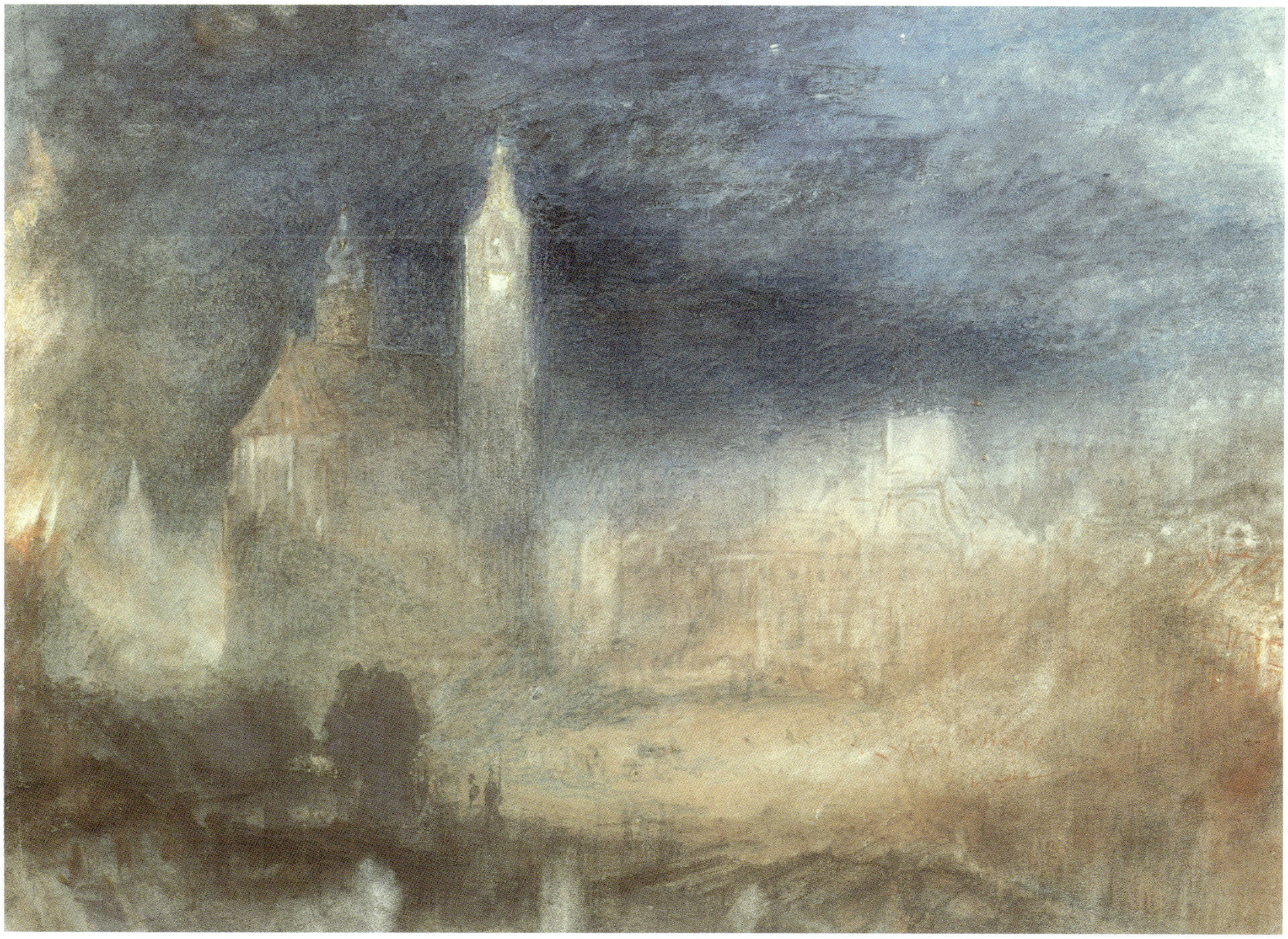

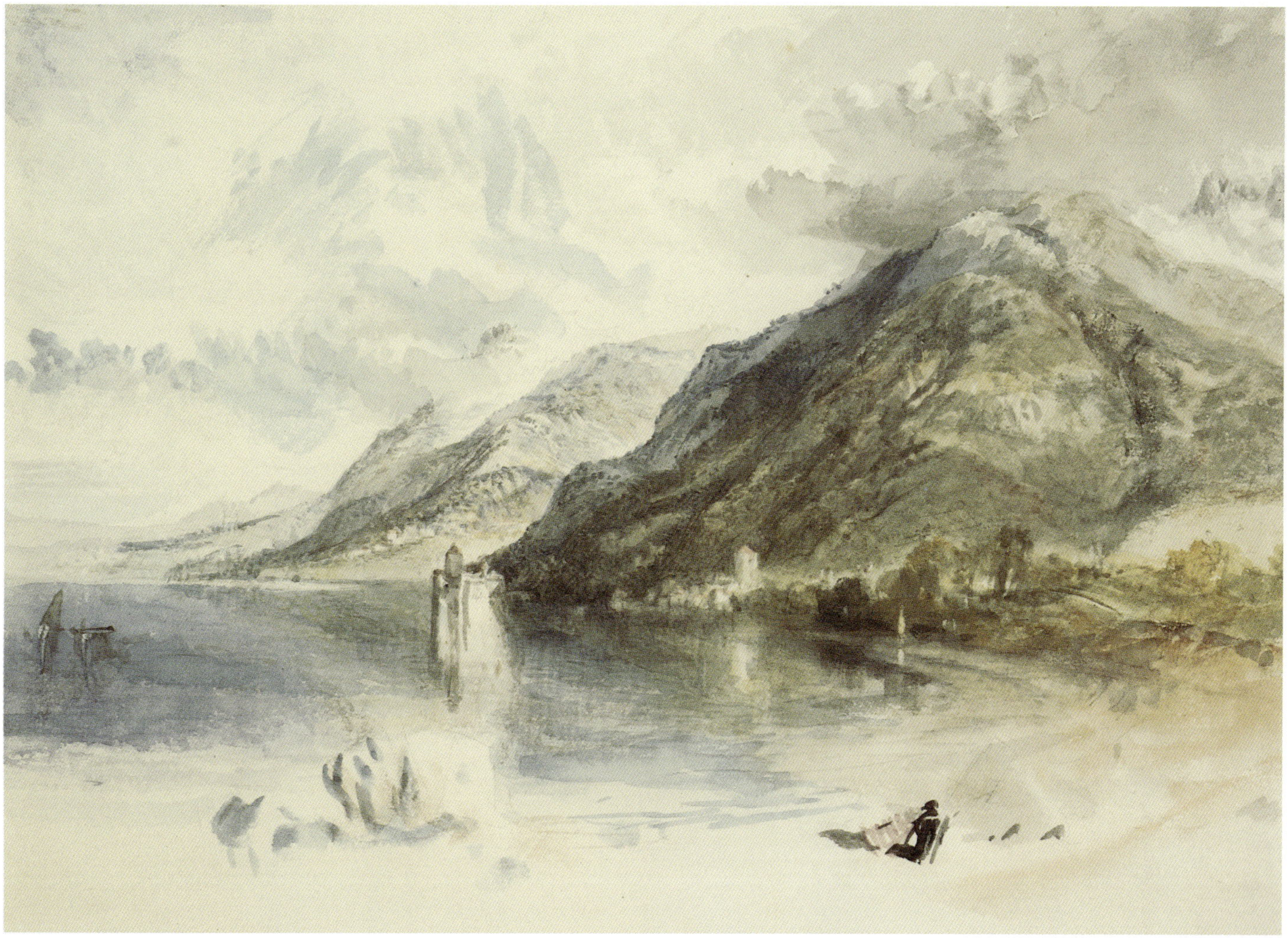

64 Landscape [formerly called St. Martin's Precipice] c. 1836

pencil, watercolor and bodycolor,
on buff paper
138 x 192 mm.
Bequeathed by James Blair in 1917
(MCAG 1917.115)

This watercolor with added bodycolor was previously thought to be a view of St. Martin's Precipice, near the town of Innsbruck in Austria, and has been connected to a work now in the Indianapolis Museum of Art, of Martinswand, near Innsbruck. Both these attributions have now been refuted by the director of archives at Innsbruck in a letter to Cecilia Powell while she was researching her exhibition *Turner in Germany*. A search through sketchbooks and loose sketches in the Turner Collection at the Tate Gallery has not resulted in a positive identification of the location, but stylistically this work relates to cats. 65 and 66 in this exhibition and could also be a representation of Sisteron or the surrounding area visited by Turner in 1836.

It shares the same dimensions as these works and is on the same buff paper. Turner would often fold standard-sized paper into halves or quarters and would use them for additional jottings or to work up pencil sketches in color from his notebook. There are numerous small pieces of paper in the Turner Bequest still awaiting positive identification, many of which show motifs of hills surmounted by ruins.

Never a purist, Turner was always experimenting with watercolor techniques. In traditional watercolors the white ground is used as a conveyor of luminosity, but even in his early career he was experimenting with washes of color on paper to give a unity and richness to his work. He often had these colored pages bound into his sketchbooks, or even prepared a whole sketchbook in this way (for example, the Wilson sketchbook). He first began to work on colored ground for more finished works in 1817 when the paper he used for his fifty Rhine views (see cats. 39 and 40) was prepared with a gray wash. For later series he used colored paper rather than covering the paper with a uniform wash. Working on buff paper, as in this work, gave him a middle tone. First, he had to work through to the darks and then work up the highlights in white, which gave a chalky appearance. In other series on blue paper, the same principle holds but here the color of the paper becomes both tone and color, which necessitates the heightening of other colors to bring them up to the key of the blue. The technique then becomes more like gouache, i.e. opaque colors as in the Luxembourg series of circa 1839.

65 Sisteron from the North, c. 1836

black chalk, pen and ink, watercolor and
bodycolor, on buff paper
140 x 192 mm.
Bequeathed by George Beatson Blair
(MCAG 1947.109)

Previously called *Landscape: a town with a fortress on a high cliff*, this watercolor can now be positively identified as a view of Sisteron based on a drawing in the *Genoa to Grenoble* sketchbook (T.B. CCXCV p. 102). See cat. 66.

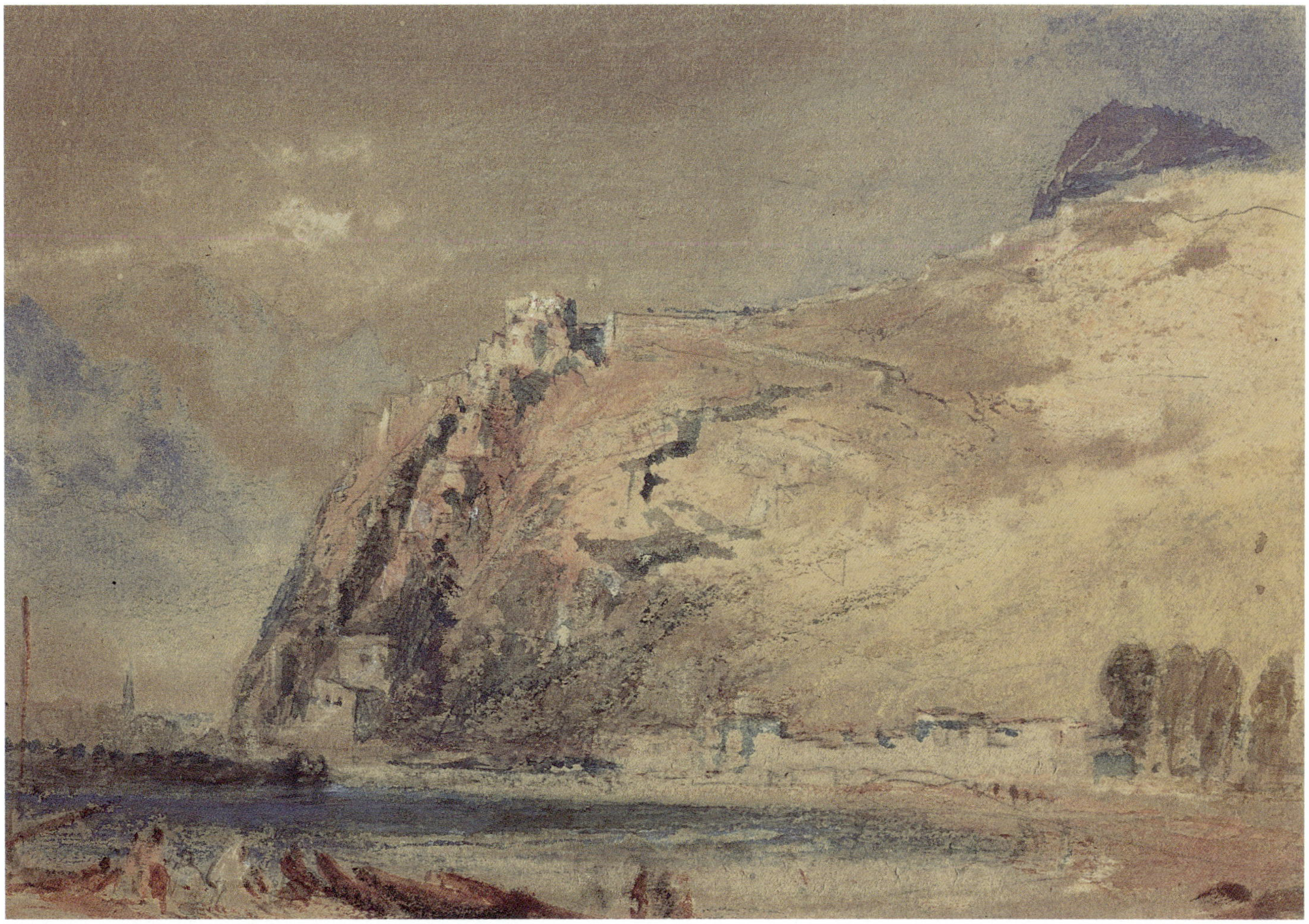

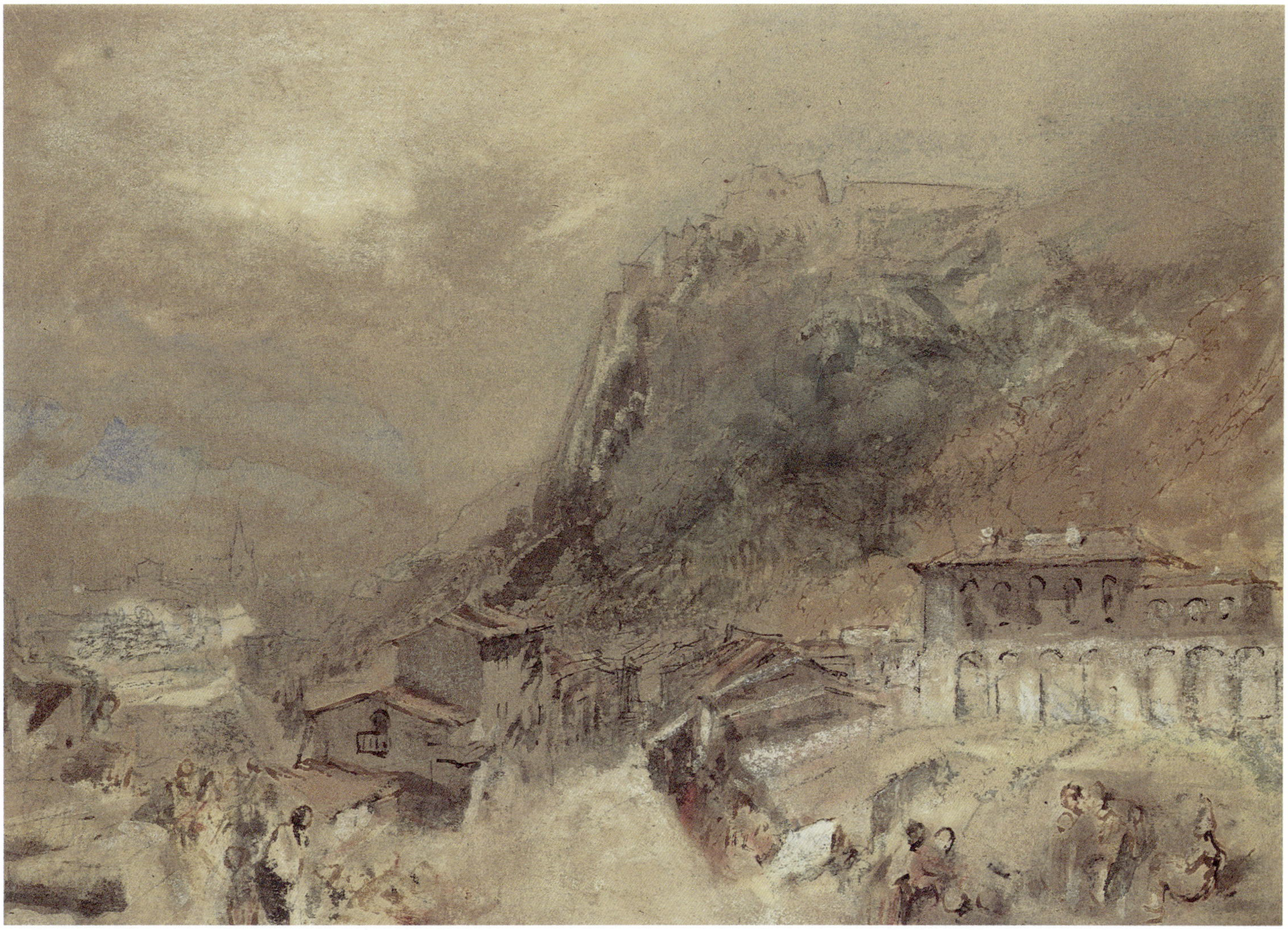

66 Sisteron, 1836

pen and brown ink and watercolor heightened with white, on buff paper
138 x 185 mm.
Probably purchased from Colnaghi's by John Edward Taylor in 1865
Presented by John Edward Taylor in 1892
(WAG.D.1892.115)

This is one of a group of views of Sisteron in southern France on sheets of similar size and color that until recently were not securely dated. Some derive from pencil sketches in the *Genoa to Grenoble* sketchbook (T.B. CCXCV). Others include a watercolor in the Victoria and Albert Museum (Wilton no. 1012), a similar version of which was sold at Sotheby's on April 3, 1996, lot 185 (Wilton no. 1011), and a watercolor in the Manchester City Art Galleries, cat. 65 in this exhibition (Wilton no. 1028), formerly called *Landscape: a town with a fortress on a high cliff*. There is also a watercolor of Sisteron, formerly in the collection of the artist Myles Birket Foster but not recorded in Wilton, which was sold at Sotheby's on November 10, 1994, lot 172; the profile of the fortress as shown in the Sotheby watercolor is the same as that shown in the Whitworth watercolor.

Although Finberg dated the *Genoa to Grenoble* sketchbook to 1835-40, it is possible to be more precise and date it to 1836, on Turner's return journey from Switzerland and after he had parted company with Munro in Turin. Turner's itinerary can be followed in the *Genoa to Grenoble* sketchbook: he traveled along the Riviera coast from Genoa to Nice, and then headed northward inland to Sisteron. He approached the town from the south and sketched the fortress (this is on page 97 of the sketchbook, inscribed "Sisteron"). He then made several sketches of the fortress from the north, including pages 102 and 103, the second of which is close to the Whitworth and Manchester City Art Galleries drawings.

67 Fire at Fennings Wharf on the Thames at Bermondsey, c. 1836

pencil and watercolor
294 x 441 mm.
Presented by John Edward Taylor in 1892
(WAG.D.1892.100)

An inscription on the reverse of the old mount (not in Turner's hand) read: "Fire on the Thames / burning of either the Houses of Parlt or Fennings Wharf." Turner was certainly present at the spectacular burning of the Houses of Parliament on the night of October 16, 1834; he made pencil studies of the event (T.B. CCLXXXIV) and a series of color studies (T.B. CCLXXXIII). He also made an unfinished watercolor possibly intended for engraving (T.B. CCCLXIV - 373, also listed as Wilton no. 522), a vignette that was engraved in 1835 (Museum of Outdoor Arts, Englewood, Colorado, Wilton no. 1306), and two oil paintings exhibited in 1835 (Philadelphia Museum of Art, Butlin & Joll no. 359, and Cleveland Museum of Art, Butlin & Joll no. 364).

Certainly, his observation of the events at the Houses of Parliament stimulated great interest in the themes of fire and water, as can be seen in his *Fire at Sea* oil painting (Tate Gallery, Butlin & Joll no. 460) of circa 1835. It is very probable that this interest led him to depict the fire at Fennings Wharf, which took place on August 30, 1836, and caused £250,000 worth of damage. Presumably, his eye-witness experience of the Houses of Parliament fire helped him to produce the Whitworth watercolor, as he cannot have been present at the later event, because he was in Switzerland at the time. In spite of its considerable fading, the Whitworth watercolor echoes in composition and style the unfinished Houses of Parliament watercolor (Wilton no. 522). Indeed, a "color beginning" entitled *? A burning Warehouse* (T.B. CCLXIII - 89) may be a study for either composition.

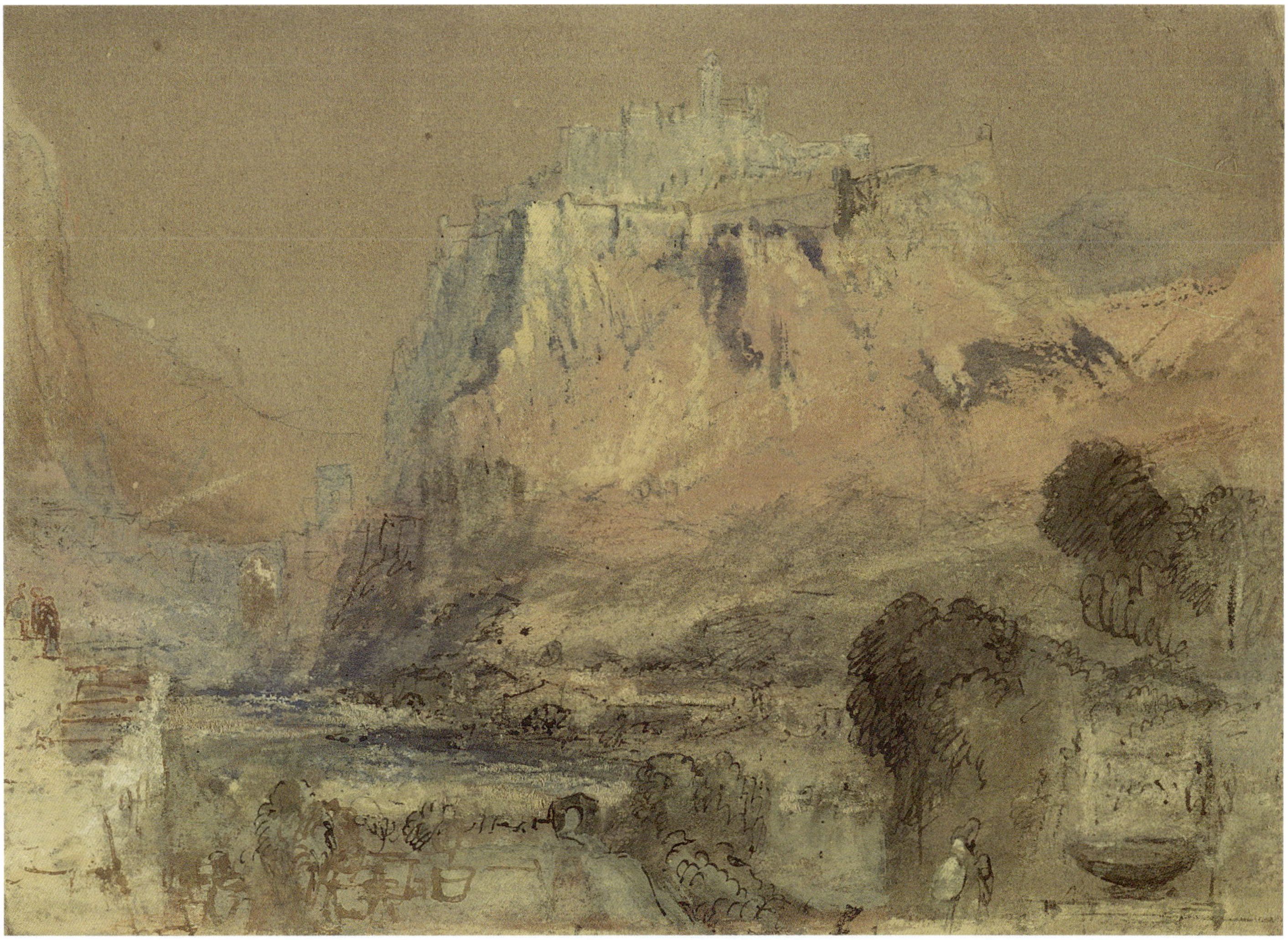

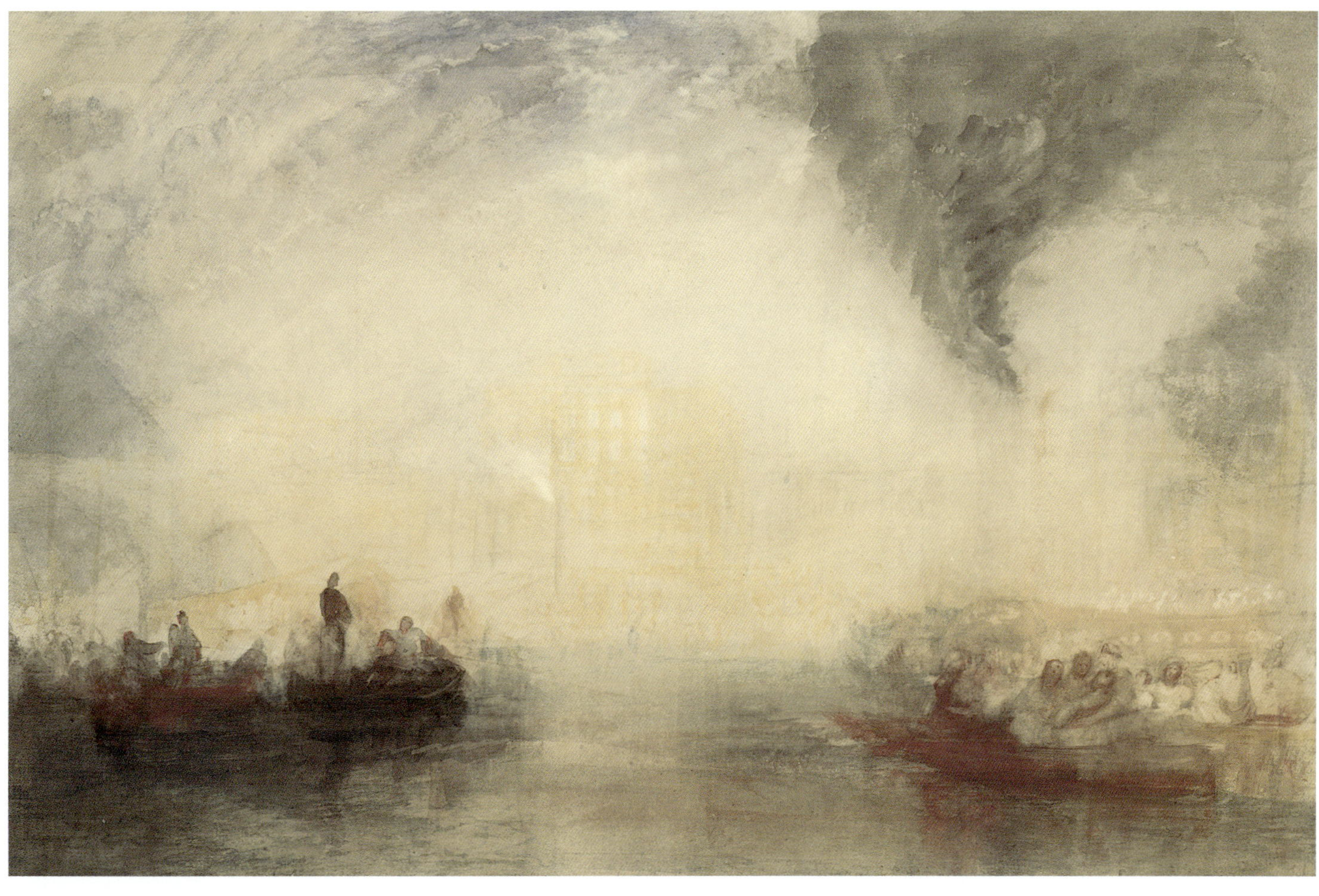

68 Venice: San Giorgio Maggiore from the Entrance to the Grand Canal, c. 1840

inscribed at length on the
reverse (illegible)
watercolor
195 x 276 mm.
Presented by John Edward Taylor in 1892
(WAG.D.1892.114)

Turner first visited Venice briefly in September 1819, spending most of his time (he was in the city for at most five and possibly as few as three days) recording the architecture in pencil. Only four brilliant watercolor studies showing distant general views of the city and the sea are known in the Turner Bequest (T.B. CLXXXI - 4, 5, 6, and 7). It is still not finally resolved when he visited the city for the second time, although a majority of scholars now agree that it was 1833—the *Gazzetta Privilegiata di Venezia* recorded the arrival of "Turner, gent. inglese" from Vienna on September 9, 1833. Internal evidence from the *Venice up to Trent* sketchbook (T.B. CCCXII) suggests he stayed about ten days. There may have been later visits in the 1830s, but there is no firm evidence for them. His last recorded visit to the city was in 1840, from which a comparatively well documented journey the Whitworth drawing probably derives.

The *Gazzetta* records his arrival on August 20 and departure on September 3, which makes it easily his longest visit. Turner put his time to good use and was at work early and late. William Callow, the watercolorist, recorded (*An Autobiography*, 1908, pp. 66-7) meeting Turner on this visit: "The next time I met Turner was at Venice, at the Hotel Europa, where we sat opposite at meals and entered into conversation. One evening whilst I was enjoying a cigar in a gondola I saw Turner in another one sketching San Giorgio, brilliantly lit up by the setting sun. I felt quite ashamed of myself idling away my time whilst he was hard at work so late." Some have doubted the authenticity of the Whitworth drawing, but its impeccable provenance (Taylor had an excellent collection of Turner watercolors) and the fact that the illegible verse on the reverse has been identified by Andrew Wilton as being in Turner's handwriting support its attribution to Turner.

The size of the sheet corresponds roughly to the smaller-sized sheets in the Turner Bequest, such as T.B. CCCXVI - 3 and 28, and CCCLXIV - 106. Although the handling of these sheets is much looser and less finished than in the Whitworth drawing, the application of the blue washes on the left of T.B. CCCXVI - 28 is very similar. In spite of the large number of Venetian studies in watercolor, no finished watercolor was ever completed that derives from them, as was to be the case with the later Swiss studies (see cats. 71-78). The vast majority of them remain in the Turner Bequest, and only a handful of the more finished sketches were sold to more discerning patrons, presumably through his agent Thomas Griffith. The handling of these, which are all on larger sheets, is in places similar to that in the Whitworth drawing (see *Venice from the Lagoon*, National Galleries of Scotland, Wilton no. 1371; *A Storm at Sunset*, Fitzwilliam Museum, Wilton no. 1353; and *A Storm on the Lagoon*, British Museum, Wilton no. 1354). Views related to the Whitworth drawing are in the *Venice* sketchbook (T.B. CCCXIV pp. 2 and 27) and on the roll-sketchbook sheet of this size, already referred to.

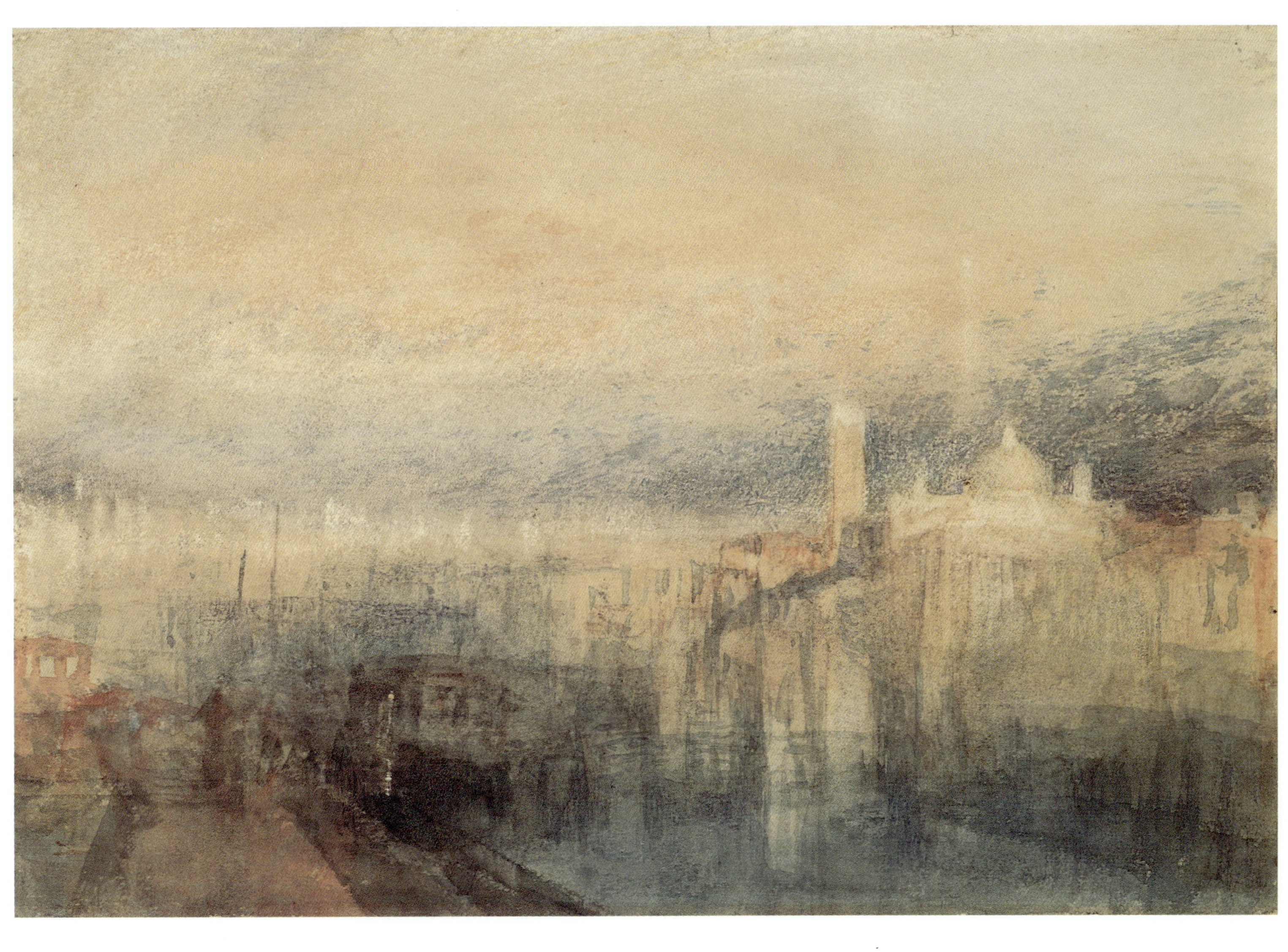

69 Sunset at Sea with Gurnets, 1838-40

black chalk, watercolor and bodycolor, on
brown paper
218 x 284 mm.
Probably John Ruskin
Purchased from Colnaghi's by John
Edward Taylor in 1865
Presented in memory of John Edward
Taylor by his nephews in 1912
(WAG.D.1912.8)

This drawing almost certainly has a Ruskin provenance and later belonged to John Edward Taylor, who bought it from Colnaghi's in 1865. It was presented to the Whitworth in Taylor's memory by his nephews, who purchased it at his posthumous sale at Christie's in 1912. It is one of a number of drawings that employ bodycolor on brown paper and feature marine subjects, many with sunsets (some of them are listed as Wilton nos. 1382-1397). Many of the group are sheets from a sketchbook bought by Ruskin from Turner's Margate landlady and London housekeeper Sophie Caroline Booth (J. Ruskin, *Works*, Vol. XIII, p. 470, entry for no. 113, and see also E. Yardley, "A Margate Sketchbook Re-assembled," *Turner Studies* (Winter 1984), vol. 4, no. 2, pp. 53-6).

Mrs. Booth took Turner in as a lodger from the time she settled in Margate in 1827 with her second husband John Booth, who died in 1833. She remained in Margate until 1846 when Turner moved her up to London into a small house in Chelsea, 6 Davis Place, Cremorne New Road, now the western end of Cheyne Walk. Before this date, Turner used to visit Mrs. Booth regularly, taking the fast packet, which departed from London Bridge Wharf three times a week. It is not known how Mrs. Booth acquired the sketchbook, nor when Ruskin acquired it from her, although the words Ruskin uses to describe the event seem to imply that it occurred after Turner's death.

The majority of the group of drawings to which this belongs can be dated to the late 1830s, and the Whitworth drawing is particularly close to *Sunset over a Beach* (Bacon Collection, Wilton no. 1387), which shows the same scene but without the fish. Despite its visionary and fantastic qualities, the Whitworth drawing is undoubtedly based on something Turner actually saw, and can be related to other fish studies, such as *Study of a Gurnard* (Victoria and Albert Museum, Wilton no. 1404). Turner was to develop the themes of fish and sunsets in two later oil paintings, *Slavers throwing overboard the Dead and Dying*, of 1840 (Museum of Fine Arts, Boston, Butlin & Joll no. 385), and *Sunrise with Sea-Monsters*, of circa 1845 (Tate Gallery, Butlin & Joll no. 473).

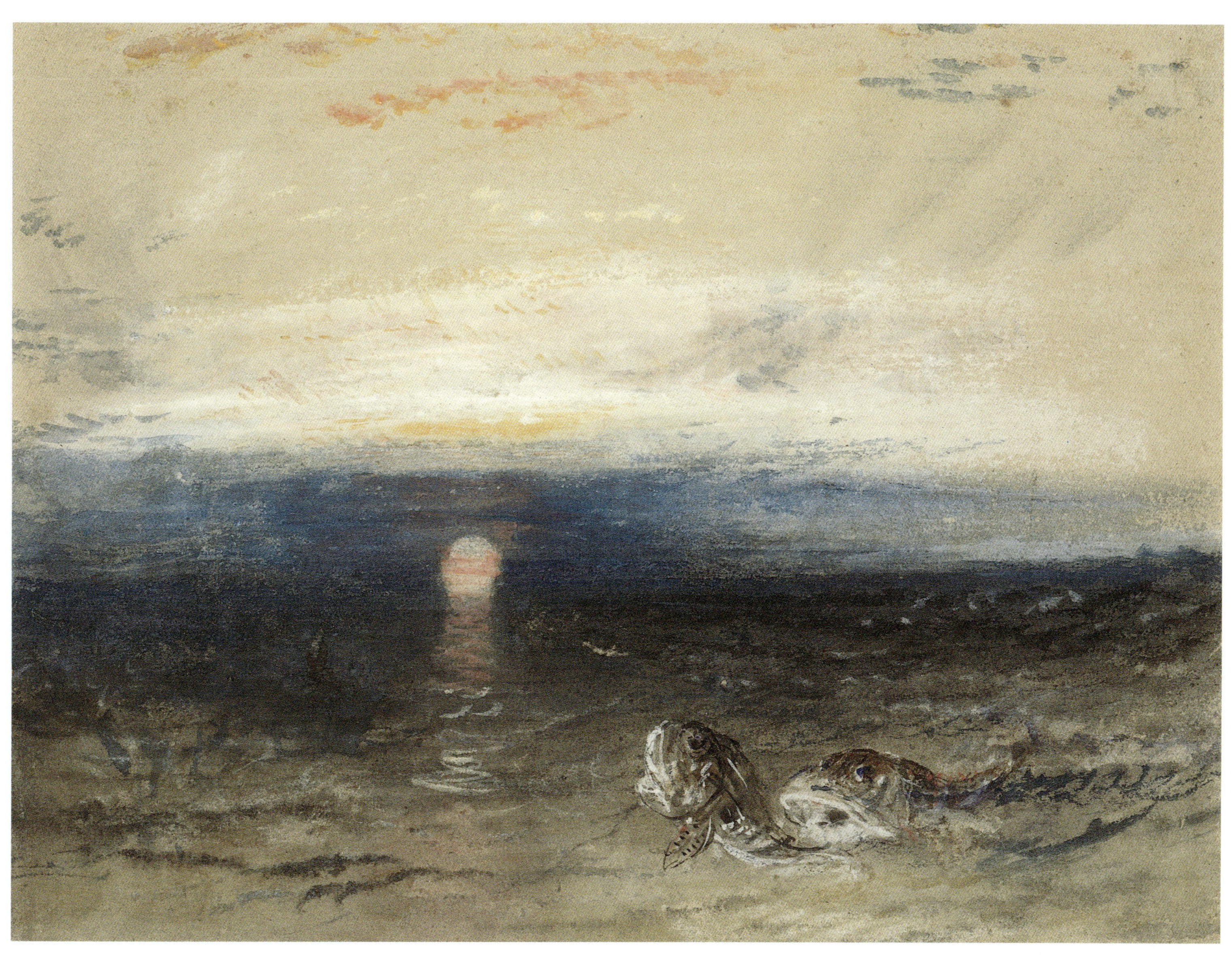

 **Heidelberg: Sunset,
c. 1841**

pencil, watercolor and bodycolor
381 x 560 mm.
Owned by John Heugh and then by John
Pender, sold by him in 1873
Bequeathed by James Blair in 1917
(MCAG 1917.106)

"Of all the grandly romantic spots, by nature, art and interesting circumstances . . . Heydelberg is the first. On the heights overlooking the university stands a castle! - a dream, a relic of Ariosto, left by him to be once seen by Lord Byron and Walter Scott . . . then the students meeting you in every street, in dresses like those of Andrea del Sarto, and the Florentines of Michael Angelo's time, all of them with port-feuilles under their arms, seem to bring forward in daylight vision, another and the most interesting age that painters can languish to have known."

Turner would surely have shared the sentiments expressed by his close friend Sir Thomas Lawrence in this letter from Heidelberg, which was published in *The Life of Thomas Lawrence* by D.E. Williams in 1831.

The picturesque town situated on the verdant banks of the Neckar river epitomized the German Romantic movement and fostered the talents of such writers as Clemens Brentano and Achim von Arnim, known as the Heidelberger Romantics, whose collection of folk poetry, *Des Knaben Wunderhorn*, inspired the Brothers Grimm and later Mahler. The Renaissance garb of the students, mentioned by Lawrence, has led commentators to see this work as a depiction of the most opulent time in Heidelberg's history—the reign of the Winter Queen—as seen in a related oil painting *Heidelberg in Olden Times* (Wilton P 440), which shows the castle before its destruction. It was, in fact, normal for German students at this time to dress in this archaic way as Turner had noted in an earlier sketchbook (T.B. CCXCI p. 29).

The Winter Queen, Elizabeth Stuart, daughter of James I of England, came to Heidelberg at the age of seventeen to marry the youthful Elector Palatine, Friedrich. Her five-year sojourn was known for its extravagance before the court's exile to Prague. The brief period of happiness followed by the destruction of the castle by the French in 1689 may have been seen by Turner as another example of the transience of wealth and power and the fallacies of hope. The equipoise between day and night, the glorious sunset and the rising moon, again evoke Byron's lines from Canto IV of *Childe Harold*, "The moon is up, and yet it is not night," (verse XXVII).

It was perhaps all these associations that led Turner to depict Heidelberg repeatedly in his sketchbooks, as well as in finished oils and watercolors toward the end of his life. The view in this particular watercolor, taken from the north bank of the Neckar looking across to the castle and the Heiligkirche, was frequently used in travel memoirs and guidebooks. It was also the basis for *Heidelberg with Rainbow* (Wilton no. 1377, at present on loan to the National Galleries of Scotland). This was produced at the request of Thomas Abel Prior as a subject for engraving, circa 1841, and engraved in 1846. There is a "color beginning" for the Manchester version inscribed "10 Mar 41" (T.B. CCCLXV - 34) and so it would seem that the two versions were painted around the same time. Wilton (1979) p. 231 talks of the "large dignity of composition" of the Manchester work and sees it as "a moment of pause between the experimental mixture of classical and topographical forms in the *England and Wales* series, and the expansive cortex that characterizes the later drawings."

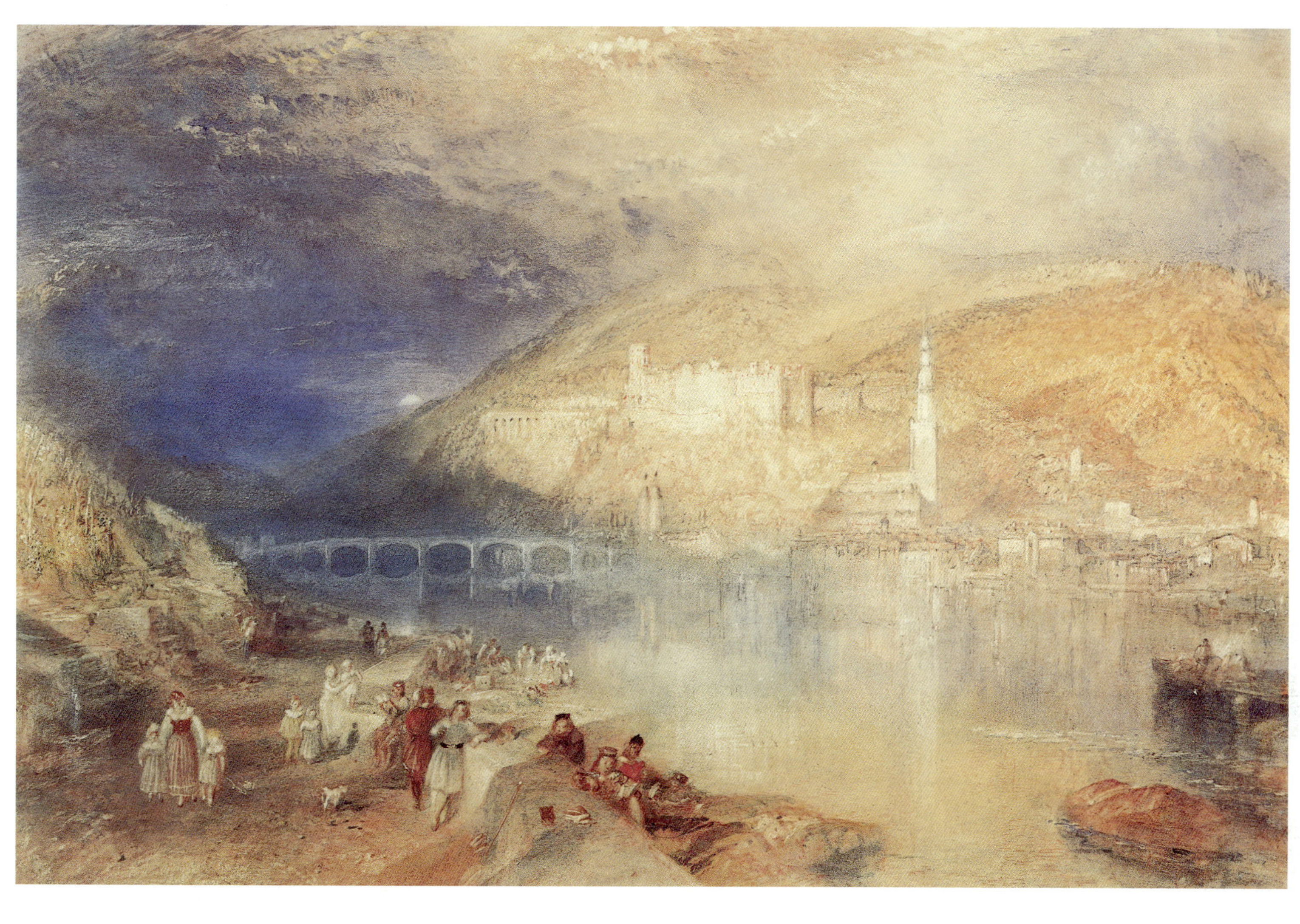

THE SWISS WATERCOLORS OF 1841-1845

Turner visited Switzerland every year between 1841 and 1844. Returning from his first trip, he embarked on a novel system of marketing his watercolors. According to Ruskin, early in 1842, he took to his agent Thomas Griffith a set of fifteen "sample studies," chosen from watercolors made in the Alps a few months before. From these he proposed to make finished versions and had already made four "to show his hand" when he proposed to make six more, making a set of ten. He asked Griffith to find buyers for the ten watercolors—Ruskin describes the arrangement and history of the commission in some detail (J. Ruskin, *Works*, Vol. XIII, pp. 475-482). The drawings are listed as Wilton nos. 1523-7 and 1529-33. Ruskin surmises, probably correctly, that the reason Turner adopted this new way of selling his work (after all, he had never asked prospective patrons to choose work before) was "uncertainty whether anybody would care to have them at all." Griffith did, indeed, not find it easy to sell the drawings.

In spite of this, Turner clearly liked the idea of working on sets of drawings (his experiences of the various engraving projects he had worked on may have led him to prefer this way of working) and produced a further set of six drawings in 1843, based on sketches of the previous year (Wilton nos. 1534-9 and see cat. 76 in this exhibition) and a final set of certainly nine and possibly ten in 1845 (Wilton nos. 1540-1549, including cats. 77 and 78 in this exhibition). Ruskin described the initial conversation between Griffith and Turner about the 1842 Swiss set of watercolors: "I have no reason to doubt the substantial accuracy of Mr. Griffith's report of the first conversation. . . . Says Mr. Griffith to Mr. Turner (after looking curiously into the execution, which, you will please note, is rather what some people might call hazy): 'They're a little different from your usual style' (*op.cit.*, pp. 478-9)." The hazy nature of all these Swiss drawings meant that Griffith found it difficult to sell them, and, of the 25 watercolors known for certain to have been in the 1842, 1843, and 1845 sets, Munro and Ruskin accounted for twenty between them. Turner's assiduous patrons of the past, notably Benjamin Godfrey Windus, who collected works of Turner's middle period, in particular the *England and Wales* watercolors, did not like the looseness of the style. According to Ruskin, he immediately said "the style was changed, he did not quite like it." In the end, however, Windus did buy two Swiss watercolors from the 1845 set.

Ruskin wrote his account more than 30 years after the events described and during one of his bouts of mental illness. It therefore contains a number of inconsistencies and is not totally reliable. In addition, recent research, notably by Ian Warrell in his catalogue *Through Switzerland with Turner* (1995), has shown that the original number of sample studies may have been as many as twenty, and has pieced together, as far as can be done, the whole history of the Swiss commissions of the 1840s. However, Ruskin's account, despite its errors and omissions, is nevertheless valuable as an outline and as a first-hand account of one of Turner's principal clients.

71 Moonlight over Lake Lucerne with the Rigi in the Distance, 1841

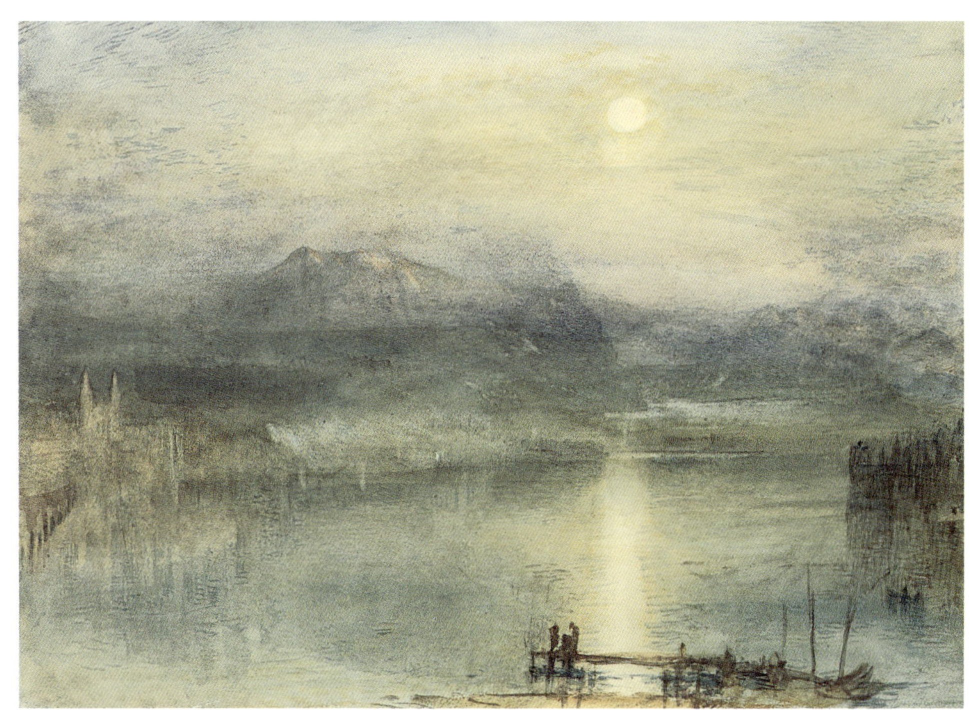

watercolor and bodycolor
230 x 307 mm.
Probably Thomas Griffith
Purchased from Thomas W. Wright in 1891 with a fund presented by the Guarantors of the 1887 Manchester Royal Jubilee Exhibition
(WAG.D.1887.16)

Ian Warrell has suggested that the Whitworth drawing may have been one of the first set of twenty sample studies deriving from the Swiss visit of September and October 1841 (*Through Switzerland with Turner*, 1995, Appendix II, p. 149). The Rigi is a mountain group eight-and-a-half miles long and around four-miles broad, between the lakes of Lucerne, Zug, and Lowerz. It was clearly visible over the lake from the town of Lucerne; Turner produced many views of it at different times of day and under different atmospheric conditions. Three of the ten finished watercolors in the 1842 set show the Rigi: *The Dark Rigi* (Wilton no. 1532), *The Blue Rigi* (Wilton no. 1524), and *The Red Rigi* (Wilton no. 1525), sample studies for which are in the Turner Bequest, T.B. CCCLXIV - 279, 330, and 341. All of these may be compared with the Whitworth drawing, which, as Ian Warrell points out (*op.cit.*, p. 75), probably left Turner's collection via his agent Thomas Griffith.

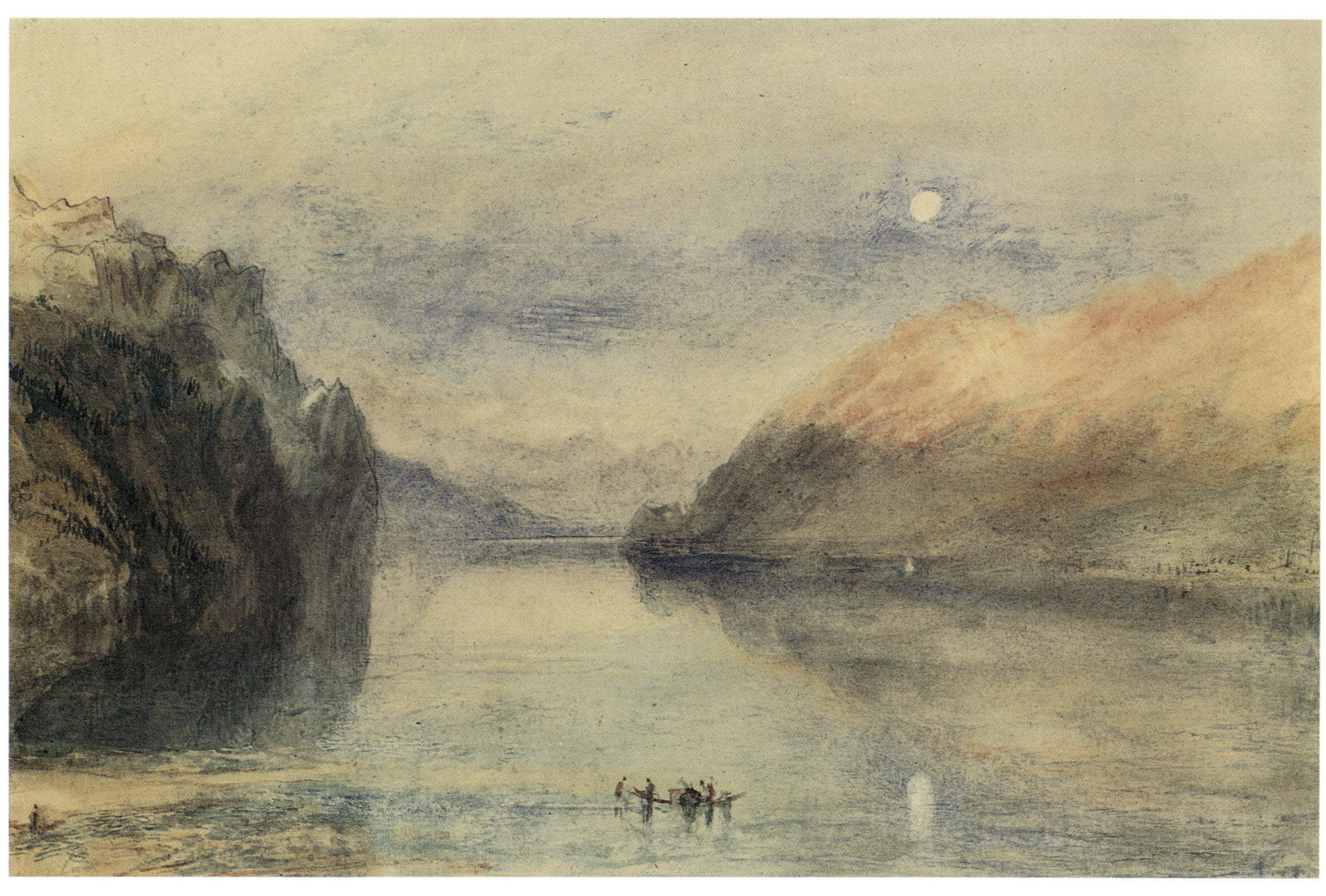

72 Lake Lucerne, Switzerland, c. 1841

pen and ink and watercolor
249 x 365 mm.
Bequeathed by James Blair in 1917
(MCAG 1917.102)

By the middle of the nineteenth century, Lake Lucerne had become a popular tourist spot. The splendor of its surrounding mountains rising directly from the water was praised by the guidebooks, and its association with the independence movement and the growing legends of William Tell made it even more attractive. Turner had always been fired with enthusiasm for noble subjects, but in his old age he saw the lake more as a vehicle for his observations of atmospheric conditions and how they could be translated into artistic form. He was to make many sketches of the lake on his Swiss tours of the 1840s. This particular sketch was probably one of twenty sample studies produced by Turner on his 1841 tour, to show clients in order to obtain commissions. Its size makes it likely that it was a sheet from one of the roll-sketchbooks used frequently by Turner at this time. Although he had not abandoned altogether his small notebooks with their frenetic line drawings, he became increasingly dependent on these larger books that could be rolled up and put in his pocket and on which he could paint his direct impressions to be worked up later for clients.

The exact location of this view cannot be positively identified but there are two distinct possibilities. Either it could have been taken from the village of Brunnen on the east side of the lake or a spot several miles away near the village of Fluelen at its most southerly point. He painted many watercolors from both spots, and if this second possibility were the case, he would have taken a similar viewpoint to that of John Robert Cozens in 1776. (*Fluelen*, *Lake Lucerne*, B.M. 1900-4-11.12). A version of this watercolor was given to Turner by his friend Richard Colt Hoare and he was to keep it all his life. The Turner Bequest owns a version of this watercolor painted possibly by Turner and Girtin in their youth (T.B. CCCLXV 20) and found in Turner's studio after his death. In Cozens' day this position from near Seedorf was barely accessible as there were no roads on either side of the bay and there was no steamer service until 1837. By Turner's time, however, it was part of the tourist's itinerary as a stop before the St. Gothard Pass en route to Italy. Ruskin despaired at the violation of the lake's peace by the influx of visitors and the growth of unsightly hotels.

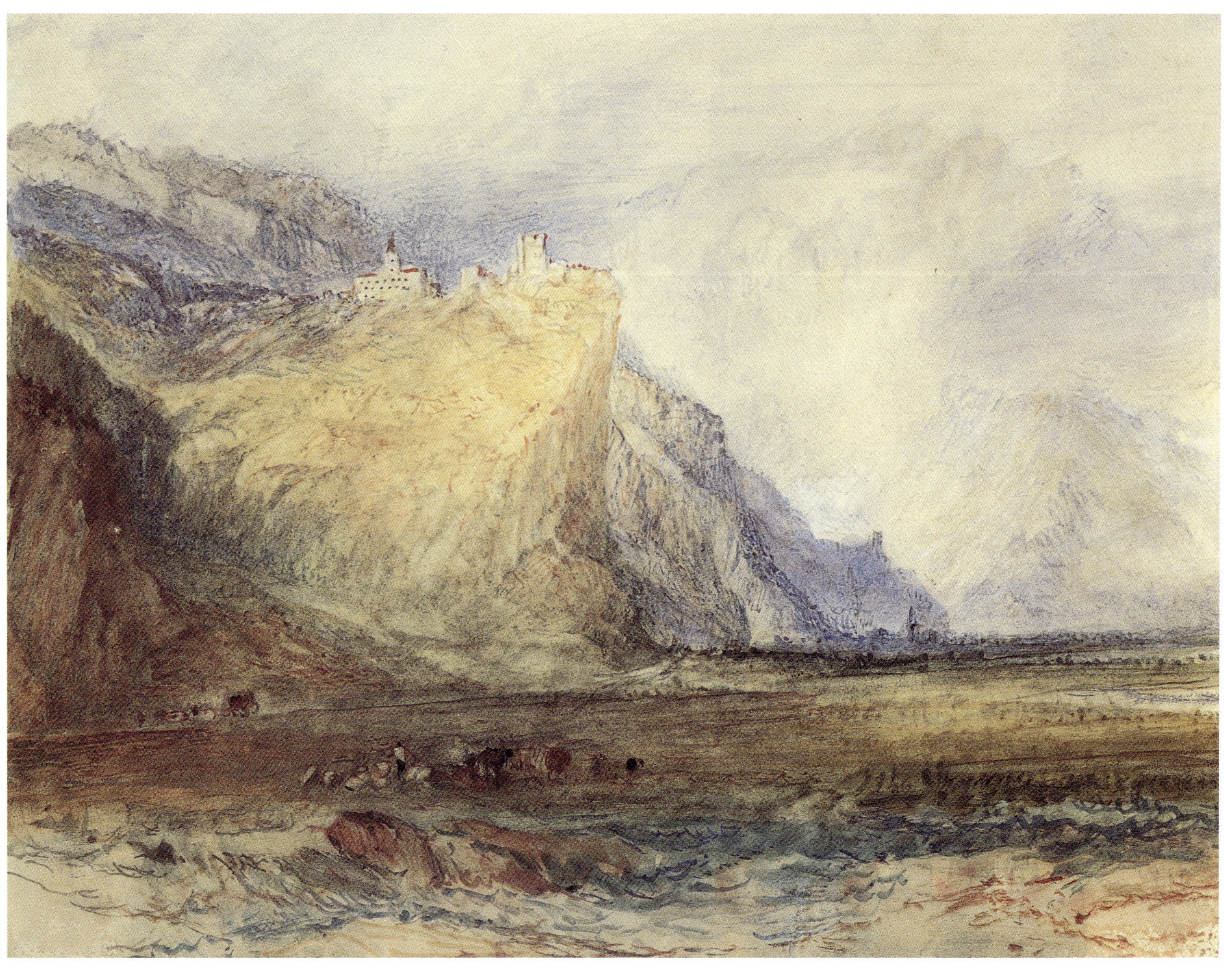

73 Alpine Landscape, formerly known as The Rhine Valley above Coire, c. 1843

pencil and watercolor
230 x 289 mm.
Bequeathed by Dr. David Lloyd Roberts
in 1920
(MCAG 1920.587)

This watercolor was sold by Frederick Nettlefold in 1913 as *Reichenbach* and then was later named *The Rhine Valley above Coire* for reasons not recorded. Turner may have visited Coire (or Chur) in 1841 and Reichenbach in 1844, as they were on his route, but no other sketches from these locations have been identified on either tour.

Ian Warrell has put forward a more plausible theory in a recent letter to the gallery. He has suggested that it could be the same view as the *Alpine Landscape* in the Fitzwilliam Museum, Cambridge, taken from the opposite direction (Wilton no. 1511). He has also linked it with *Valley of St. Gothard* (Wilton no. 1502) and *A Swiss Alpine Valley, possibly St. Gothard* (Oldham Art Gallery, not in Wilton). As they all are of similar dimensions, he felt that they could all be part of the same roll-sketchbook and have 1843 as a possible date. He also suggested that *Swiss Pass* (cat. 75) could have originally been part of this same roll-sketchbook.

This would link it to the 1843 tour, when Turner went through the St. Gothard Pass and produced his sketch for the *Pass of the Faido* (T.B. CCCLXIV-209) and other sketches in the Bellinzona region (see cat. 74). He also points to an association between this watercolor and *The Foot of the St. Gothard* (Leeds City Art Gallery, Wilton no. 1522), which he sees as a possible later version of this watercolor and one of a series of reworkings of Alpine motifs.

74 Bellinzona no. 11, Switzerland, 1842-3

pencil, pen and ink, watercolor and
bodycolor
228 x 289 mm.
Owned by John Ruskin and sold by him in
1869
Bequeathed by James Blair in 1917
(MCAG 1917.100)

Bellinzona is situated near the Italian border at
the meeting point of three cantons—Uri,
Schwyz, and Unterwalden. It was not a popular
tourist spot in Turner's time, but clearly it had
a fascination for him with its three ruined castles dominating the skyline. He made sketches
from various viewpoints on his tours of 1842
and 1843. In this particular view, taken from
the south-west, the Ticino river is seen in the
foreground and the Marmonta range of mountains is in the background (Lake Como lies
behind them).

The dominant fortress in the center is the
Castel Grande, which was used as a prison in
Turner's time. This was the oldest of the three
castles and was situated in the canton of Uri.
To the right are the ruins of Castello
Montebello, or Castel Nuovo, in the canton of
Schwyz. On the far right on the hill is the
Castello di Sasso Corbaro in Unterwalden,
which had been built in a few months by the
Milanese in 1479. The Castle Grande's walls
with their sixteen towers leading down to the

river were important examples of military
architecture but were soon to be dismantled
after Turner's visit.

This work was probably one of the ten
sample studies produced by Turner after his
1842 tour of Switzerland, recorded by Ruskin
in his diary for January 16, 1843, and as such
was probably once part of a roll-sketchbook
(see cat. 75). The studies were marked with
numbers. Three were views of Bellinzona and
marked as such on the back. The City Art
Galleries' example is marked number 11; there
is one in the Turner Bequest, inscribed number
12, and one in Indianapolis, inscribed number
10. Only five of the works were commissioned
from the sample studies. Four of these were for
Munro of Novar including *Bellinzona from the
Road to Locarno* (Aberdeen Art Gallery) and
Manchester City Art Galleries' *Küssnacht* (cat. 76).

Ruskin once owned this watercolor and
intended to include it in a set of facsimile
reproductions of Turner's drawings to be
engraved by George Allen.

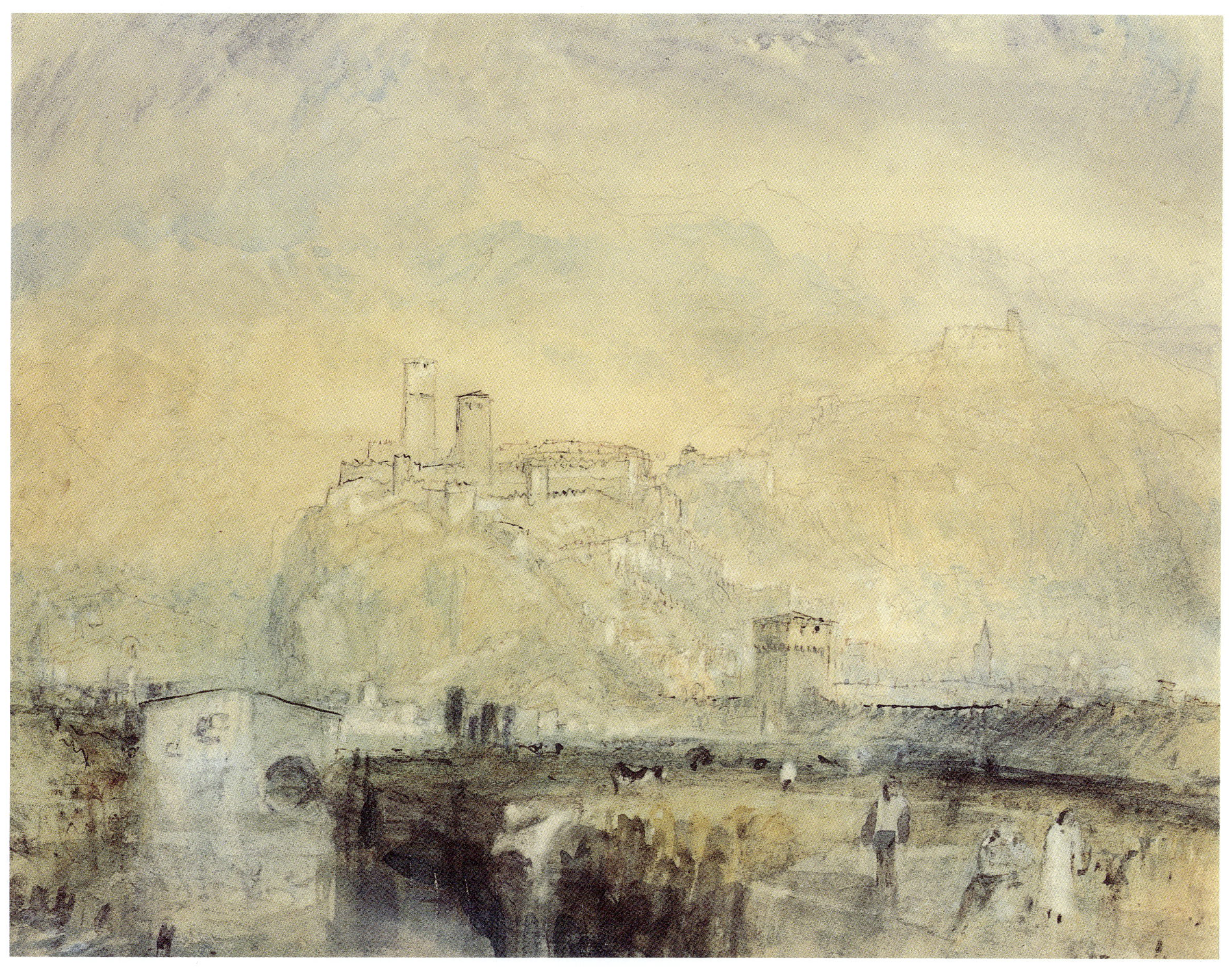

75 Swiss Pass, c. 1842-3

pencil and watercolor, on Whatman paper
dated 1840
232 x 291 mm.
Bequeathed by James Blair in 1917
(MCAG 1917.111)

The exact location of this work has not yet
been positively identified but its size suggests
that it was probably part of a roll-sketchbook
used by Turner in 1842 or 1843. It possibly
depicts a site in the Bellinzona region. Research
by Nicholas Serota in an unpublished thesis has
reconstituted some of the sketchbooks and
loose sheets in the Turner Bequest. He has suggested that this sketch could be seen as part of
a roll-sketchbook that he calls the *Goldau to
Bellinzona* sketchbook, as also is *Bellinzona no. II,
Switzerland* in the MCAG collection (cat. 74). If
this is so, then the fast-flowing river is probably the Ticino, which flows through the St.
Gothard Pass to Bellinzona. It is a work similar
to *Pass of Faido* (Wilton no. 1538), which is the
same size and was produced as a finished work
in the following year. This was praised by
Ruskin who wrote to Charles Eliot Norton that
Turner had selected "the Ticino as his expo-

nent of Alpine torrent of rage." *Swiss Pass* does
not have the same drama but there is a feeling
of power as the river rushes against the rocks
and through the Alpine pass, overlooked by a
dramatic tower catching the light on the right
hand side with a fleeting cloud sending a
shadow over the narrow road. In the far distance between the clefts of rock another tower
can be seen, and directly above, there is an
indication of a high mountain pass.

Ian Warrell has suggested that it could be
in the same vicinity but possibly the following
year (see cat. 73). An alternative location has
been suggested by Andrew Wyld after a recent
viewing of the work. He believes it was a view
of the Brünig Pass, with the tower in the distance indicating the village of Meiringen.
Turner visited this area on his 1841 tour, but
not in 1842.

76 Küssnacht, Lake Lucerne, 1843

watercolor and bodycolor, watermark
Cansell 1828
305 x 473 mm.
Bequeathed by James Blair in 1917
(MCAG 1917.103)

This finished watercolor was commissioned by
Munro of Novar from the sample studies
brought back by Turner from his 1842 journey
to Switzerland. It shows the little village of
Küssnacht located at the most northerly tip of
Lake Lucerne. It is seen from the lake nestling
among the mountains. The sample study on
which it is based is in the Turner Bequest
(CCCLXIV) and is inscribed on the back
"Kusnacht and Tells Church and Gesler
Castle/Lake of Lucern" and "Mr. Munro."

In both the sample study and the finished
work the emphasis is not on references to
William Tell and his fight for freedom (in fact,
neither of the monuments noted by Turner are

visible from the viewpoint he has taken), but
on the picturesque little village with its baroque
church of St. Peter and St. Paul next to the
town hall and schoolhouse, their whitewashed
walls standing out against a backdrop of lush
green hills.

The sample study indicates several boats in
the foreground and is a reminder that Lucerne
was a busy lake both for commercial transport
and tourism. In the finished work these take on
a prominence and lead the eye back, together
with the steep perspective of the hills, to the
village that appears to float above its own
reflection and bathed in a soft light giving the
image a feeling of warmth and contentment.

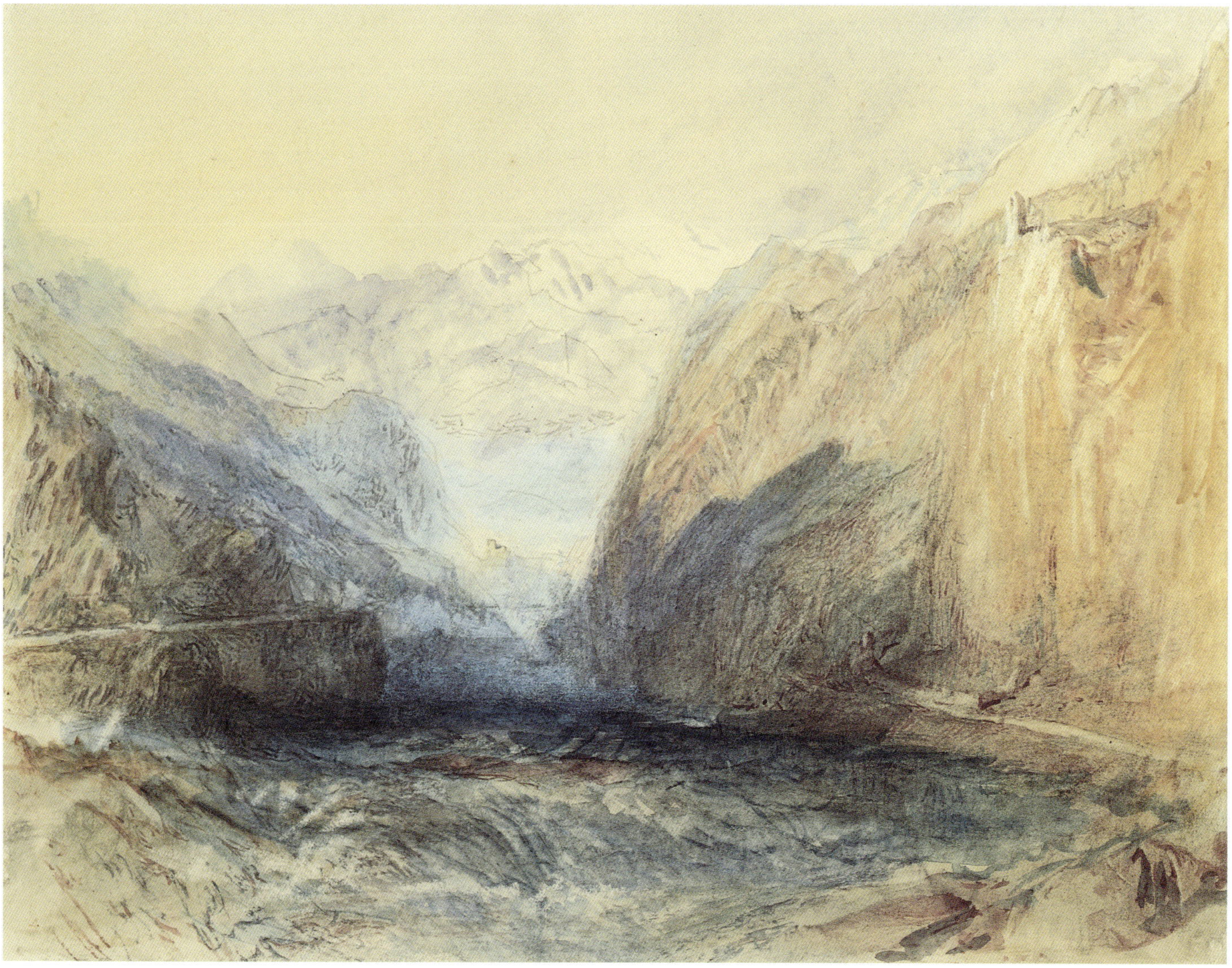

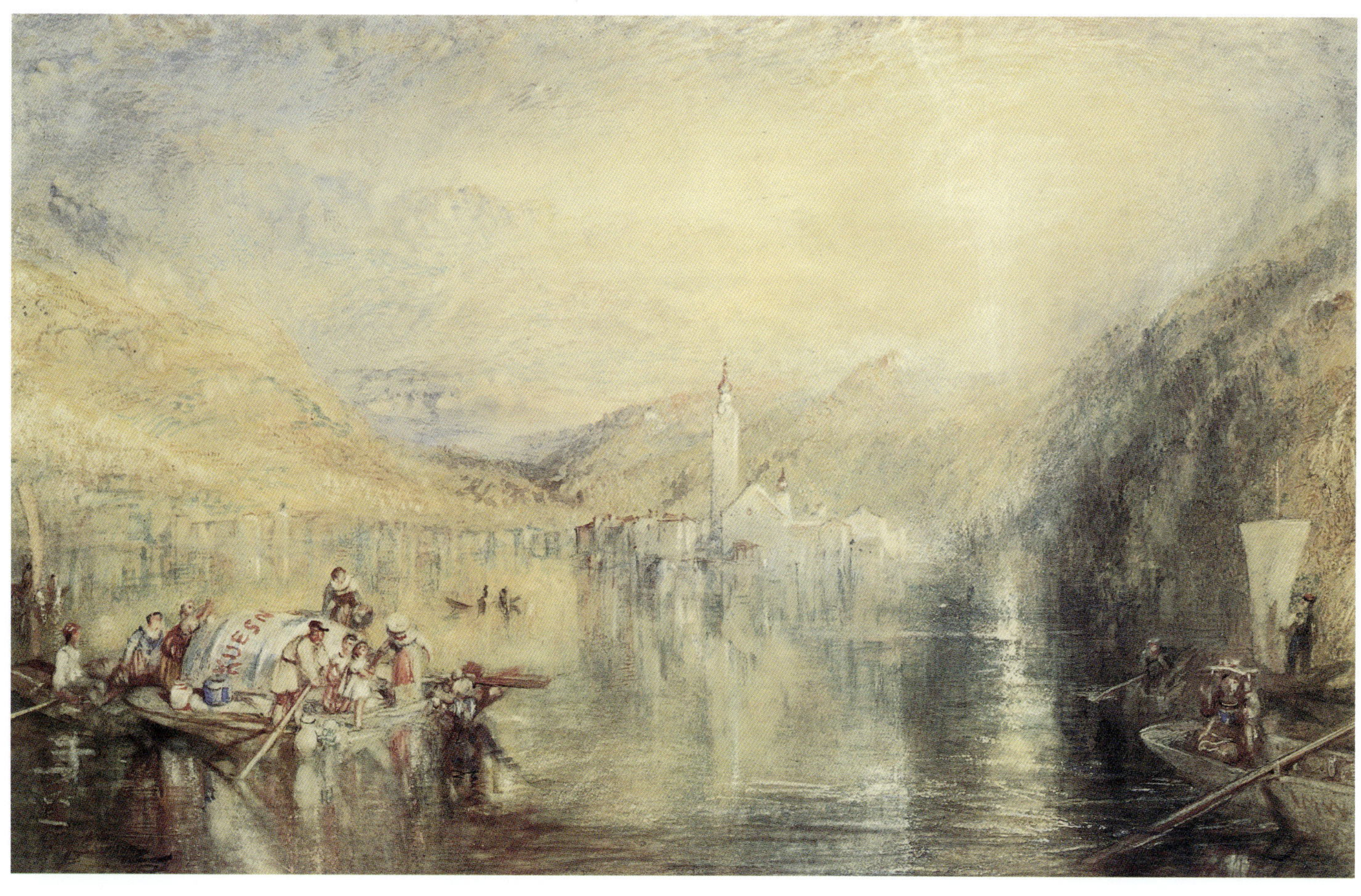

77 Lake Lucerne, Sunset, 1845

watercolor
292 x 477 mm.
John Ruskin
Abraham Haworth, by 1887
On loan to the Whitworth Art Gallery
(WAG.L.1995.1)

A Ruskin commission, this drawing from the 1845 set of Swiss drawings derives from the "sample study" T.B. CCCLXIV - 338. With the benefit of hindsight, it seems strange that such marvelously luminous drawings as the Swiss series of 1842, 1843, and 1845 should find so few buyers (Elhanan Bicknell was the only other buyer apart from Ruskin and Munro), but in the context of the time they were most unusual and unfashionable. At a time when fashion demanded sharply defined outlines and seemingly accurate depictions, such hazy and ill-defined images were totally out of place. Their lukewarm reception, except by a dedicated few, should be seen in the light of the criticism of his oil paintings at the time, described by various contemporary reviewers as "pictures of nothing and very like" . . . "neither referring to fact, nor appealing to the imagination," and "soapsuds and whitewash" . . . "the fruits of a diseased eye and a reckless hand." Credit should therefore be given to Ruskin and Munro for their adventurous taste, which posterity has surely vindicated. This watercolor, along with *Storm in a Swiss Pass* (cat. 78), *Chain Bridge over the Tees* (cat. 54), and *Warwick Castle* (cat. 51), was lent to the Manchester Royal Jubilee Exhibition of 1887 by members of the Haworth family, a wealthy Manchester textile family whose collecting interests were typical of members of the entrepreneurial classes; their contribution represented a quarter of all the Turner watercolors in the 1887 exhibition.

78 Storm in a Swiss Pass, 1845

watercolor
290 x 470 mm.
John Ruskin
H.A.J. Munro of Novar
Purchased from Thomas Agnew & Sons by Jesse Haworth in 1872
Bequeathed by Jesse Haworth in 1937
(WAG.D.1937.23)

Also part of the 1845 set of Swiss drawings, this drawing—also known as *First Bridge above Altdorf*—shows a view in St. Gothard Pass. The sample study on which it is based (T.B. CCCLXIV - 283) is inscribed "Altdorf" and has Ruskin's initials to indicate for whom the finished version was intended. Indeed, of the 25 watercolors known to have been in the sets of 1842, 1843, and 1845, Ruskin commissioned eight. Ruskin exhibited the study in 1857, describing it as *Scene on the St. Gothard*, and wrote in the catalogue: "And certainly, before we have much passed Altdorf, it comes on to rain to purpose. Fine things in the way of precipices and pines at this part of the road, as far as we can see them from under our umbrella. This sketch was realized by Turner for me in 1845, but I having unluckily told him that I wanted it for the sake of the pines, he cut all the pines down, by way of jest, and left only the bare red ground under them. I did not like getting wet with no pines to shelter me, and exchanged the drawing with Mr. Munro," (J. Ruskin, *Works*, Vol. XIII, pp. 205-6). The drawing that Ruskin received in exchange from Munro is *Lake Lucerne: Brunnen and Schweitz Mountains*, also known as *Fluelen* (Wilton no. 1541, Yale Center for British Art).

Four years later, in 1861, Ruskin wrote to his father: "I walked three times yesterday to the bridge with the pines, which Turner cut away, when he made the drawing which I exchanged with Munro. In many respects, I find that the realised drawing was always liker the place than the sketch; though in this instance the pines were cut down; the bridge is really carefully drawn in the finished drawing; and being a formal and ugly one, disappointed me—the sketch having suggested one far more picturesque," (*op.cit.*, p. 206). In addition to formalizing the bridge and removing the pines in the finished drawing, Turner has turned the impending storm in the valley into a vortex—a hanging cloud of approaching rain from which the figures on the bridge, one of whom is on crutches, appear to be fleeing. The same hanging cloud of rain appears in another of the 1845 set, *Fluelen, from the Lake of Lucerne* (Wilton no. 1549, Cleveland Museum of Art), the appearance of which has been transformed from the sketch (T.B. CCCLXIV - 381) in a way similar to the Whitworth drawing.

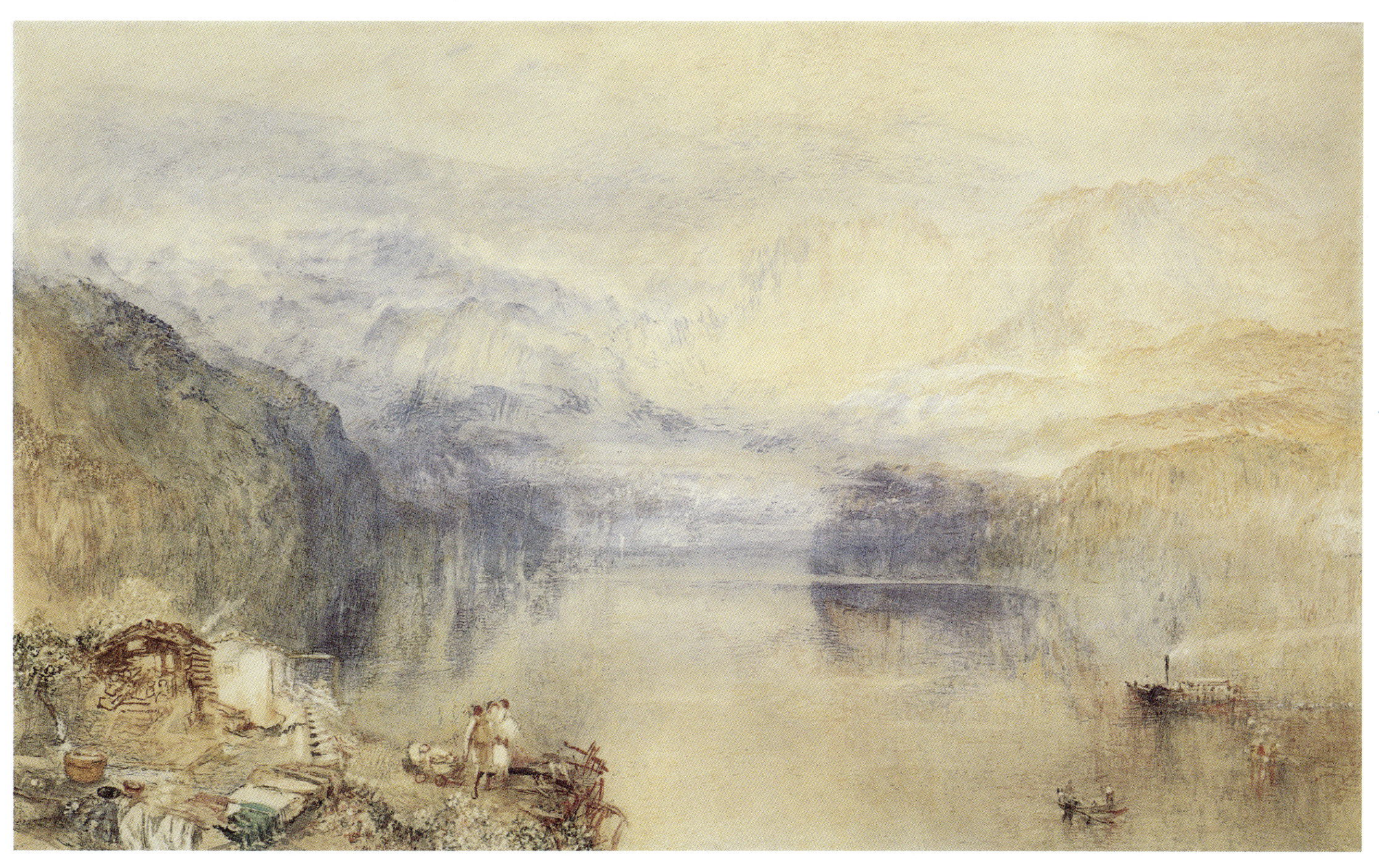

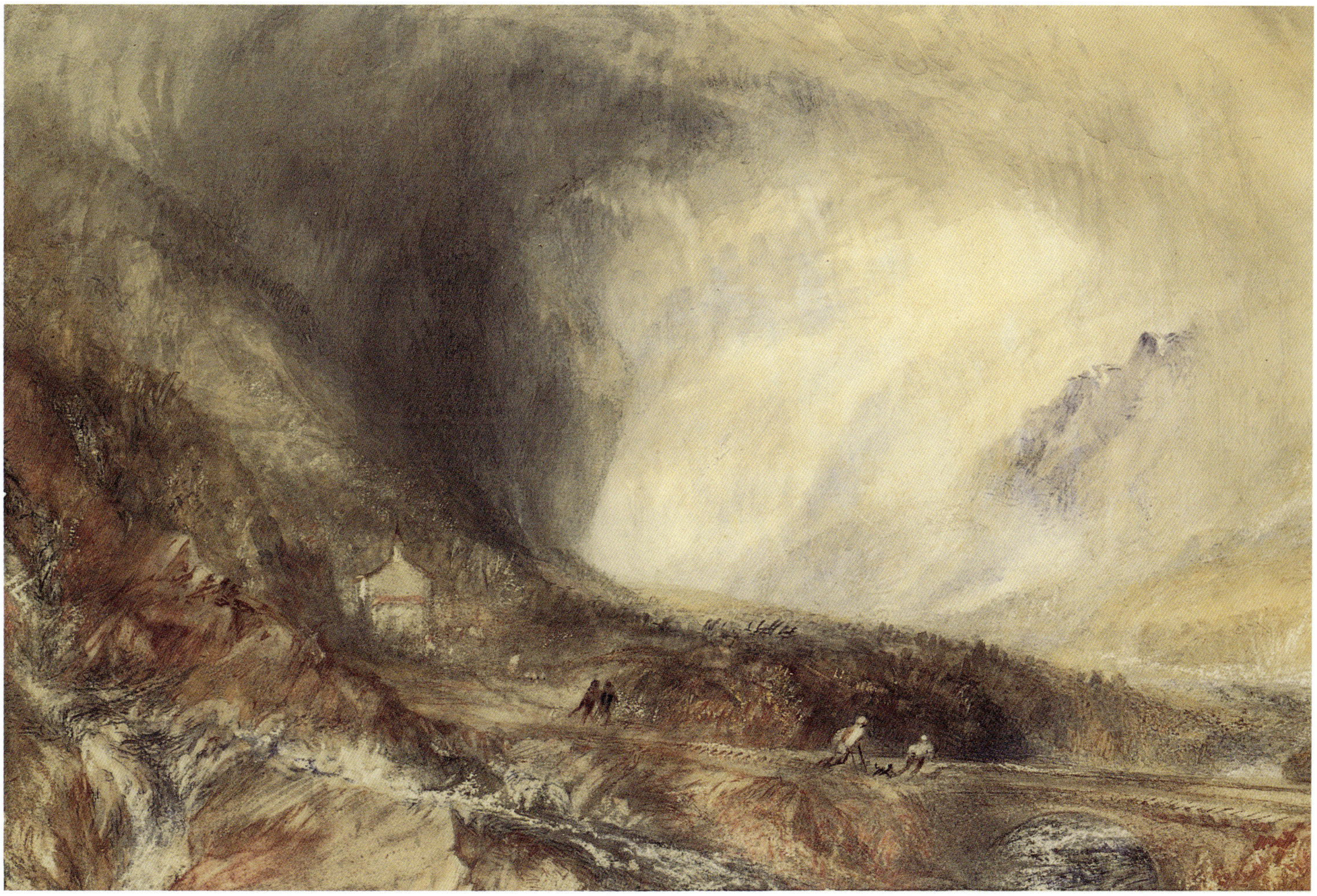

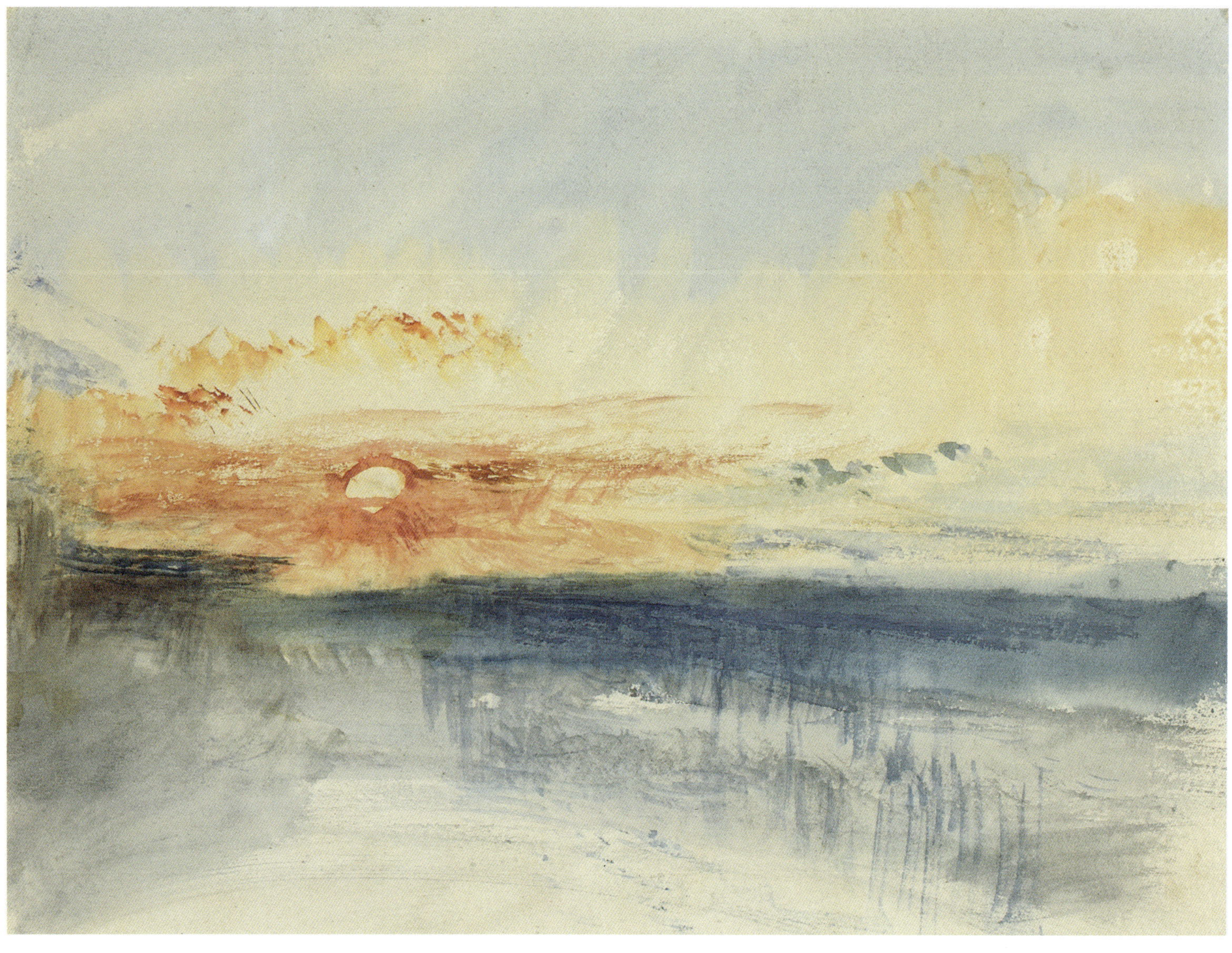

79 Sunset, c. 1840-45

watercolor
226 x 297 mm.
John Edward Taylor
Bequeathed by Dr. David Lloyd Roberts
in 1920
(MCAG 1920.594)

Turner's energy and curiosity did not abate even when he was in his seventies. This directly observed study of clouds and the sea is related to a group of works on loose sheets of paper probably painted by him in the Margate area on one of his retreats from London. Ruskin wrote: "He knew the colors of the clouds over the sea, from the Bay of Naples to the Hebrides; and being once asked where, in Europe, were to be seen the loveliest skies, answered instantly, 'In the Isle of Thanet'." (i.e. the Kent Coast). (Ruskin, *Works*, XXVII, p. 164.)

This work can also be related to other studies made on the French coast in 1845, examples of which can be seen in the *Ambleteuse and Wimereux* sketchbook (T.B. CCCLVII) and to a group of oil studies (see Butlin & Joll nos. 486 - 500). On his final trip to France later that year Turner was reported to have said that he was "looking for storms and shipwrecks,"

(Richard and Samuel Redgrave, *A Century of Painters of the English School,* 1866, II, p. 86).

All these works share an interest in cloud formations and the effects of weather conditions which Turner had closely observed all his life but which, in these final years were executed not just as studies for future paintings but stemming from a deep necessity to translate his reactions into paint. All the works painted either on the French or the Kent Coast share a common format of horizontal planes of sand, sea, and sky with no other features to break the monotony save the occasional rough indication of a figure. These works are highly prized for their spontaneity and abstract qualities. Turner would not have understood the twentieth century terms of reference, but he shared with some contemporary artists a love of color as form painted for its own sake and for no other reason (see also cat. 80).

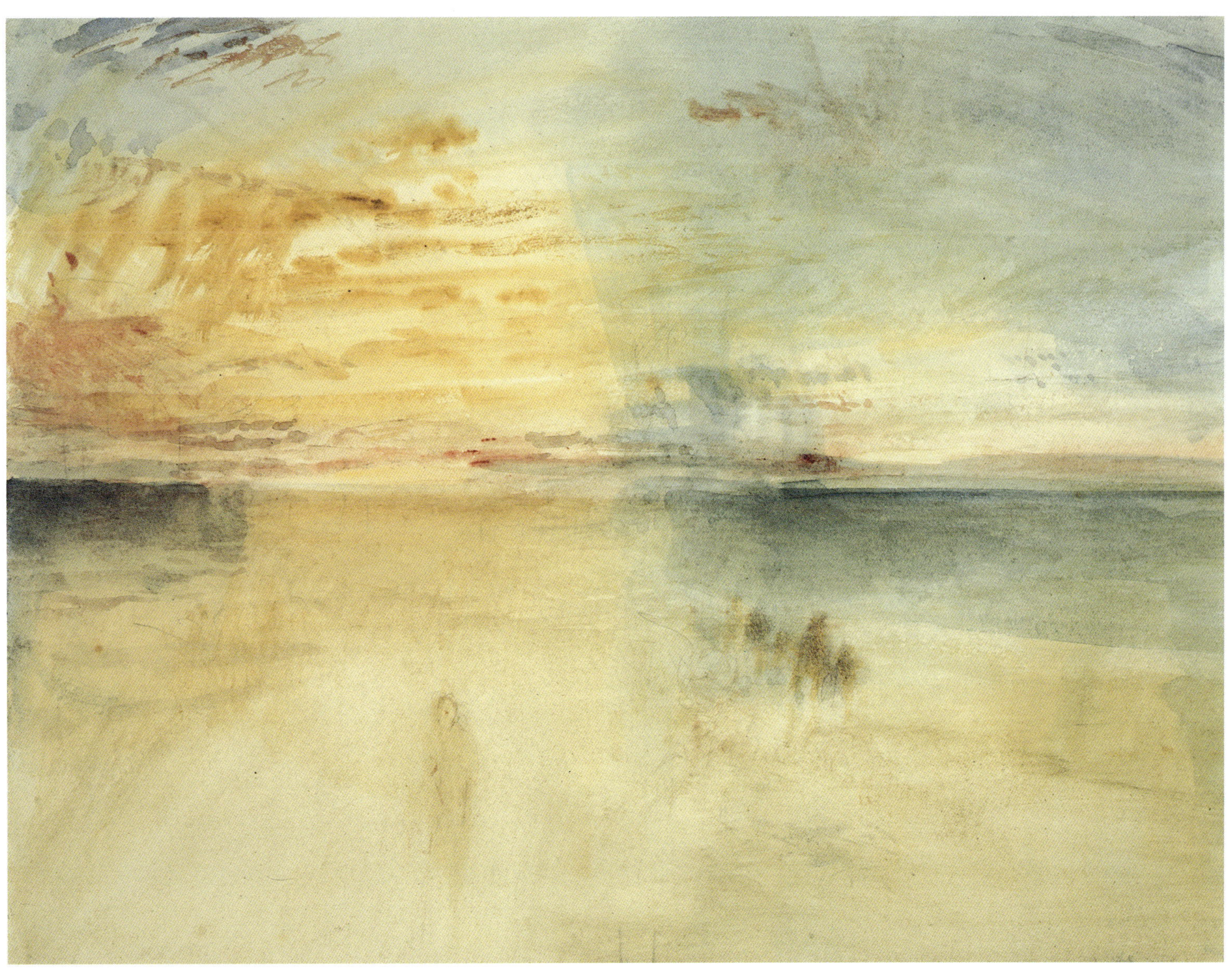

80 Sunset on wet Sand, 1845

pencil and watercolor
229 x 292 mm.
Presented in memory of John Edward
Taylor by his nephews in 1912
(WAG.D.1912.7)

After his annual visits to Switzerland between
1841 and 1844, duties at the Royal Academy
intervened: the infirmity of its President Sir
Martin Archer Shee (1769-1850) meant that
Turner had to act as Deputy President and
chair meetings on academy business, a task that
he found tiresome and unpleasant.
Notwithstanding these duties, he was able to
visit northern France in the spring of 1845 and
again in September of that year, his last visits
abroad. This drawing is one of a group of studies of clouds and water that may have been
made on one of his trips to France in 1845 or
at Margate which he visited regularly in the
1840s. The whole group (Wilton nos. 1411-
1429), many of which are in the Bacon collection, "are distinguished by their slightness, or
by a general perfunctoriness of handling which
suggests a very late date,"(Wilton, 1979, p.
469). They do not seem to be preparatory to
any other work and show the artist in his old

age using watercolor to record fleeting effects
of light on water in a way quite unlike anything
else being produced in England at the time.
The provenance of the group is generally
obscure—they probably left Turner's studio via
Ruskin, who no doubt acquired them through
Mrs. Booth. This drawing, along with *A
Conflagration, Lausanne* (cat. 62) and *Sunset at Sea
with Gurnets* (cat. 69), belonged to John Edward
Taylor. All three drawings were included in his
posthumous sale, being purchased by his
nephews and presented to the Whitworth in
his memory. Also included in the sale was the
drawing now in the Manchester City Art
Galleries, cat. 79 in this exhibition—the two
sheets are remarkably similar both in size and
technique. They may be compared to watercolors dated May 1845 in the *Ambleteuse and
Wimereux* sketchbook (T.B. CCCLVII), in particular pages 2 and 4.

81 A Village in the Alps [formerly called Sion near the Simplon Pass] after 1846

pencil and watercolor, on Whatman paper
dated 1846
381 x 560 mm.
Bequeathed by Dr. David Lloyd Roberts
in 1920
(MCAG 1920.591)

The title of *Sion near the Simplon Pass* traditionally given to this work would appear to arise from some confusion with a work called *Simplon Pass* now in the Fogg Museum at Harvard, with which it shares some of the same provenance. There is no documentary proof that Turner visited Sion in the 1840s, but several works have traditionally been assigned to this area. Stylistically, with its broad concepts and unresolved areas, it can be dated with a last set of watercolors that Turner probably produced between 1845-51 and with which it shares the same dimensions (c.f. *Genoa*, cat. 35, also in the collection of MCAG).

There is a sketch for the Manchester picture in London's Victoria and Albert Museum (Wilton no. 1494), now called *An Italian Town (in the Alps)*. It is smaller than the Manchester work and, although the paper has a watermark of 1841, it has been suggested by Ian Warrell that it should be grouped with sample studies for 1843-4, which relate to this final set. It may be through this sketch, which is more clearly defined than the finished watercolor, that a positive location for the Manchester work can be achieved; but for the moment, as for many of the late Swiss subjects, this can only be a matter of conjecture.

The Victoria and Albert sketch is thinly painted with linear details in scratchy pen and ink. It shows a wide road with low walls on either side. On each side of the road is a swiftly flowing river, and on the bottom right a furious cascade of water flows into the river. Against a backdrop of high mountains can be seen a small village, with the tall tower of a church on a hill dominating the landscape. A bridge crosses the river on the right-hand side among a jumble of cottages. Along the road walk a bedraggled set of people with an oxen, a cart and several animals. This gave the work its original title in 1865, *A View in the Tyrol - Going to Market*.

Many of the elements of this view can be seen in an illustration in *La Suisse Pittoresque* by William Bartlett, published in London in 1836, depicting the village of Splügen (fig. 18). Turner visited this area in 1841 when he produced a watercolor sketch called *The Pass of the Splügen* (and again in 1843). This work impressed Ruskin because its composition was "very remarkable as an example of Turner's occasional delight in a perfectly straight road seen for four or five miles of its length at once," (J. Ruskin, *Works*, XIII, p. 218). The finished watercolor was sold to Munro of Novar much to Ruskin's annoyance, but it was eventually presented to him by a group of friends. Andrew Wilton has suggested that the Manchester painting could be a reworking of a Splügen motif, produced after the success of the first version. With Turner's ability to synthesize experience and to use the work of others as an aide-memoire, the Bartlett engraving, or something similar, could have provided some sort of catalyst.

As with many of the works of the "last set," the mood seems to transcend the place. The figures in the Victoria and Albert sketch look desolate and isolated—the blues and browns give a feeling of dismal dampness. In comparison the gold color in the Manchester painting unifies the people, the animals, and their surroundings. The feeling of an exodus is intensified by the steepened perspective and straightening of the road in the finished work. A strong diagonal movement starting at the top right-hand corner gives a powerful sense of unity and power to the image.

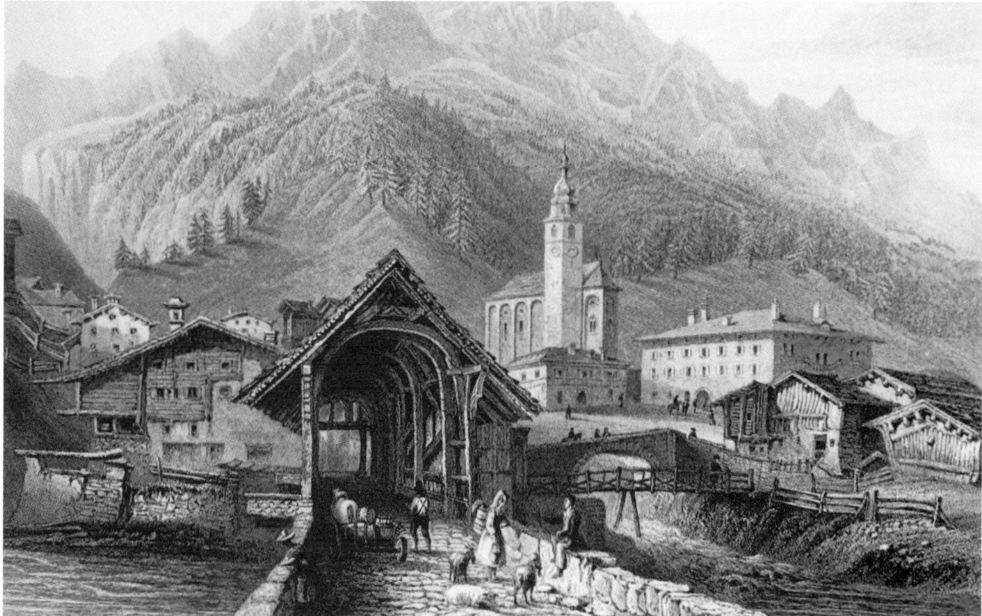

Figure 18. *The Village of Splügen*, from *La Suisse Pittoresque*, London, 1836, Manchester Public Libraries

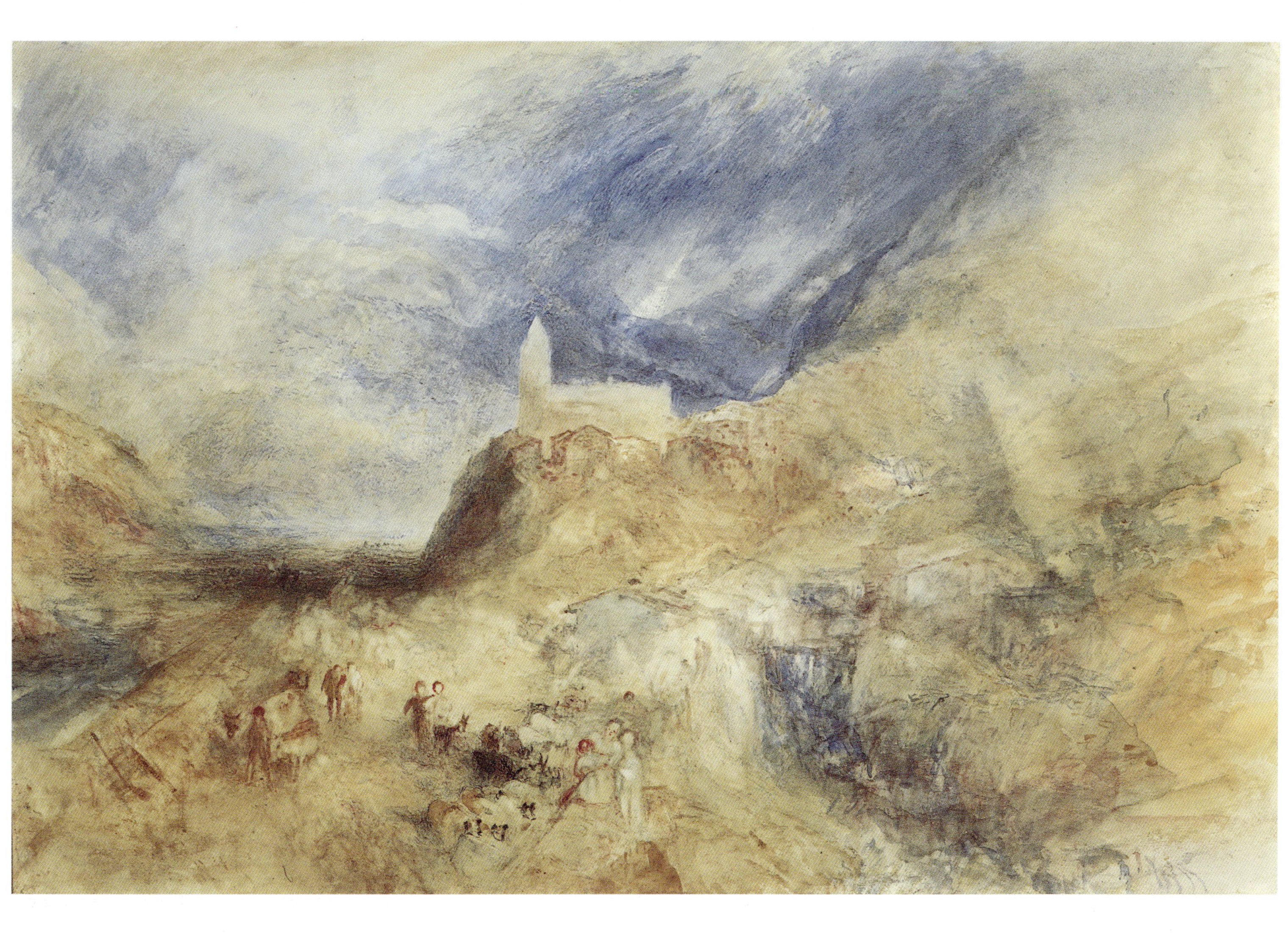

82 Genoa, c. 1850-1

pencil and watercolor
370 x 543 mm.
Bequeathed by James Blair in 1917
(MCAG 1917.101)

This is one of a group of watercolors which Turner produced in the last years of his life. It has been speculated that he was attempting to amass another set of watercolors as he had with the Swiss subjects in the early 1840s. The location of most of these works is problematic, but they appear to be a mixture of Swiss, German, and Italian subjects and have more in common with each other as a set than with specific locations. They are mostly expansive views of water and cityscapes, often including arched bridges and churches, and have a festive atmosphere. They are unified by color and design and have a sense of space that seems entirely pictorial rather than realistic. Manchester City Art Galleries owns two of this "last set" (see also cat. 81).

This work is now known as *Genoa* but was called *Geneva* in the late nineteenth century. The landscape does vaguely resemble some of the earlier views of Genoa on the Mediterranean coast of Italy (Wilton nos. 1015-17). This is probably the only one of the "set" to have some sort of narrative content, showing marching soldiers watched by a small group of people on a hill. A letter in the City Art Galleries files from W. Y. Carman, an expert on military uniforms, suggests that these are Neapolitan foot-soldiers and the view is that of the Bay of Naples. On the other hand, the women in the foreground have head-dresses similar to those

in Normandy, where Turner visited in 1845 on his last trip to the Continent. The figure group in the foreground is reminiscent of the work of Watteau, whose work influenced Turner in the late 1820s. The group is seated on a hill overlooking a large city with several churches, bridges, smoking chimneys, etc. There appears to be a steamer on the water in the background to the left. In mood and style it is most like *Florence* in the same set. It also shares with *Florence* and with *Oberhofen on Lake Thun* the artificial platform or terrace overlooking a cityscape. Other works in the set relate to each other: *Heidelberg* and *Zurich* depict sunset on a fête day and the *Brünig Pass* and *Swiss Pass* are reminiscent of Alpine scenes of the 1840s (see Ian Warrell, *Through Switzerland with Turner,* for details of this final set).

Ruskin said of this last period of Turner's work: "In 1845 his health gave way, and his mind and sight partially failed. The pictures painted in the last five years of his life are of wholly inferior value," (J. Ruskin, *Works*, XIII, p. 99). Is it not rather that we are seeing a glorious finale? The distillation of a lifetime's experience where people and landscape exist as part of a homogeneous whole. A larger landscape based on memories of things past where location is no longer important and color and mood are of the essence.

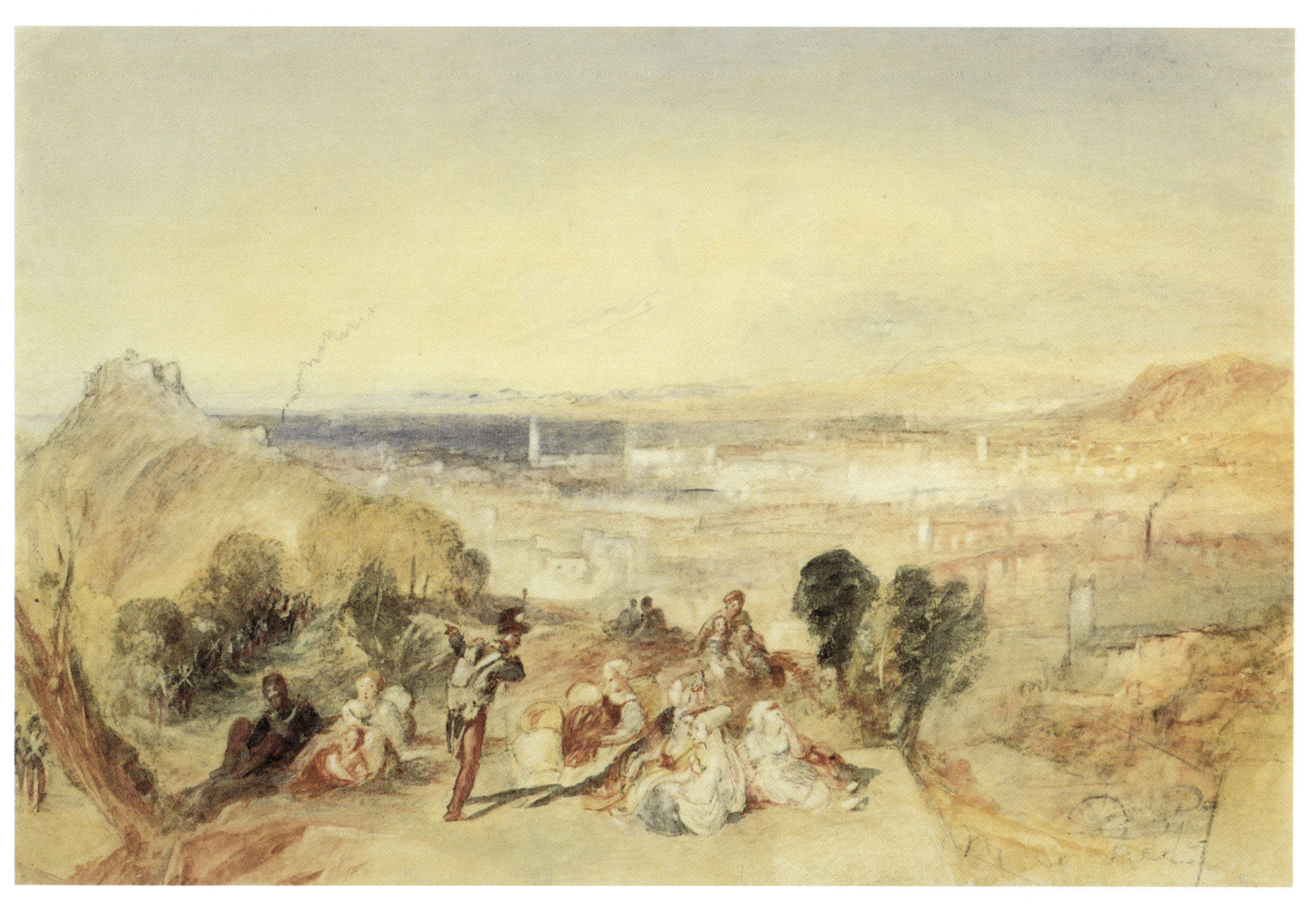

Abbreviations used in the text

Butlin & Joll   Refers to the numbering in M. Butlin and E. Joll, *The Paintings of J.M.W. Turner*, revised ed., 1984

Finberg (1909)   Refers to the text of A.J. Finberg, *A Complete Inventory of the Drawings of the Turner Bequest,* 2 vols., 1909

Hartley (1984)   Refers to the text of C. Hartley, *Turner Watercolours in the Whitworth Art Gallery,* 1984

MCAG   Refers to the Manchester City Art Galleries (initials preceding an accession number)

Rawlinson   Refers to the numbering in W.G. Rawlinson, *The Engraved Work of J.M.W. Turner,* 2 vols., 1908 and 1913

J. Ruskin, *Works*   Refers to the text in *The Works of John Ruskin,* ed. E.T. Cook and A. Wedderburn, 38 vols., 1903-12

T.B.   Refers to the numbering in A.J. Finberg, *A Complete Inventory of the Drawings of the Turner Bequest,* 1909

WAG   Refers to the Whitworth Art Gallery, University of Manchester (initials preceding an accession number)

Wilton (1979)   Refers to the text in A. Wilton, *The Life and Work of J.M.W. Turner,* 1979

Wilton   Refers to the numbering in the catalogue of watercolors in A. Wilton, *The Life and Work of J.M.W. Turner,* 1979

Select Bibliography

Aberdeen Art Gallery, *Turner in Scotland*, exhibition catalogue, 1982

M. Campbell, *Turner in the National Gallery of Scotland*, 1993

T. Clifford, *Turner at Manchester*, 1982

B. Dawson, *Turner in the National Gallery of Ireland*, 1988

J. Farington, *Diary*, ed. K.Cave, K. Garlick and J. Macintyre, 14 vols., 1978-84

G. Finley, *Landscapes of Memory: Turner as Illustrator to Scott*, 1981

J. Gage, *Color in Turner: Poetry and Truth*, 1969

_______ *Collected Correspondence of J.M.W. Turner*, 1980

_______ *J.M.W. Turner: 'A Wonderful Range of Mind'*, 1987

W. Hauptman, *Magnificent Switzerland: Views by Foreign Artists 1770-1914*, 1991

D. Hill, *Turner in Yorkshire*, 1980

______ *In Turner's Footsteps, through the hills and dales of Northern England*, 1984

______ *Turner in the Alps: the Journey through France and Switzerland in 1802*, 1992

M. Lloyd (ed.), *Turner*, 1996

C. Powell, *Turner in the South: Rome, Naples, Florence*, 1987

Royal Academy, *Turner 1775-1851*, catalogue of bicentenary exhibition, 1974-5

E. Shanes, *Turner's Picturesque Views in England and Wales 1825-1838*, 1979

_________ *Turner's Rivers, Harbours and Coasts*, 1981

_________ *J.M.W. Turner: The Foundations of Genius*, 1986

_________ *Turner's England*, 1990

_________ *Turner's Human Landscape*, 1990

L. Stainton, *Turner's Venice*, 1985

A. Wilton, *Turner in the British Museum*, 1975

_________ *Turner and the Sublime*, 1980

_________ *Turner Abroad: France, Italy, Germany, Switzerland*, 1982

_________ *Turner in Wales*, 1984

_________ *Turner in his Time*, 1987

_________ and J. Russell, *Turner in Switzerland*, 1976

Tate Gallery Exhibition Catalogues

P. Bower, *Turner's Papers*, 1990

D.B. Brown, *Turner and Byron*, 1992

M. Butlin, I. Warrell, and M. Luther, *Turner at Petworth: Patron and Painter*, 1989

A. Chumbley and I. Warrell, *Turner and the Human Figure - Studies of Contemporary Life*, 1989

M. Davies, *Turner as Professor - The Artist and Linear Perspective*, 1992

G. Forrester, *Turner's "Drawing Book" - The Liber Studiorum*, 1996

A. Lyles, *Turner and Natural History: The Farnley Project*, 1988

_________ *Young Turner: Early work to 1800*, 1989

_________ *Turner: The Fifth Decade, Watercolours 1830-40*, 1992

_________ and D. Perkins, *Color into Line: Turner and the Art of Engraving*, 1989

D. Perkins, *Turner: The Third Decade, Watercolours 1810-20*, 1990

_________ and I. Warrell, *Turner and Architecture*, 1988

J. Piggott, *Turner's Vignettes*, 1993

C. Powell, *Turner's Rivers of Europe: The Rhine, Meuse and Mosel*, 1991

_________ *Turner in Germany*, 1995

R. Upstone, *Turner: The Second Decade, Watercolours 1800-10*, 1989

_________ *Turner: The Final Years, Watercolours 1840-51*, 1993

I. Warrell, *Turner: The Fourth Decade, Watercolours 1820-30*, 1991

_________ *Through Switzerland with Turner*, 1995

A. Wilton, *Painting and Poetry - Turner's Verse Book and his Work of 1804-12*, 1990